695
6

GOLDEN PHOENIX

THE BIOGRAPHY OF
Peter Munk

GOLDEN PHOENIX

RICHARD ROHMER

KEY PORTER BOOKS

Canadian Cataloguing in Publication Data

Rohmer, Richard, 1924–
    Golden phoenix : the biography of Peter Munk

Includes index.
ISBN 1-55013-912-6

1. Munk, Peter, 1927– . 2. American Barrick Resources Corporation.
3. Businessmen – Canada – Biography. 4. Executives – Canada – Biography.
I. Title.

HD9506.C22M86 1997   338.7'622'092   C97-931312-0

THE CANADA COUNCIL | LE CONSEIL DES ARTS
FOR THE ARTS | DU CANADA
SINCE 1957 | DEPUIS 1957

The publisher gratefully acknowledges the support of the Canada Council for the Arts and the Ontario Arts Council for its publishing program.

Key Porter Books Limited
70 The Esplanade
Toronto, Ontario
Canada M5E 1R2

Design: Jean Lightfoot Peters
Electronic formatting: Frank Zsigo

Printed and bound in Canada

97 98 99 00 6 5 4 3 2 1

To my mainstays in a long life: my wife, Mary Olivia Whiteside Rohmer, and our daughters, Catherine Rohmer-Dyer and Ann Rohmer-Barker.

CONTENTS

BUDAPEST TO BERGEN-BELSEN TO BASEL

The setting sun threw long shadows across the city of Budapest, Hungary. It was the end of a warm, humid day—Thursday, June 29, 1944. Sixteen-year-old Peter Munk sat astride a knobby, sway-backed horse that was pulling the rickety cart his grandfather had rented. Earlier that day, he and his grandfather Gabriel Munk had filled the cart with family members' luggage and belongings from their home. Now they were on their way to the Columbus Street siding. There they, their family and hundreds of other Hungarian Jews would board a Nazi train that would transport them out of Budapest. Peter Munk recalls:

> I think it was the first time in my life that I ever rode through the streets of Budapest on a horse. I was on top of the world. Our carriage carried the elegant Munk family luggage. I felt like a conqueror; I was young; I was tough; I was rich; I was supremely confident. The others were old and frightened.

The round-faced, red-haired teenager had no idea that what he thought was a carefree adventure could be part of Nazi Germany's plan to round up the Jews of Hungary and transport them to camps to be exterminated in accordance with Hitler's intent that Europe should be free of all Jews—*Judenfrei*. Peter's grandfather Gabriel Munk, a tall, white-haired, deeply religious patriarch, had heard the horrifying rumours about the gas chambers at the concentration camps, but he saw no reason to worry young Peter or the other family members. Besides, he was reasonably confident that he had found a way to escape the fate that awaited so many.

Three months earlier, on March 19, 1944, Hitler's troops had occupied Hungary. With them came the beginning of the end for that country's 825,000 Jews. The Final Solution was about to be implemented. Lieutenant-Colonel Adolf Eichmann, Hitler's supreme organizer of the Final Solution, arrived in Budapest shortly after the initial invasion force. His men immediately met with the leaders of a Jewish group called Judenrat and promised them that Hungary's Jews would not be harmed. Eichmann's likely motive was to prevent a repeat of the Warsaw uprising.

In addition to the Judenrat there was a Budapest organization of Jews called the Va'adat Ezra Vehatzala (Aid and Rescue Committee—Va'adah for short). Its purpose had been to help persecuted Jews in other countries, but that purpose changed dramatically with the arrival of Hitler's troops. The extensive activities of Va'adah before the German occupation had been supported by money from an American-based organization that had been established during the First World War—the Joint Distribution Committee, the JDC, whose basic purpose was to raise and deliver money from American Jews to provide relief to their fellow Jews throughout Europe.

Rezsoe Kasztner, one of the Va'adah representatives, was a thirty-eight-year-old lawyer and journalist born in Kolozsvar. He had gone to Budapest in 1940, where he continued his profession. An ardent Zionist, skilful negotiator and eloquent bargainer, Kasztner was reputedly dedicated to saving as many Jewish lives as possible out of the mass deportations that were certain to follow the Nazi occupation.

Kasztner had been working closely with Joel Brand, a Zionist who was a glove manufacturer by trade. Both he and Kasztner had participated in the January 1943 creation of the Va'adah.

On March 24, Kasztner and Brand met with Captain Wisliczeny of the SS to present a proposal similar to one that earlier had allowed 2,500 Jews to escape from Slovakia. If bribery worked in Slovakia, the men reasoned, it might also succeed with the SS in Hungary. Kasztner and Brand offered Captain Wisliczeny SFr 2 million, of which two hundred thousand francs would be an immediate down payment, to save Hungarian Jews from the death camps. Kasztner implied that the funds would come from a source of intriguing interest to the German—the United States of America.

The negotiations did not progress until April 25, 1944, when Adolf Eichmann made an offer that was received by Joel Brand in Budapest. This was just before Eichmann's death machine began its mass deportation of Jews out of Hungary to Auschwitz and other death camps. Eichmann offered Brand the release of one million Jews. The price? Mountains of coffee, soap, tea and cocoa, and ten thousand trucks. Eichmann was prepared to allow Brand to go abroad to contact Jewish groups among the Allies. To sweeten his offer the Nazi death master indicated that as soon as the Allies agreed to deliver the trucks, a group of several thousand Hungarian Jews would be allowed to leave the country for safe haven.

This Eichmann proposition was of enormous significance to Brand and Kasztner. It meant that the Nazis were indeed prepared to bargain the lives of Jews in exchange for equipment, goods or money.

Brand left Budapest for Ankara—on a German private plane—to make contact with the Western Allies to pass along the Eichmann offer. He had to have quick proof that the Allies did not reject the proposal.

On May 22, 1944, in an apparent attempt to underscore his serious intent to negotiate, Eichmann agreed to release a group of six hundred Hungarian Jews who held Palestinian immigration certificates. They would not be permitted to travel to Palestine because that would offend Arab states that were supportive of the Nazi regime, but they could go to any neutral or Allied country. On one of the accepted lists were fourteen members of the family of Gabriel Munk.

The Kasztner organization eventually persuaded Eichmann to increase the number from six hundred to some thirteen hundred.

The matter of the route continued to be negotiated by Va'adah and the Eichmann officials. Eichmann ultimately decreed that the transport would proceed through Germany, occupied France, Spain and Portugal, where the participants would go by ship to West Africa. Where they went from there, whether to Palestine or to any Allied country, was not his concern.

As Peter Munk rode to Columbus Street that fateful night, he knew nothing of these events. However, he was worried about the safety of his beloved mother, Katharina Adler, who had been divorced from Peter's father, Louis, shortly after Peter was born. A few weeks earlier she had been ordered into the Nazi Budapest compound as a hostage. Peter was living with his father and stepmother, but he had gone to his mother's apartment and carried her pitifully small valise as the two of them took a streetcar to the designated place.

As Peter Munk tells the story:

> I took her into the Hungarian camp where she had been ordered to go. I was sixteen years old. I carried her bag because Grandmother was too frail to go with her. I promised her that I was going to look after her. I realize now that they could have taken me in with her in one second. But I thought that I could protect her. When the Munks, a month later, said they were going to leave Hungary together, I said, "I'm going to stay with my mother. You go." But Grandfather said, "But you're the last male Munk! You cannot not go." And I said, "Well, I'm not going." Then I actually talked on the telephone to my mother in the camp … and, boy, do I remember this … I talked with the camp commander personally. He said to me, Don't worry, your

mother's a very special person, and I thought, Gee, the
commander! My mother sits with the commander! My
mother spoke to me then and said, "I want you to go with
the Munks, and I don't want any kind of nonsense from
you. Just go."

Peter was aware that Grandfather Gabriel had paid heavily to
secure a place for the Munk family on one particular train. Some
weeks earlier in the living room of Louis's flat in Gabriel's huge house,
Peter had watched his father remove a large painting from the wall.
Behind it, embedded in the wall, was the grey metal face of Gabriel's
safe. Eyes bigger than ever, Peter looked on as his father took a long
key from his jacket pocket to unlock the safe. Swinging the door open
Louis proceeded to empty into a valise the contents of the deep hiding place. Gold coins, bank notes, precious stones and gold-encrusted
jewellery came out by careful handful after handful.

Peter then followed his silent father, who carried the heavy valise
downstairs to deliver it to Gabriel. Peter is sure that the enormously
valuable treasure trove in that valise, a collection that had been gathered and handed down over many generations of Munks, was at least
part of the heavy price that Gabriel Munk had to pay to the Germans
so Kasztner could obtain passage for the family on the special train
that became known as the Kasztner Transport. As Peter recalls:

Sometime in May, my grandfather and my father, the two
male members of the Munk family, delivered the valise with
the gold coins and the dollars to Kasztner's office to pay for
passage on the train for all fourteen of us.

The cart finally arrived at the Columbus Street siding where the
train waited. Its windows and metal could just be seen in the increasing darkness. There was no panic among the hundreds of Jews who
had come from all parts of Budapest to claim their place on the

Kasztner Transport. They stood quietly in lines as they waited patiently for their names to be checked off the list of approved persons by the Nazi SS guards and Kasztner's own Va'adah assistants.

Peter dismounted and helped lift the baggage off the cart. Then, struggling with their luggage, the family joined the nearest line: Grandfather Gabriel; Peter's father, Louis, his wife, Olga, and her son John; Gabriel's daughter, Ernestine Merey, and her husband and son, John; Gabriel's daughter, Gizi, with her influential Zionist husband, Dr. Kahan, and their daughter, her husband and child.

As the Munks had been making their way to the Columbus Street siding, the tall, strapping Erwin Schaeffer had been escorting his own parents to the Kasztner train. Former school friends, Erwin and Peter had not seen each other for some years. To avoid being apprehended by the Germans, Schaeffer had dyed his hair blond and made himself look like a Hungarian Nazi, even changing his name to Julius.

That night Erwin was terrified that one of his old classmates would unwittingly reveal his identity. If Peter Munk acknowledged the identity of his Jewish friend, a watchful SS or Gestapo officer might have realized that Julius was actually a Jew. He would have been taken into custody immediately, and would probably have joined the four hundred thousand other Hungarian Jews who were sent to concentration camps that summer and exterminated.

Peter Munk recognized Erwin Schaeffer in the brief moment when the two passed each other in the crowd of Jews struggling to get on the Kasztner train. But his friend's appearance—blond hair, Gestapo raincoat—was so altered that Peter instantly understood that it was a disguise that could easily be destroyed by the wrong gesture or by words of greeting. Peter fought his natural impulse to embrace his dear friend and walked calmly away. It would be eight years before Peter and Erwin saw each other again.

All the authorized passengers were on board well before midnight, but the train's departure out of the Columbus Street siding was delayed for four hours by an air raid. During that time, some

Jews from Budapest's Bocskay Street Synagogue who had found out about the transport to a neutral country stormed the train and forced their way onto the lightless coaches. They too wanted to escape with their lives.

The all-clear signal finally came in the dawn light. The engineer hauled on the lever that fed power to the massive pistons. Slowly the huge steel wheels began to turn and pull the cars of the Kasztner Transport. Crammed in them were 1,684 Hungarian Jews and, in their own coach, their SS guards.

Peter Munk, oblivious to the enormous dangers under which they were travelling, was settling in for his great adventure, which would take them west and south to Spain and Portugal through Austria and Germany. He was delighted to find that he would be sharing that journey with a beautiful girl about his own age, Kitty Frank, whose father, a doctor, felt he couldn't leave Hungary. Instead he asked Louis Munk to look after his daughter on the train. Peter was more than happy to share that responsibility.

During the days that followed, the passengers on the train that pulled out of the Columbus Street siding changed trains many times, from passenger cars to freight trains to cattle cars, whatever was available. Peter recalls that they transferred from train to train seven or eight times because the rail systems belonged to different jurisdictions, or because the trains were commandeered by local officials, or because the tracks were bombed out and they had to switch by truck from one train to another. He recalls:

Often we were on a regular passenger train, but squeezed. Sometimes there was one cabin for the luggage and another one for the people, and sometimes we were all pushed in together. I preferred the slow freight trains. They couldn't go fast because of all the damage to the tracks. We could open the whole side door, and I would sit on the floor with my legs hanging out of the train. Grandfather sat inside, reading,

while I was out where I could see everything, getting a suntan.
I thought it was fantastic. I got to know those cars well,
because I had so much time in them. You could climb up on
the roof, there was wind in your face and you could see all
these places....I was really happy.

Peter Munk may have had a grand time on the train, but most of
the adults suffered severe discomfort and, in the cattle cars, a total lack
of privacy. One woman on the Kasztner Transport recalls they would
"sit day and night cramped on wretched luggage—and we young
mothers held our children on our knees....We travelled in freight
wagons that were intended for six horses or forty people but we were
eighty people of all ages."

Peter Munk hadn't travelled for years. With the war on Hungarians
couldn't go anywhere.

So to travel into Austria, into Germany, was fantastic. I
remember that we were stopped at the Austro-Hungarian border for three days waiting for the papers we needed. We went
to Vienna, then to Linz and north toward Hanover.

In Vienna there were huge signs saying "Judenfrei," declaring the
city to be free of Jews.

Every German city had them. They were proud, because they
had deported their last Jews. It was an eerie feeling to walk
around in Vienna. When we left Budapest the SS told us to
take off our yellow stars—that was how I had made money in
Budapest: I had sold these stars. And now we had to take
them off. I put mine in my passport, and I still have it.

Why did the Nazis ask us to take them off? Because they
were embarrassed, going through city after city with a train-
load of Jews, when these cities were all declaring themselves

"Judenfrei." But the SS had orders to deliver us wherever they would get the big money payoff.

At Linz, Austria, Peter and the others were subjected to their first showers and disinfecting procedures. The Germans ordered them off the train and marched them to a nearby building, where all were told to strip. Peter's aunt Ernestine remembers that first shower very well. She had heard the rumour that the showers in the camps were not showers at all but lethal gas chambers. "But I had to go to the shower because my husband was not in very good health and my son was four years old. They couldn't go but at least I had to go. So I went every time to the shower, and thank God I survived."

There was one part of the long train ride that Peter Munk remembers clearly.

The American bombers! After Linz and around Hanover the sky was filled with what looked like hundreds and hundreds of airplanes. The earth shook, and it was like a distant sound of thunder because there were so many bombers. And the sound amplified and the earth vibrated. It was incredible. I wanted so badly for the Nazis to be killed. I hated them.

From Linz, the Kasztner Transport headed for its final destination, which, despite Eichmann's promise, was not Portugal but the Bergen-Belsen concentration camp. The train and its hundreds of suffering Jewish passengers arrived on July 8, 1944.

Part of the camp complex was a fenced-off "transit camp" where candidates for exchange with the Americans and their Allies were housed. The rest of the camp included the concentration camp, with its barracks and crematorium. The adult passengers on the Kasztner Transport were once again in fear for their lives. Being marched into a Nazi concentration camp in the heart of Germany between Berlin and Hanover was not the outcome for which they had traded all their savings and possessions.

Peter Munk remembers Bergen-Belsen well.

We slept in huge rooms, each of us in a wooden bed. The ladies' camp was separate. I was stuck with my father, and I remember stealing cigarettes from his suitcase. He would only smoke a particular Turkish brand, and I discovered that it was a currency that I could give to the guard in exchange for some privacy with Kitty Frank.

On the far side of two sets of barbed-wire fences I sometimes saw a group of men in prison garb. They were terribly emaciated.

We had to stay in our own compound. Father got the food every morning, bread and soup, sometimes sausages, and even jam or butter. I still had no doubt at all that we were on our way to Spain. All I cared about was getting to be alone with Kitty. For me Belsen was an interesting interlude on the way to where I wanted and expected to be, far away from Hungary, the war, the Nazis and the special restrictions for Jews.

I didn't know that my mother was in Auschwitz by then. I didn't know what Auschwitz was. We didn't know that Jews in Hungary were being murdered.

Peter Munk and his family did eventually arrive in Switzerland. They owed their good fortune to two American agencies, the JDC and the War Refugee Board; to Rezsoe Kasztner's dealings with Eichmann's men; and to Saley Mayer, the Swiss representative of the JDC.

By Executive Order No. 9417, signed January 22, 1944, President Roosevelt had created the War Refugee Board (WRB), whose mission was to organize and implement programs for the rescue, transportation, maintenance and relief of the victims of enemy oppression, and to establish havens of temporary refuge for such victims.

The American WRB representative in Switzerland was Rosell McClelland. By 1944 the JDC funds for the relief and rescue of European Jews were substantial—$884,786. Movement in Mayer's crucial bargaining for the release of the Kasztner Transport people imprisoned at Bergen-Belsen began at the end of July.

After weeks of difficult negotiation, Mayer knew that the SS were ready for an agreement. The German Seventh Army in Normandy was boxed in by Canadian, British and American forces. The Russians were coming from the east. The end was near for the Nazis. On August 21, the day that the defeat of the German Seventh Army was complete, Mayer and Kasztner stood on the bridge at Saint Margarethen, which spanned the border between Switzerland and Austria. They had come to meet Kurt Becher, the high-ranking SS officer who was authorized to deal for Himmler and Eichmann. The SS asked for ten thousand trucks and other machines "for agricultural purposes," which were to be brought from the U.S. on American ships. The Jews in Bergen-Belsen would be permitted to leave on the same ships. Preposterous as the demand may seem, the Germans were serious. Mayer stalled, saying that, although he was a JDC representative he did not have the authority to deal on behalf of the Swiss organization. He would have to get instructions. If the Nazis would demonstrate some form of good faith, he was sure he could get them the trucks.

The Germans moved quickly. Later that same day, August 21, 1944, an SS officer arrived at Bergen-Belsen and announced the names of 318 Jews who were to depart immediately for Switzerland. The Munk family were on the list—all but Ernestine and her husband and son, perhaps because their surname was different. Peter Munk had no idea why he was chosen or how it was that the Nazis were going to release any Jews at all. Kitty Frank, too, was one of the lucky ones.

A passenger train was already at Bergen-Belsen, and the chosen 318 quickly gathered up their belongings and were marched to the waiting coaches. They went first to Frankfurt, then headed south toward the Swiss border. It seemed that their escape was imminent, but would the Swiss admit 318 Hungarian Jews into their country? No one knew.

> The train halted. And the Swiss authorities didn't want to admit us. They had never seen a proper train carrying Jews who wore good clothes, who had passports and suitcases. So they thought there was something fishy going on there. They suspected us of being Germans, spies, SS fugitives, anything but what we were. And I don't blame them.

The Swiss were dubious, but they relented, and the train was allowed to proceed. In Basel the travellers were taken directly to a hotel in Montreux on Lac Lucerne. There they were placed in military quarantine for two weeks while the authorities checked their credentials and assured themselves the arrivals carried no communicable diseases.

Although Ernestine Munk Merey and her little family were not among the first group to be rescued, their release came a few months later, when Mayer at last secured the freedom of all the remaining passengers on the Kasztner Transport. On the night of December 6, they too departed by train from Bergen-Belsen; they crossed the Swiss border on December 13, 1944.

In the last few months before the Allies arrived at Belsen, some thirty thousand Jews died there: those who were not shot, beaten, or starved to death fell victim to epidemics of typhus and other diseases. Peter Munk owes his life and the lives of his family of fourteen to Rezsoe Kasztner, Joel Brand and Saley Mayer. If it had not been for them, all the Hungarian Jews of the Kasztner Transport would have been shifted out of the transit camp at Belsen to the other side of the barbed-wire fence.

Would Peter Munk have been consumed in that Holocaust? To use his word in answer to that question: *absolutely!*

CHAPTER TWO

THE EARLY YEARS
IN HUNGARY

Peter Munk was born on November 8, 1927, to Louis Munk and his wife, Katharina Adler, after three years of marriage. When Peter was four, Katharina left the marriage, and took her baby son with her to live with her widowed mother "in Budapest, but down the Danube," as Peter describes it.

> The Munks were very powerful. There were four of them: two brothers, two sisters, a grandfather and grandmother. There was wealth, respect, a close-knit family structure, and religion. My mother had lost her father. She was guilty of adultery, but she was very courageous about it, and never denied the truth. I was in love with my mother.

While he lived with his mother and grandmother, Peter started school. The boy who sat next to him in class was Erwin Schaeffer, and they became close friends. More than that, the much taller Erwin often defended his little redheaded pal from attacks by schoolmates. Eventually, Peter learned how to fight and defend himself.

Peter's father, Louis, had started a number of businesses that subsequently failed: a stock brokerage firm and a bank business; then two manufacturing companies, making candy and gramophones. After the fourth failure, Gabriel refused to bail out his son. But Louis still had an income from real estate holdings, which he had inherited. And his second wife, Rosie Waltner, was a very wealthy woman.

Rosie was not able to have children, but she longed for a child she could call her own. She decided to ask that Peter, her husband's son, be returned to his father. And so, at the age of eight, Peter was removed from his mother's care and taken to live with Louis and Rosie in Gabriel's house. Grandfather Gabriel had a flat on the first and second floors; Louis and his wife were on the upper floor. Peter recalls:

> When my father married for the second time, in '38 before the war, they took me back from my mother, because under Hungarian law at that time the man always had custody of a male child.

Peter lived there until 1944, when the family left Budapest on the Kasztner Transport. He and his stepmother did not get along.

> If I misbehaved—and I always misbehaved—the punishment was that I wasn't allowed to visit my mother. I became obsessed with the injustice of it, and the one thing I would not tolerate was for Rosie to call me *her* child. Once when we went shopping in a fancy area of the city, and she introduced me in the shop as "my son," I lost my temper. I was beside myself. I was quite small, ten years old, but I attacked her physically.

As a result, Peter's father sent him to a disciplinary Calvinist boarding school in Miskolc, a provincial city. There Peter completed his first and second years of high school. But that was only half of his punishment. The other half was that at no time was he allowed to visit his mother. Life at the Calvinist school was a living hell for the banished Peter Munk.

I didn't know anybody there. I was Jewish and this was in '38, '39, just when Nazi ideas were starting to get a real grip on Hungary. A lot of the senior lecturers or professors were strong Nazis. One teacher used to call me Jew-Munk. "Come out here," he'd order me, and he'd pull my hair and say, "If you're a Jew, why don't you wear sidelocks?" That would encourage some of the kids to be cruel, imitating the example of the teachers. And they would tease me after classes. I had to fight constantly. I tried to run, but at the end they always caught up with me. As a result I became a really good fighter. In fact, I took up boxing, and I was good at it. I became tough and muscular.

Those traumatic two years had a profound and positive effect on the young Peter Munk. In addition to making him tough, self-reliant, and ready to defend himself against attackers, they taught him the first lessons of self-respect and self-confidence.

I became a proud Jew, which I hadn't been before. I knew that when they said *dirty Jew*, I was proud. And I was ready to fight.

In 1939 the Waltners, Rosie Munk's family, moved to Switzerland, on their way to New York. Louis Munk went to Switzerland with them, but when they offered to take him to New York he decided he wanted to go back to Budapest and stay with his family in his own home. Then he and Rosie divorced.

With Rosie gone, Louis brought his son home from Miskolc. Peter Munk's life immediately changed for the better. He was sent to a Jewish high school where his uncle, Dr. Bernard Munkacsi, a recognized scholar, was a member of the board. He could see his mother whenever he wished, and he was back in the bosom of the Munk family, with his grandfather Gabriel at its centre, and all the rest of his old crowd.

My grandfather ruled his family absolutely. No one dared not to kiss his hands on meeting him. Mother often said that his reputation was not based on brilliance, but on the fact that he was a man of tremendously high moral and ethical standards. He was completely committed to his family. The moral guidance he gave me has stayed with me throughout my life, and I have tried to pass it on to my children.

His grandfather was also a deeply religious man.

My grandfather was determined that all the grandchildren would go to the synagogue every Saturday morning. After he'd seen you in his synagogue, you had to recite the prayers you had learned, and only then would you receive your pocket money for the week. I was never particularly religious or very committed to Judaism. I became more Jewish when they tried to beat it out of me in school, but as a religion it wasn't that significant to me.

Although young Peter loved and admired his grandfather, his relationship with his father was distant.

My relationship with him was not that good at the beginning. During the four or five years when he was not married, he would sit at the head of the table with the newspapers on his left, and he would start reading. I ate and he read the papers. I was not allowed to leave the table until I had finished everything on my plate. And if I didn't eat it for supper, I got it for breakfast. Every time I left something, he'd say, "People in China are starving." I never understood how my leaving some food in Budapest would have an effect on Chinese kids.

During the war years Louis continued his varied business activities.

From 1940 until 1943, father was in the wholesale oil business. He was an executive of Shell. My grandfather gave him permission to use the basement of the Munk house as an oil warehouse, so he could buy engine oil wholesale. Then he would sell that and gasoline to drivers, from the house. I worked there one or two summers. Just before the Germans came in, my father got married again, to a very charming and very beautiful widow with a young son.

The Munk family's comfortable Budapest lifestyle was to cease abruptly during the early summer of 1944.

The sixteen-year-old Peter Munk who stepped off the train at Basel, Switzerland, on the pleasant, sunny afternoon of Thursday, August 24, 1944, was at that moment the last male inheritor of a family name that proudly traced its history back to Worms, Germany, in the sixteenth century. He was to carry the name to a new life in Canada, taking with him as one of his most prized possessions the original leatherbound copy of the Munk family genealogy published in 1939 in Budapest. The paternal line of Munk intellectuals and businessmen is detailed in this remarkable document, titled "The Genealogy of the Munk Family of Hungary," and compiled over a lifetime by Dr. Bernard Munkacsi, the scholarly elder brother of Gabriel Munk, who had Hungarianized the Munk name when he became the first Jewish scientist to be elected to the Royal Hungarian Academy of Sciences. As Ernestine Munk Merey has said, "In Peter's background [on his father's side] there are two strands: the intellectual and the commercial. The commercial is represented by Grandfather Gabriel, the intellectual by Gabriel's father, Adolf, and by Gabriel's elder brother, Bernard Munkacsi." It was Bernard's scholarly education that diverted Peter's grandfather Gabriel from the intellectual Munk inheritance into the commercial line. As Ernestine's son, Dr. John Merey, explains:

When our great-grandfather Adolf took his second son
[Gabriel] to the high school to be educated, the principal said,
"Mr. Munk, you already have one son educated. I think your
second son should be an apprentice." And so his academic
career ended and a commercial career began.

Given the considerable natural intelligence lodged in that
remarkable red head, it would have been difficult to predict which
strand of the Munk inheritance would ultimately capture Peter
Munk's attention.

As for his courage of conviction and facility for understanding
what motivates people—a skill that has proved important in both
his private and business lives—that can be traced to his maternal
forebears, the Adler family.

CHAPTER THREE

SWITZERLAND

The Swiss were highly suspicious of the passengers on the Kasztner train. Peter Munk was dreaming of a life of freedom in the charming Swiss city of Basel, and imagining scenes in which he and Kitty browsed in luxurious shops, idled away time in restaurants and munched on delectable chocolates, but all that was not to be, at least for some weeks. The Swiss had other plans for the Jewish refugees. Peter was put in a hostel for students, while his father, his stepmother and most of the other Munk family members were taken to the Hotel Belmont at Montreux, which served as the military internment camp for refugees.

For months their fate was uncertain. Then, in April 1945, the Swiss threatened to send all the Kasztner Transport passengers to Algeria. The Hungarian Jews refused to go, telling the Swiss they would take public action, even go on a hunger strike, to stop this unwanted move. Unwilling to risk the publicity such protests would attract, the Swiss backed down. Finally, all the members of the Kasztner group were told they were free to stay or to go to destinations of their choice. That included permission to settle in Switzerland, which is what the Munk and Merey families decided to do. They would become Swiss residents.

At the outset, money for the family came from Gabriel's other son,

Nick, who had emigrated to Toronto, Canada, in the 1930s and had become a successful car parts manufacturer. Uncle Nick was to be the main force in Peter's move to Canada in 1948.

The war in Europe was in its final days. Black market activity flourished in Switzerland as American soldiers, who were by then occupying parts of France, Italy and Germany, came to Switzerland on leave. Lacking local currency, the soldiers carried only military scrip, and so Louis Munk entered the money-changing business, paying Swiss francs for scrip from Canadian, U.S. and other military personnel, then converting it into various currencies. He also started an operation to assist Hungarians in America and Canada to send money or food parcels back to their starving families in Hungary.

To his great joy, Peter received a letter from his mother, Katharina Adler, written from Budapest in August 1945, just a few days after she and the other inmates of Auschwitz had been freed by the American army. She, too, had survived the Holocaust.

> That was probably the most important document I ever received. The emotional impact on my soul was profound. You could not reproduce such circumstances, in which an only child receives word from a mother who has come back from the tomb.

Katharina wrote:

My only darling Peterke!

I cannot tell you how I feel now, sitting at a desk writing to you. I feel as if you were sitting right here, across the table. I can see your red hair, your beautiful grey eyes, and I feel as if I was holding your big hands. I hope you have no bitten nails now, but well-kept hands of a man. My dear little angel, so I am alive. After a lot of difficulties and a very long time, I arrived home on June 12th.

I arrived in Budapest, but I cannot put in words the feeling that I had when I stood there before the Budapest Western Station and I saw the bombed-out Berlin Square. I was at last home and free, without a soldier with a bayonet behind me.

With my pack sack I strolled down the Lipót Boulevard, which you loved so much, and went to the Pannonnia Street address, which was the last address of your grandmother. I cannot tell you that I was full of joy, only that I was excited to know who would I find at home. There was no place for excitement, as the arrow-cross people took Grandmother away in November, and she never came back again. Peter, you must know how I felt, as you must have buried me as well.

I wish to talk over with you and deal with your future plans, to find jointly some kind of solution for you. In your telegrams you are asking me if you should come home or not, or travel on. If I can answer in one word, I would say travel on. You must believe me how hard it is for me to say this. I would give up half my life if I could see you here now, and that you could be with me, but common sense tells me you must not sacrifice your life and your future for the feelings of your sentimental mother.

Go to North America to be a free man. Get a decent, nice job and earn a lot of money. If you have money, the world is yours; you can travel, live decently and enjoy arts, and you can further improve yourself. You can achieve these only if you live in a completely free country like America.

I know I must be patient and I must wait a long, long time, and I hope I will have enough strength and persistence to wait for that wonderful moment when I can embrace you again.

The reason I am writing this is to tell you that the past fourteen months have not broken me in body or in soul. So do not think of me as an old mother. My one and only dearest, I wish to say good-bye to you now, and it is very hard to put my pen down, as I have so much to tell you. Please write.

I embrace and kiss you a thousand million times,

Mother

Now that the Munk family was settled and thriving in Zurich, it was time for Peter to return to school. His father wanted him to study engineering at a Swiss university, the famous Eidgenossische Technische Hochschule (ETH), the European equivalent to the Massachusetts Institute of Technology. There was no dispute about this. Both father and son were old-fashioned enough to accept the parent's right to decide his child's future.

The thought was probably conceived some time in '42 or '43 by my family in Hungary, where the strong anti-Jewish laws excluded Jews from most professions and from professional schools. In those days a Jewish person of middle-class background who wanted an education had to leave Europe, and the only professions that were totally transferable were engineering and the sciences. With law or medicine, you had to requalify if you went to another country. To tell the truth, I did not really want to be an engineer. But there was no discussion.

Peter was therefore sent to Juventus, a high school, and subsequently to Dr. Junod's, the best preparatory school in Zurich for the ETH entrance exams. It was there that he met a "little Hungarian kid" named Steve Friedlich, who was to be a lifelong friend. "He was so frightened and alien in Switzerland," Munk recalls, "I sort of looked after him."

Peter was not among the top students in school, competing as he was against the brightest kids from all over the continent. But he was having too good a time in Zurich to care.

My father gave me a good allowance, and I lived in my grandfather's apartment, where I had a beautiful room. But I also made enough money of my own to pay for tea dances and entertain all the dates I wanted. I went on long skiing holidays with friends up in the mountains, in winter. And in the summer we went up to the Italian part of Switzerland. Steve Friedlich was with me all the time and we had a great time—international kids whose parents could afford to send their children to the only country in Europe not in total devastation.

After school, Peter went to the cafés, where all kinds of things were bought and sold. He and a group of twenty or thirty other young men made money by handling rare stamps, nylon stockings and foreign currency. It wasn't the black market, but it wasn't exactly a proper retail operation either. Peter spent the money he made on luxuries: he had his shirts and suits custom-made in Zurich, and he and his friends often went to the Baur au Lac Hotel. There they would buy the cheapest wine, but make it look as though it was champagne by having it served in an ice bucket, covered with a white cloth.

Finally his father said, "This can't go on. You're going to dances instead of promoting your career. You've got to get down to work." Knowing that Peter would never be accepted by a Swiss university, he arranged for Peter to apply to the University of Toronto. His uncle Nick in Toronto helped. Eventually Peter was accepted at the University of Toronto, subject to passing senior matriculation in Ontario.

The idea of going to Toronto was "like a death warrant." An unknown city, so far away, was an awful prospect, but the decision had been made. He was allowed to go back home to Budapest to say goodbye to his mother. Steve Friedlich went with him, and they planned a little money-making scheme they could try out on the way. They loaded up on nylon stockings, the international currency of the times, and hid them under the carpet of the train.

I told Steve there was no danger. If somebody at customs found them, I would just say, "What the hell? Who knows who used this carriage before us?" In Budapest we exchanged the stockings for rare stamps that we could sell to collectors in Switzerland. On the return trip we put the stamps under the carpet. We made quite a bit of money on this. It wasn't difficult.

Seeing his mother before he departed for Canada in 1948 was an emotionally wrenching experience for Peter. She had survived the unspeakable horrors of the Nazi death camp at Auschwitz, and now she was living in poverty. It gnawed at Peter's conscience then, and it still does. He says:

I loved my mother so much. She was courageous and strong, but she was all alone. Her mother had been murdered by the Nazis and her father had died years earlier. She had no family, no real home; she lived in a tiny room. She had no photographs, no dresses, no income. I brought her what I could, things like nylon stockings (which she could sell). Dr. Tibor Lucas, her sister's husband—they still lived in Budapest—supported her. They were wealthy people and gave my mother something like a thousand florins a month. I promised that when I finished school I would repay them that money. After I came to Canada I was able to send her four or five dollars a week that I borrowed from Uncle Nick, and she lived quite well on that money—enough in those days—for several years. That's why I had to work so hard when I came to Canada. I would owe quite a bit of money by the time I finished university here.

Reluctantly, Peter Munk said his farewells to his mother and to Europe. It was time to travel to an unknown future in Canada.

CHAPTER FOUR

TORONTO

Louis Munk accompanied his son on the first leg of his journey, from Zurich to London, where they visited for two or three days with some of Louis's friends. Their hosts took them around the city to show them some of the sights that had survived Hitler's bomber aircraft, the German V1 pilotless buzz bombs and V2 rockets. The centre of the British Empire was still blighted by war damage. When the brief holiday was over, Peter said goodbye to Louis and boarded a train for Liverpool, the port from which his ship was to depart.

He arrived in Halifax on a rainy day in early March, 1948. After Zurich and London, Halifax struck Peter as unutterably dreary. "It was dirty," he recalls, "and it was raining, and people were all bundled up in parkas. No one had a decent suit." Peter took a train to Union Station in Toronto. There in the crowded station was Nick Munk, Peter's uncle, with his wife, Hedy. To Peter's astonishment, Nick did not have a car. They carried Peter's luggage themselves, and went home by bus and streetcar.

Uncle Nick owned a factory in Toronto, and at that time he must have employed four or five hundred people, and everybody who worked for him had a car. But Uncle Nick went from his home to his factory in a streetcar.

When they got to Nick's house at 438 Avenue Road, just below St. Clair Avenue, Aunt Hedy showed Peter to his room on the third floor of the house, and Uncle Nick had a talk with him. "Peter, you've arrived in Toronto," he said. "You're in my house. This is the last time we'll speak Hungarian or German, because in Canada we're Canadians. As of today you speak only one language and that's English. And tomorrow morning we'll get up early and go to Lawrence Park Collegiate, where you have been enrolled, to meet the principal, Mr. MacKellar."

At Lawrence Park, arrangements had been made for Peter to take the high school courses that he needed for his admission to the Faculty of Applied Sciences at the University of Toronto. Peter made a memorable first impression on his classmates.

> In those days no one of that age in Toronto had met any Europeans. In the movies they saw evil Germans, but they didn't see European immigrants; it wasn't like Toronto now. Mr. MacKellar took me to the classroom. Of course I wore my suit: my English Harris tweeds and my Oxford shirt and my wine-coloured tie. And the boys were in shirts and sweaters and the girls had on white sweaters and nylon stockings. They just stared at me. "Please be considerate of Peter," the principal said. "He just arrived from Switzerland and he doesn't speak English very well."

Peter had always been interested in girls, but in Hungary and Switzerland, where co-educational schools were unheard-of, his contact with them had been restricted. At Lawrence Park, he found girls beyond his wildest dreams.

> I thought I'd hit paradise on that March morning. Lawrence Park High opened up a world of friendship for me—and the girls! In Switzerland, if you got within a hundred yards of a

girls' school, you were expelled. And girls in Europe had to wear dreary uniforms, yet here I sat in class with girls dressed in tight cashmere sweaters!

Then an even more astonishing thing happened.

When we went back to the classroom, somebody passed me a note. It was from a girl. She wrote, "I am the girl three rows down on the left. I wonder if you'd like to come home and have dinner with us." Now, I am a sociable guy, and in Switzerland I had enough money and I spoke Switzerdeutsch and German like the locals, but the Swiss would not take anyone home with them, not even a prime minister's son or the child of an aristocrat, unless he was a cousin—and even then it would take twenty years.

Here I had got off the train the night before, arrived at school in the morning, and at noon girls were inviting me to their home. By the afternoon I had three of those little white folded notes.

Nick and Hedy Munk took Peter to see New York. In later years Peter Munk would come to know the city well, and raise hundreds of millions of dollars there, but on his first trip the problem that arose was the money he spent.

New York in 1948 was fantastic. We had Passover evening at Aunt Hedi's aunt and uncle's, and their daughter, who was my age, brought home a girlfriend called Judy Gastner. I had never met any American girls before. The next day Judy and I walked down to Central Park, and in the evening we went to the movies. Judy showed me all over New York. We had little dinners in the Divan de Paris on 64th Street, we went to the Tavern on the Green, and we went to the revues down in

Rockefeller Plaza. I was in love with her—truly, it was the first big love affair of my life. We still keep in touch.

Unfortunately, the only money Peter had to spend in New York was the $360 Louis had given him to pay his university tuition. By the time he arrived back in Toronto, he had only $80 left. The rest had gone into exploring New York and courting Judy Gastner. Uncle Nick, true to the old-fashioned Munk values, refused to lend Peter the money for his University of Toronto tuition, telling him, "You created the problem. You must solve it. I can't help you." Peter had no choice but to look for work. He became a part-time driver for a travel agency that looked after Hungarian immigrants, but he made very little money doing that.

Then somebody told me there was only one way to make big money in a short time in Ontario: picking tobacco. I didn't even know they grew tobacco in Canada. I was told, "Go to Guelph, to the Ukrainian-Hungarian church at the end of July. They hire labourers there for the one-month harvest period. They pay twelve to thirteen dollars a day, plus board. If you can hold out for thirty days, you make $390." So I looked up Guelph on a map, took a bus there and lined up in the church with Mexicans, itinerate field labourers and other people. The farmers and their wives came in their trucks and hired however many people they needed for the harvest. They asked, "Are you experienced?" And I said, "It's all I've done all my life." But my hands didn't look like a farmer's hands, and I wasn't dressed like a farmer. No one took me. Finally, when it was getting dark in the church and very few growers were left on the picnic grounds, a man named Mr. Goering came in. He didn't believe that I had any experience either, but he hired me anyway. "Listen," he said, "just come along. If you're no good, I'll kick you out." So he threw me in the back of the

truck with six others, and the next morning they got us up
at four.

Those few weeks were a tough physical challenge. The scorching
summer heat was nearly unbearable. With his fair skin, Peter suffered
from sunburn, and his hands and arms were infected by the nicotine
juices. Some of the scratches became open sores, but he worked on, all
day, every day, from four in the morning until dark, and in the end it
paid off. He went back to Uncle Nick and Aunt Hedy's with $350—
enough to cover his annual tuition fees. And he had discovered his talent for focusing on the job in hand, and getting it done.

Focus is one of my specialties—in conversation, in business,
in the sports I do. I think the reason I became focused is that
I was ambitious, but I don't have exceptional talents or an
exceptionally high IQ. If I had to do anything more difficult
than algebra in school I had to have it explained three times
over. Focus, I guess, became my way of compensating for my
lack of talent. I'm focused above all else.

In June, Peter wrote the Lawrence Park exams. He stood among
the highest in the class, and the University of Toronto accepted him.
The only remaining problem was his English. However, because it was
the only language he heard at school or at home, he was learning fast.
By the time he began his engineering course in September 1948, his
quick natural ear had brought him a more than adequate fluency.

The engineering faculty of the University of Toronto had
accepted an exceptionally large first-year class—many of them
young veterans who wanted to become engineers. The downtown
Toronto facilities were stretched beyond their capacity, and the
engineering department had no choice but to move. The only available site was at Ajax, a small community east of Toronto, where war
surplus buildings were available. The distance from Toronto was a

major handicap for students who couldn't afford to commute. Fortunately there was living space available in the Ajax on-site barracks, and Peter Munk was one of a number of first-year students who moved in.

As soon as he was settled at Ajax, Peter began a campaign to get some of his school chums from Switzerland to join him.

> I kept writing to them that this was paradise. I told them they all had to come; they had to leave Europe. All that Swiss sophistication and dances was nonsense. I sent Steve Friedlich and Paul Szasz visas.

Peter Munk's integration into Canadian society included getting his photograph in Canadian newspapers. In the *Evening Telegram* of September 29, 1948, the photo of Peter Munk of Switzerland is immediately above a picture that includes his friend Paul Szasz of Hungary. The caption reads: "In the Ajax Division of the University of Toronto this year with 1500 students enrolled in engineering, there are 26 countries represented." The Toronto *Telegram* reported that: "P.M. Munk came to Canada from Zurich, Switzerland, because he wanted to study in an English-speaking university. His home university is a German language one. He is studying electrical engineering and, since all of Switzerland runs on waterpower, even its electrical railways, he knows he can find a job at home."

Over his summer holidays, Peter worked for Ontario Hydro, and at various engineering jobs.

> In electrical engineering, you had to work so many hundred hours, as part of your course, at Ontario Hydro, Toronto Hydro or Bell Telephone. It was just at the time Hydro was establishing the Pickering substation, and the first summer I worked for them clearing the bush. The second year I worked up in Brent for Canadian National Telegraph, laying

telegraph wires and again, clearing bush on both sides of the wire. We lived in a caboose.

Peter also worked every August for the Canadian National Exhibition in Toronto. The work there was very much to his liking, not only because the CNE job was his introduction to sound installations and equipment, but also because of the beautiful young women he met there when he was installing sound systems for the Women's Building—he got to meet all the models. "Bob May, whom I knew from fraternity and from school, was really good in engineering. His father was a big shot at the CNE and introduced me to the man in charge of sound installations in the various buildings. So they gave me a job."

The final three years of Peter Munk's four-year electrical engineering course were not in remote Ajax but at the University of Toronto campus in the centre of Toronto. To get to class, he walked the few blocks south from the Munk house at the crest of Avenue Road just below St. Clair. Grandfather Gabriel Munk had arrived in Canada by this time and he too was living there; it was a true Munk family residence.

Peter worked hard at his classes and enjoyed the social life of the downtown campus and the Sigma Alpha Mu fraternity, with its Jewish orientation, but he also took on plenty of part-time jobs. He worked at the car wash at the northeast corner of Bathurst Street and St. Clair Avenue. He sorted Christmas mail at the Front Street post office. Anything to make a much-needed dollar, for his own needs and to send to his mother in Budapest. His first entrepreneurial activity in Canada took place in Uncle Nick and Aunt Hedy's front yard. Peter was sure he could make a success of a small Christmas-tree business during the 1949 season. "Uncle Nick reluctantly loaned me $250. I bought wholesale trees and sold them from the front yard—and made good money."

Peter already had the successful businessman's instinct to expand.

The next year he got permission to use the corner of the parking lot of the Dominion store just to the east of Bathurst on St. Clair. Once again, he was successful. He teamed up with a fraternity brother, Gerry Heifetz, a law student. The next year they planned to hire more of their friends from school and operate ten or twelve lots. Heifetz and Munk incorporated under the name Student Co-op Sales Limited. "We had an office, my first, at 107 King Street East," Munk recalls. "We even had stationery."

Munk and Heifetz bought Christmas trees in the Penetang area in summer and then, in season, hauled them down to several Dominion Store lots. Munk had $1,700 of borrowed money invested in trees, ready for the big Christmas season.

Then a huge snowstorm hit Toronto. It was catastrophic.

Nobody showed up to buy trees; they were left covered with snow. All of those costly trees were worthless. That was my third year in the Christmas-tree business and I just barely made it. But I repaid the loan.

In the spring of 1952 Peter passed his final examinations in electrical engineering, and the chancellor of the University of Toronto bestowed upon him the degree of Bachelor of Science. The twenty-five-year-old immigrant from Budapest—via Bergen-Belsen, Basel and Zurich—was now an engineer.

It was time for Peter Munk, B.A.Sc., P.Eng., to begin his professional career. But in Hungary or Switzerland?—or would he stay in rapidly changing Canada?

CHAPTER FIVE

THE BIRTH OF CLAIRTONE

With graduation behind him, Peter Munk quickly found a job at Canadian National Telegraph's Bay Street, Toronto, office, making drawings for the installation of new telegraph lines and the upgrading of old ones. It was a nine-to-five job at about $100 a week, a good salary for the time. But Munk found the work tedious. After a few months he was looking for something more interesting.

When a family connection mentioned Atlas Radio, Munk realized it might be the next rung of the ladder. Atlas was owned by D. Lou Harris, a good friend of Peter's uncle Nick; the firm was in the business of distributing imported antennae, speakers, hi-fi and electronic components. Lou Harris hired Peter Munk as his assistant chief engineer, and before long he was putting together his CNE sound experience and his access to parts at Atlas. The quality of sound recording and reproduction was improving quickly in those years, and demand for hi-fi sets was increasing. Peter was soon telling his friends, "Don't go to somebody's store. I'll do it for you 'custom-made.'" As an Atlas employee, he had the right to buy components at cost, so customers could come to him, rather than going to some retail shop on Bloor Street. "I would give them a quotation," he recalls, "then put together the amplifier, tuner, speaker, and record player, and there it would be: what was eventually known as a Peter Munk hi-fi set."

When Lou Harris saw how successful Peter's hi-fi sets were, he encouraged the young engineer to become a master assembler of components. Peter would find the right components at the right price, and assemble them, hiding the electronic works in attractive wood cabinets, and adding doors, legs and dials. The sets would be sold as products of Atlas Radio Corporation, not of the man who had designed, engineered and put them together, but Munk was happy at Atlas. He was building his sound equipment techniques and his hi-fi knowledge by hands-on experience.

It was in this 1952–53 period that Peter Munk and a compatible group of young men and women started to gather for parties, travel, skiing, tennis and the fun of high-powered, idea-rattling discussions. It was a happy group made up of Rosedale types, such as Shelagh Van Sittart, George Huvos and Gerry Heifetz, and persuasive new arrivals like Munk. The gang would meet every weekend at someone's house or a drinking hole and have a grand time together.

Huge parties were organized at Number 72 Roxborough Street East, a soon-to-be demolished seven-bedroom mansion that Gerry Heifetz had found. He made a deal to rent the place dirt cheap until the wrecker's ball arrived a year later. Some of the team, including Munk and Heifetz, moved in. There were other young swingers frequently about—such as Zoltan de Tariczky, Joe Feller, George Thiery, Dave Crysdale, Des Bouge, Joe O'Brien and George Feyer. Among Peter Munk's many new acquaintances was David Gilmour, an elegant young man he met in 1952 at the Diana Sweets restaurant on Bloor Street, a University of Toronto students' hangout. Munk and Gilmour were total opposites in every way, yet they took an immediate liking to each other, and their friendship would later become one of the closest, most lasting, and most compatible partnerships in Canadian business history. The man who introduced them was George Huvos, a professional photographer and fast-moving man about town, who worked at the CBC.

David Gilmour, tall, pencil-thin, fit, handsome of face and always impeccable in dress and bearing, was twenty-one in 1952. He was the only son of Adam Harrison Gilmour, a veteran officer of the First World War. David himself, after attending Trinity College School in Port Hope, had been a postwar lieutenant in the Governor General's Horse Guards, the élite military regiment. He now was in his first year at the University of Toronto as a student in institutional management. His bachelor apartment, close to Varsity Stadium, put him at the geographical centre of the U of T's social whirl, and only a few steps from Diana Sweets. Though very young, he was already familiar with the sophisticated life of London and other European centres. He also had advantages slightly beyond the norm of those days: skiing, horsemanship, tennis and sports cars. Gilmour soon became part of the social circle of parties and dancing of which Peter Munk was one of the leaders.

Alas, the wrecker's ball eventually did arrive at 72 Roxborough. But by then Peter Munk had met a highly intelligent, bright-eyed beauty named Linda Gutterson. Peter was falling in love, and he was also happily aware that Linda's father, Bill Gutterson, was a wealthy pharmaceutical entrepreneur. This was a connection that the Munk family would approve. Gutterson himself took an immediate shine to this dynamic young Hungarian, from an old and respected Jewish family, who was courting his daughter.

As Peter became more seriously involved with Linda he was careful to keep his mother, Katharina, fully informed in frequent letters. Katharina had moved from Budapest to Paris, where she was living with her new husband, Dr. Tibor Abranyi, for whom Peter had the highest affection and regard. (In later years Dr. Abranyi would devote himself to administering the complicated and considerable financial affairs of his stepson, Peter Munk.)

The marriage of Peter Munk and Linda Joy Gutterson took place on Monday, September 3, 1956, at twelve o'clock at Holy Blossom Temple, with a reception afterwards at the Banquet Hall of the Royal York Hotel. The best man was Gerald Heifetz. Among the ushers were

Peter's cousin John Merey, who had been on the Kasztner Transport, and his old friend, Steven Friedlich.

To the groom's delight, his mother had flown in from Paris to be at his wedding.

> Linda's father, Bill Gutterson, was very generous. I had no money, and my mother and her husband couldn't afford to come to Canada for the wedding. So Mr. Gutterson paid for my mother to come to the wedding and bought her a fancy French gown. That's the kind of man Gutterson was and is.

Peter's father, Louis, and his wife—by then resident in Canada—were also among the five hundred guests who drank toasts and enjoyed the speeches and the celebrations at the Royal York.

Impoverished or not, Peter Munk cut a fine figure in his white-vested morning suit and formal striped grey trousers. And Linda was radiant in a gown and Mary Stewart headdress of handmade Calais lace that her father had brought from Paris. For Peter, who had lived the happy-go-lucky life of a young bachelor ever since his arrival in Canada eight years before, the magnificent wedding and his marriage into the Gutterson family marked a critical turning point.

> Gutterson was one of the first Americans to attend the London School of Economics. He and his father and brother made fortunes in the late 1920s stock market boom. He remembers flying over to London, and throwing parties in the Waldorf Astoria in New York. Later he lost much of his fortune in the crash of '29 but he still walked away with a million dollars. He bought Webber Pharmaceuticals in Canada, who specialized in vitamin E. His was a different mentality from the Munks'. The Guttersons were in love with the idea that the Munks were an old family, even though we had no money. At the wedding the rabbi made a speech about the

Munk genealogy, how we were one of the oldest and most prestigious Jewish families in Europe, and what an honour it was to know us and all that. It made the Guttersons feel good. The rabbi didn't mention that we were refugees—why should he? Everyone there knew it.

Not long after, when the bride and groom came home from their honeymoon, Bill Gutterson sat Peter down in the library and gave his son-in-law some fatherly advice. He recognized that Peter Munk, with his entrepreneurial approach, should not be working for someone else. He should be out of Atlas and in his own business.

"You know hi-fi," he told me. "You could make a good hi-fi set. You could make excellent money." And I said, "What do you expect me to say? I'm not exactly Atlas Radio. I don't have capital." "What kind of capital would you need?" he asked. "A smart guy like you could figure that out. Just think, everybody's building new homes. Everybody wants a custom-made hi-fi set. Why don't you try it?" I told Linda about it on the way home. It certainly appealed to me.

I needed about six thousand bucks. When I went back and told Bill Gutterson, he just got up, moved a painting from the wall, opened his safe and took out a bundle of cash. My eyes popped! And he said, "You need six thousand dollars? Here is three. The condition is that you get the other three from your father and your uncle."

Peter Munk talked to his uncle Nick, but he was reluctant, partly because Peter still owed money he had borrowed for an engagement ring. But Louis and Nick could not lose face; they had to match Bill Gutterson's offer, and finally they came through. The start-up money—*big* money, so far as Peter Munk was concerned—was committed.

He talked first with the kindly owner of Atlas Radio, Lou Harris, who agreed to extend credit on easy terms. Peter Munk Associates Limited would be a new customer, and Peter, after all, *was* a Munk.

Other plans soon fell into place as Peter made deals for component parts assembly, for sales, legal advice, and factory space. On January 17, 1957, the newborn corporation was in business, with a factory and showroom at 26 Sable Street, Toronto.

At this critical moment Peter Munk made a marketing decision that was clearly characteristic of the way he would do business forever after. He put some eight hundred precious dollars into advertising: a brochure and letter campaign, and in February, Peter Munk Associates Ltd. sent letters to carefully selected potential customers, inviting them to read the splendid company brochure for the "Custom Built Peter Munk High Fidelity Sound System" with "Eugene Ormandy conducting."

An observer might recognize a major flaw in the Pro Forma Opening Balance Sheet of the Munk corporation: the complete lack of working capital. The balance sheet was prepared by a man who was then recognized as among the top entrepreneurial chartered accountants, David Perlmutter.

The balance sheet of the company six months later showed what Peter Munk, with the assistance of his bride, Linda, had done with the money advanced to him by Bill Gutterson, and Louis and Nick Munk. The net profit for the period, from start-up, was $875.64. Not bad at all. And the management salary was $750 for the entire period. Linda and Peter were living on not much more than love!

Peter Munk Associates Ltd. flourished from the moment of start-up. Munk struck a deal with Slavic Brudnitsky of Design Trends in Scarborough, who manufactured custom kitchens. His company could make more cabinets than they could sell. Whenever Munk sold a hi-fi set, Design Trends would make the cabinet to Munk's customers' specifications. Brudnitsky had a small store on Balmuto Street near Creed's, and he put one of Munk's specially designed hi-fi sets on display there. Peter was delighted. Being that close to Creed's and Holt Renfrew on Bloor was "like being close to God," he said.

The next move, again encouraged by Bill Gutterson, was to obtain the exclusive Canadian rights to the best-quality speakers for the hi-fi sets. Munk arranged to import Duode speakers from England and make money on the deal as both importer and wholesaler.

The first employee at the offices of Peter Munk Associates Ltd. was Helen Campbell, a young woman who was everything—secretary, receptionist, bookkeeper, whatever was needed. The next employee was a youth who had just immigrated from Poland, Michael Choynacki. He eventually became Munk's vice-president of production, a post he would hold until the day—ten years later—when Peter Munk left the sound manufacturing business forever.

Meanwhile, Munk was mining new business through his friends, among them the top-flight architects of the day, John Parkin, Harry Kohl, Jim Crang and George Boake, to name just a few. They all had well-to-do clients for whom Peter Munk was the right source of high-quality, custom-made high-fidelity sound systems.

Munk's reputation and that of his hi-fi sets grew quickly, and his business expanded. But he was still short of cash. Then along came David Gilmour, Munk says, "with a fancy idea."

It was in the spring of 1958, and Gilmour had just come back from Scandinavia with a beautiful, long, low teakwood cabinet for his sister Shelagh Van Sittart's shop on Bloor Street.

David asked me to fit out the cabinet with a hi-fi system. "We'll take a chance," he said. "We'll put it in the window."

It was a new concept. Up till then I had always gone to the prospect's house or office. I gave them a quotation and we negotiated; they gave me a deposit; and I produced and installed it. David was asking me to build a hi-fi on spec and he would sell it in a retail shop. He supplied the cabinet; I supplied the hi-fi parts. When it sold Shelagh got her 30 percent retailer's mark-up, he got repaid for the cabinet, I got repaid for the cost of components and we shared the profit. I designed a set with sliding doors and damask cloth. We called it the "S100" and sold it in a week for $700. That was a big price. Volkswagens were selling then for a couple of thousand.

We decided to give the company a name. We were sitting in my father-in-law's library, David and I, with our wives and my father-in-law, and David kept saying, "Call the company Peter Munk. Everybody knows the Peter Munk custom set." I said, "What if something goes wrong? I'm not going to ruin my name! I have a very good business here in Peter Munk Associates. I'm not going to go for $700 when I can get $1,000 or $2,000 per throw. It just cheapens my product. Why don't we call it David Gilmour?" After an all-day session we came up with Clairtone, and on June 9, 1958, Gilmour and I signed an agreement to incorporate Clairetone—yes, it did have an 'e' after the 'r.'

The agreement the two signed that day was, in effect, a partnership agreement, the foundation and cornerstone of the close relationship that Munk and Gilmour have enjoyed and in which both have flourished. That memorandum, perhaps the most important document Munk has signed, was never again read or relied on through the more than forty years of their partnership.

So what did Peter Munk do next? The unexpected: he and Linda left immediately for a three-month tour of the Soviet Union, sponsored by the National Federation of Canadian University Students (NFCUS). The cost, for the two of them, was $1,700; the package included tour guides, lectures and visits to factories and the historic cities of Leningrad and Moscow. It would be a chance to see the "Soviet miracle" at first hand.

CHAPTER SIX

TURNING POINTS

The Peter Munk who flew to Helsinki, Finland, in June 1958 was an idealistic thirty-one-year-old who, like many young people of the day, was "a little bit left-wing." His mind was filled with glorious images of Communism and its achievements for the people of the Soviet Union. Furthermore, the Soviets were heroes who had saved his mother's life and helped to defeat Hitler.

Many other people in the Munks' social group had equally strong socialist beliefs. Even though their lifestyle included many of the privileges of the upper echelons of a capitalist society, their consciences owed much to socialistic ideas. Munk had never been to the Soviet Union or any other "Socialist" country; his views were shaped by books and talk about the idyllic state of Communism. He believed that the Soviets had the right idea—as a young man who considered himself to be a decent soul, he believed everybody in the world should have an equal chance, and that wealth should be distributed in accordance with need, not achievement or talent.

As soon as the train from Helsinki to Leningrad crossed the border into the Soviet Union it was stopped, as it always was, by armed Soviet troops, and Linda and Peter had their first run-in with real Soviet authority.

Gunther's *Inside Russia* had come out that summer and I had a copy with me. The dust jacket was yellow, with a big Russian star. And these Russians came in in their uniforms, and one of them picked up the book. Ten minutes later four more guys came by and hauled me off the train. They took the book away from me! I said, "You can't take it away. I want to talk to my ambassador. It's my book—I paid for it!" That was how it started in Russia.

In those days you could only travel with a Soviet agent, they called them Interpol Guides, next to you. They told us what a paradise the country was and took us to villages set up for tourists. They always had a guide with us to act as interpreter and we could never get away. Then Walter Tarnopolsky [later a well-known Canadian judicial figure], our Canadian tour organizer, went to see his uncles in the Ukraine. They took him to see the real villagers who lived in mud huts. And they showed him all the places where their brothers had died of hunger and told them the real story of the Soviet Union.

Peter and some others wanted to get away from the guides and see what was really going on. He told the guide that he had to go to his synagogue, and another of the group said he had to go to a Catholic church; others were Protestant or Russian Orthodox. On four or five occasions they all disappeared suddenly, each saying that he or she had the address of a church or a synagogue.

All of our people came back with stories that showed how frightened the Russians were, how downtrodden. I felt morally torn, because my mother's life was saved by Russian soldiers who sacrificed their lives to defeat the Nazis. And now they were the liars and oppressors.

Exposure to the reality of life in the Soviet Union overturned

Munk's naive belief in the socialist system and Communism. His disillusionment was painful but complete, so complete that he contemplated going to university campuses across Canada to preach about what he had seen. He didn't take that step, but Linda did write a series of articles for the *Globe and Mail* about their experiences. Their unique window on Soviet life was newsworthy, and Linda's writing provided some much-needed cash flow.

Back at Peter Munk and Associates Ltd., three people whom Peter trusted completely had been minding the store: Michael Choynacki, Helen Campbell and an aggressive young salesman, Leslie Berenyi. And David Gilmour had been busy. Munk was amazed at the progress they had made in his absence. Gilmour recalls:

> Before Peter went we'd made three sets. We rented a suite in
> the Park Plaza and showed these units to the dealers: the
> Simpson company, Eaton's, Bay-Bloor Radio, and others.
> They were favourably impressed with the product, so I bit the
> bullet and ordered our first fifty sets. Peter was slightly
> stunned when he got back and saw the commitment I'd made,
> but fortunately we sold them.

In September two new sound systems, one a high-fidelity set and the other a stereophonic hi-fi, both with Scandinavian cabinets and superb engineering, were ready for marketing. Again the partners took a room at the Park Plaza, brought in their two new models and invited buyers. Then Munk and Gilmour strapped their best set onto the top of Gilmour's father's Packard and drove it to Montreal, where they repeated their in-hotel demonstration.

The demonstrations were resoundingly successful. Orders were received from 103 buyers. Then Granco Products Inc., a major U.S. producer and distributor of FM radio and stereo sets—a parts supplier to Clairtone—asked to have a model flown down to New York.

Granco liked what it saw and placed a large opening order for its 2,000 dealers in 32 states.

The sudden demand was enormous. So was the need for more capital. At Clairtone's cramped, 2,800-square-foot Sable Street shop, employees, many of them newly arrived from Hungary, worked in three shifts, twenty-four hours a day. In the first year of operation, which ended on August 31, 1959, sales were $311,068, with a not surprising net loss of $8,759. Some 1,200 Clairtone sets, an astonishing number, were sold in that first year.

But it was the 1959 First Prize award by the National Industrial Design Council that really kicked off what was to be an escalating frenzy of complimentary articles and columns about the skyrocketing success of Munk, Gilmour and their Clairtone Sound Corporation Ltd., soon known simply as Clairtone. Shortly after the award was announced, the main judge, Alan Jarvis, wrote in his "The Things We See" newspaper column in the Toronto *Telegram*:

> It is immensely gratifying to be able to tell the story of these
> young men's success for it bears out all that the experts have
> been preaching about industrial design in Canada for years: that
> good design can mean good business and that design must be a
> vital factor in any attempt to increase Canada's export trade.

The young partners and Clairtone had arrived. Sales were escalating. Money was flowing in, in large bundles. But it was also running out, in even bigger bundles.

One Friday in February 1960 a representative of the Federal Collector of Sales and Excise Tax called Munk and demanded $27,000 in overdue sales taxes. He wanted it by Monday, or else, and he told Munk: "This is our money you've collected—or should have—in cash. So you pay us by Monday or I'll shut you down. I'll send the bailiff."

Munk promised to pay, but he was at his wit's end. He realized that if his volume kept on growing, he would have another big payment to make in about thirty days, and the taxman would be at his door again. How could he find that kind of money on short notice? The bank turned him down flat. Clairtone was already well over its credit limit. Next Munk got on the phone to his buyers at Simpson's and Eaton's. He told them the tax man was going to shut him down. Could they order enough sets for future delivery but pay him now? About thirty sets between them would be enough.

The buyers understood perfectly. They were making good profits on their Clairtone sales and didn't want the little company to fail. They placed their orders and wrote their cheques. Munk and Gilmour's Clairtone was saved—but for only the briefest of moments.

The lack of capital and sufficient equity still threatened to destroy their embryonic company. It was the penalty for their enormous quick success. Gilmour recalls:

> We were a victim of our own success in the initial days. The more orders we got, the more inventory we had to create, the more credit we had to provide for our dealers, and the more capital it required. The banks were reluctant to help us because we were small and unknown, and we were a start-up situation. I have to quote a famous banker once at one of our first interviews when Peter and I went down, hat in hand, to ask for fifty or a hundred thousand. The manager at the main branch looked at our cash flow forecasts and said, "Well, gentlemen" … he was an Englishman … "I say, there's always a chance for a slip between cup and lip," and he turned us down. Peter and I were joined at the hip at that point, and financing was a job for both of us to do. So when we couldn't get the bank financing to tide us over, I put a mortgage on my house, which provided most of the capital—$40,000.

The mortgage went on the house without Gilmour consulting Munk or asking for any covenant from him. As Munk recalls,

Gilmour walked into the office and dropped the $40,000 cheque on his desk. Gilmour recognized that Munk had "legally no risk, but the partnership was based on trust." That's the way it was then between Gilmour and Munk and the way it has been since.

Another thing that hasn't changed is Gilmour's admiration for Munk. He says:

> What first attracted me to Peter was his focus. He was a very, very focused man, which is unusual in an entrepreneur. Usually, they're all over the place, but here was a man whose mind was crystal clear. He was wonderful to work with because of his natural enthusiasm, and in intellect he was superior to anybody I'd ever met. Peter is blessed with both the mind of an engineer and the heart of a great entrepreneur. A very unusual combination.

In 1959, the capital crunch was continuing unabated, notwithstanding Gilmour's mortgage. The intense pressure was getting to Munk. His friend Erwin Schaeffer—by then a resident of Montreal—recounts:

> Every time there was a serious crisis Peter would phone at one or two o'clock in the morning, and we'd talk for an hour. I didn't tell him what to do because I didn't know anything about the electronics business. But I said, "Look, there is simply no way that you have to lose this if you tackle it the right way. You have to find somebody who can help you financially."

Munk listened to Schaeffer very carefully. Schaeffer goes on:

> A couple of months later I learned, from the newspaper like everybody else, that Clairtone was going public. The rest is history. From there on it was up, up, up.

CHAPTER SEVEN

"AMAZING" GROWTH

unk and Gilmour decided they had no choice but to attempt to approach the Bay Street investment houses. Gilmour's name as the son of the late Harrison Gilmour, a director of Nesbitt Thomson, was a door-opener but not a deal-maker. There was no interest in financing Clairtone, a new company with a short track record.

Enter Gilmour's accountant, Zigmund "Ziggy" Hahn. At a party at Shelagh's—one of the few that Munk and Gilmour had missed—Hahn cornered Irving Gould, a successful stock promoter and financier, a man with cash. Hahn gave Gould such a good sales pitch on Clairtone that Gould decided he'd like to explore the idea seriously.

Hahn called Munk and Gilmour on a Saturday night. The next morning the partners and Hahn met their prospective investor for the first time at Gould's fancy new apartment on Bathurst north of Eglinton. "We needed $80,000," Munk remembers, "but we thought we might as well go for $250,000. He said, 'You sign this piece of paper. You give me 45 percent of the company and by the end of the week, I'll get you a quarter of a million dollars.'"

Munk, the negotiator, told Gould that 45 percent was too much. The disheartened partners left Gould's apartment without a deal.

But the next morning, Monday, Gould telephoned them. He had

lined up interest on the part of a small brokerage firm, MacNames &
Company. Munk and Gilmour were at the MacNames offices at 2:30
that day. By the close of business the following day they had an executed letter of intent in their hands. MacNames agreed to underwrite
116,000 shares of Clairtone for slightly less than $250,000 and take
the company "public."

It was double celebration time for Peter Munk. The deal was
closed and the shares went on sale to the public on April 16, 1960,
the day after his son, Anthony, was born. There was a beautiful new
baby in the proud Munk family, and money in Peter's bank and
Clairtone's till. At that euphoric moment Munk and Gilmour
thought they had the working-capital dragon slain forever. The conclusion of the official Clairtone prospectus paints a picture of a gold-
en Clairtone future, with "high quality Canadian made, designed,
and engineered products" selling in the domestic market and all
over the world.

And a fact of interest to every potential purchaser of Clairtone
shares was that the profits looked equally promising. Clairtone's after-
tax net profit from the seven months of September 1959 through
March 1960 was $49,756. At March 31, 1960, total assets were
$535,785 against current liabilities of $205,584. There was no funded debt. Not surprisingly, Clairtone shares were soon trading at $4,
making Munk's and Gilmour's personal paper stake in the company
worth almost a cool million.

In 1960 Peter Munk was finally ready to repay the money he had
received from Bill Gutterson and his father and uncle.

> I was so proud. I had my father come over to Uncle Nick's
> house and I gave him a cheque for the whole amount, includ-
> ing interest. Uncle Nick kissed me and said, "Congratulations.
> It's a wonderful thing and I'm so proud of you." As I was
> walking my father home, he turned to me and said, "You
> know, you haven't given Uncle Nick enough interest. You've

given him normal bank interest, but the risk associated with giving you money was not exactly the kind of interest which banks charge. So, it's up to you, Peter. But if you want to act honourably, then you must repay the full amount. Full amount means including the interest, considering the risk which would have affected an interest rate."

I had borrowed the money from them at five percent. And I had done the calculations. So I gave him back his money at five percent. And Father didn't like it that the interest rate was not nine percent. So, that's how the Munks were, and, thank God, that's how I was brought up!

Sales were increasing not only in Canada, but also in the American market. The Granco connection that the partners had made in 1958 was paying off handsomely. Some seven hundred Clairtone sets had been sold in the United States in the year before the company went public. The partners knew they weren't being sold just in New York or Los Angeles because the warranty cards enclosed in each set were being mailed to Toronto from cities, towns and villages all across the United States. The size and speed of Clairtone's development in the U.S. market astonished both the partners. They had been conditioned to believe that it was impossible to crack the American marketplace from Canada with an all-Canadian designed and manufactured "high-tech" product. This was especially thought to be the case in the consumer electronics field, which was so totally dominated by the U.S.-based majors, such as Admiral, Zenith, RCA and Magnavox.

Munk and Gilmour decided that what was needed now was an attention-grabbing, but prestige-enhancing advertising campaign backstopped by public relations opportunities, such as speeches to influential audiences. After hearing presentations from a number of advertising and public relations firms, they retained the services of Dalton Camp & Associates, but in particular the direct involvement of Dalton Kingsley Camp himself. According to David Gilmour, when we met Camp, he left an indelible impression, because he was a thinking man. He stepped right outside the square by producing a presentation that was unique for its time. Advertising to that point in Canada had always packed as many words and different typefaces as possible into a square inch. Instead Camp made tremendous use of white space.

Dalton Camp's advertising campaign started in the *Globe and Mail* on Monday, April 4, 1960 (before the MacNames deal was done and Clairtone shares began trading), and in the Toronto *Telegram* on Monday, September 19. The ads were all full page and always on page 3. The April 4 *Globe and Mail* advertisement was a photograph of the two partners in their tailored suits, casually talking with each other, and in eye-catching large print the opening words: "April 4: A MOST REMARKABLE CANADIAN SUCCESS STORY—have you heard?"

The September 19 *Telegram* full-page ad again featured a photograph of Munk and Gilmour opposite the boldface heading: "INTERNATIONAL TRIUMPH—(CONT'D)"; while the third ad in the series (*Globe and Mail*, October 19) was headlined at the top of the white space this way: "*AT HOME AND ABROAD* CANADA'S most successful sound." Below those words was a picture of Munk casually leaning against a chair occupied by an attentive Gilmour, who was apparently listening to every word with care.

Camp had recognized that Munk and Gilmour were a pair of charismatic characters. Their outgoing personalities could be sold as the identity marks of Clairtone, much like a trademark. It was a personalized campaign that RCA, GE, Admiral and the other Clairtone competitors could not match. Peter Munk, never a shrinking violet, was and still is always prepared to nurture his public persona. David Gilmour was equally outgoing but more shaded, and not quite so forceful. He was always ready to let Munk take the stage or the podium as the more visible player of two equal, multi-talented partners.

Through all this frenzy of growth and activity, the European influence and presence at Clairtone continued to increase. Munk saw to that.

Through a cousin of mine, we hired a bunch of guys from Hungary who had worked in some electronic factory and who were all part of the '56 exodus. Once we went to a trade show at a hotel in Houston with six or eight Hungarian guys in three Clairtone trucks. The unions from Chicago wanted to stop us unloading and setting up our displays on the weekend. These American union guys came out and said, "You're not supposed to move products. That job belongs to one of our state unions." And the lead guy, Bertie Hahn, said, "You just try and stop us." The Hungarian guys were water polo players, all at least six feet tall. No one was going to get in their way, either Saturday or Sunday. We were the only stereo and hi-fi display in the whole weekend trade show.

Those guys would die for Canada. They hated Hungary. They hated Russia. In Canada they had a job, they had profit sharing, they had stock options. And we all made money. It was a fantastic time!

Indeed, in the summer of 1960 sales were moving so fast in the United States that Munk and Gilmour began to discuss the need for a hands-on presence in New York, to take advantage of its ready air access to other American cities. Munk wanted to stay in Canada, his adopted nation. Also, he was in charge of the engineering and manufacturing divisions, both situated in Toronto. They agreed that when the time to move arrived it would be better for Gilmour to go to New York and represent Clairtone in the bright lights and the high society. After all, the U.S. job was all about sales and marketing—Gilmour's specialities.

Offices were quickly established in New York (on Fifth Avenue),

Los Angeles, Chicago, and San Francisco, with David Gilmour at the helm even though he was still based in Toronto. Clairtone ads appeared in late fall editions of *Time* magazine, proudly announcing the new offices.

The next year, 1961, was also a stunning success. And that meant that Clairtone needed a further infusion of capital. In June 1961, Clairtone sold 60,000 shares at C$9 per share to S.J. Brooks & Company of Toronto (on behalf of Armac Securities Ltd. as underwriter); C$540,000 was raised.

In 1961 Clairtone made its first acquisition, a furniture manufacturer, Strathroy Industries Ltd. and its subsidiary, to ensure an ongoing supply of cabinets that met Clairtone's high standards. And it also opened the door for Clairtone to make cabinets for American buyers.

Meanwhile Dalton Camp was putting together a new campaign that involved Frank Sinatra, Oscar Peterson and a host of Hollywood stars, all listening to Clairtone. Munk recalls the people and coincidences involved in the campaign's development:

> Eric Smith, who had joined us from General Motors, introduced us to his best friend, Oscar Peterson. That's how we met Dizzy Gillespie and Sarah Vaughan and all those people in the pictures. Oscar knew them. And then Dalton Camp developed this campaign for us: "Listen to Sinatra on a Clairtone—Sinatra does!" "Listen to Peterson on a Clairtone—Peterson does!" And that won an American competition for the best advertising campaign.

The star-studded cast included not only Sinatra, Peterson, Gillespie and Vaughan but an impoverished young Scotsman who was about to become James Bond and one of the highest-paid and most-respected film actors of his time, Sean Connery.

Peter Munk concluded the extraordinary calendar year of 1961 by writing a letter to Clairtone's shareholders of record. Their progress, he reported, had been sensational. They had established offices in the United States. Clairtone's new consolidated assembly plant and head office in Etobicoke was almost completed, and merchandising rights had been secured for radio and phonograph products of the prestigious Max Braun Company of Frankfurt, Germany. In Canada, during its third complete operational year, Clairtone had captured over 20 percent of the market, and Munk was looking for a comparable penetration in the United States.

In his letter to Clairtone's shareholders, Peter Munk left the best news to the last:

> The truly dynamic growth of your company's market penetration can be best measured by the sales figures below:

1958	6 months	$99,000
1959	full year	$642,000
1960	full year	$1,626,000
1961	full year	$3,523,000
1962	estimated	$7,500,000

In his sign-off, the word Peter Munk used to describe the results he and Gilmour had achieved was *amazing*.

CHAPTER EIGHT

PROJECT G AND
THE U.S.A.

At the beginning of 1962, the new plant and head office referred to in Munk's letter to Clairtone shareholders was under construction at 100 Ronson Drive in Etobicoke, near what was then called the Toronto International Airport.

The spanking new building, at 40,000 square feet of working space, was the physical manifestation of the spectacular success that the young partners had achieved in Clairtone's brief existence. At its official opening on July 26, 1962, the federal trade minister, George Hees, shared the platform with another Conservative, the Honourable Robert Macaulay of the Ontario provincial cabinet. Both Hees and Macaulay would be co-opted by Munk to give Clairtone a helping hand. Hees's involvement started even as the ribbon was being cut.

Munk and Gilmour needed money to finance the deal. They owed their bank more than a million dollars. Dean Nesbitt of Nesbitt, Thomson, a major Montreal-based investment house, had agreed to do a Clairtone share and debenture under-writing but had just backed off. The markets had slipped badly since the spring.

Would George Hees help? Macaulay suggested an unheard-of approach: He suggested that Hees talk to the governor of the Bank of Canada. Maybe that high official could strong-arm Dean Nesbitt. With nothing to lose, Munk decided to ask Hees if he would do it.

Hees said he would try, and put in a call to Ottawa to the governor. In short order Munk went to Ottawa and J.H. Beatty, the senior deputy governor, heard his story. The very next day Munk was invited to lunch in the Nesbitt, Thomson boardroom in Montreal.

Thus it was that on September 1, 1962, the public was offered a million dollars in Clairtone debentures (a loan that can be traded on the stock exchange) that had warrants (the right to purchase shares). Nesbitt, Thomson and Osler, Hammond & Nanton were the successful underwriters. Once more Munk and Gilmour had gone to the brink of disaster, but turned bad luck into good, as would happen many times in the future. They were saved by their ability to find people who had the right connections and their talent for presenting their case with power and detail when offered the opportunity.

Munk's successes were making him known beyond the business community. In early 1962 he was appointed to the post of advisory member of the prestigious National Research Council in Ottawa. He was only thirty-four, the youngest appointee ever. He had suddenly become a much-sought-after public speaker. Not only was he the head of an enormously successful firm, he was also a compelling, articulate orator who spoke passionately about Canada, free trade and Clairtone.

In the summer of 1962, in a speech at the annual Couchiching Conference of the Canadian Institute of Public Affairs, Munk scolded the Canadian business community. Canada, he said, was a peaceful country committed to maintaining the status quo. "We assume that Canada must present a dull, uninteresting and undramatic picture of industrial transition. This, ladies and gentlemen, is not so." He went on to note that tremendous changes were taking place in Canada. With government incentives and with the help of people who were responsible and willing to take chances, Clairtone was developing a product image and tradition; it was also promoting people who had a knowledge of foreign trade and encouraging people with knowledge of foreign languages to go out and sell Clairtone products. By becoming more competitive Clairtone would become more design-conscious, and encourage the development of top-quality designers, top-quality engineers and independent thinkers who could influence and create a highly favourable international climate for Canada. He saw an opportunity to create a commercial equivalent of Marshall McLuhan's global village, a precursor to the North American Free Trade Agreement. He concluded his Couchiching talk with some strong words:

> We, the younger generation of Canadian industrialists, are unwilling to take no for an answer. We are absolutely committed and we know we are justified in believing that in the long run Canada will have a leading role in industrial trade and production.

Munk's next major speaking opportunity came when he was invited to be a panellist and speaker at the Manufacturing Opportunities Show and Conference, held at the Royal York Hotel on Monday, November 5, 1962. At the luncheon that day the young executive was delighted to be able to chat again with Bob Macaulay, who was still the minister of economics and development. Munk saw him as a brilliant person of considerable influence, whose friendship could be very helpful. He also talked at length with the new premier of Ontario, the affable, popular John Robarts, the principal luncheon speaker. In Robarts, Munk made another important connection.

The topic of Munk's speech also provides an insight into the aggressive young entrepreneur who was just three days away from his thirty-fifth birthday. Munk wasted no time in getting his audience's full attention: he told them that if they were going to compete as manufacturers they were going to have to get off their comfortable Canadian butts in the next five years, get over their Canadian inferiority complex, develop Canadian manufacturing and commercial talent, and become much more aggressive in world trade.

He made his case forcefully, because it was based on his strongly held convictions, and effectively, because he could point to the success of Clairtone's assault on the international market as evidence of its merit. The same strong words appeared in a feature article on Munk, Gilmour and Clairtone that the highly regarded American magazine *Business Week* had run earlier in the year. Entitled "Canadian Hi-fi Maker Cracks U.S. Market," the article was a snapshot of Clairtone's domestic and international successes as well as the youthful partners' techniques and expectations:

> In 1961 Clairtone had sold 3,000 stereo radio-phono units in the U.S., with a wholesale value of about $1.2 million. In 1962 it expected to sell 10,000 sets in the U.S., valued at about $4 million. Including U.S. sales, Clairtone had built up a 1961 sales volume of $3.65 million, a big jump from $1.2 million in 1960. Munk and Gilmour predict sales of $7.5 million for '62. With U.S. sales outstripping Canadian sales after this year, the partners were looking for $20 million by 1965.
>
> Munk and Gilmour are conscious of being handicapped by being a Canadian company. Their first effort to break into the U.S. market with a New York display of two models was pretty much a fizzle, though they picked up two or three good outlets.
>
> "That year was terribly rough," says Munk. "If we had been a German company, or Scandinavian or British or from practically anywhere except Canada, our sets would have been much better received. But when we told store buyers we were from Canada, they just stared at us. So far as people in the States are concerned, Canada means wheat, fish, and endless silent forests. Nobody thinks of us as highly skilled manufacturers."

Business Week was impressed by the aggressive pair's sales tech-

niques: they "go on the floor, coach the salesmen, actually sell to customers, talk about engineering, design, display." The article gave a
tremendous boost to the partners, their employees and, of course, sales
of Clairtone products in both Canada and the United States.

The 1962 sales record was not far off the target of $7.5 million
Munk and Gilmour had predicted for *Business Week*. The final tally
was sales of $6.7 million, with a net profit of $290,000. For a company that started in 1958, that track record was impressive. But as
far as Peter Munk was concerned, the markets for Clairtone products had barely been scratched, particularly in the U.S. and Europe.
It was time to focus.

Notwithstanding the increasing sales volumes, the American operation wasn't doing nearly as well or going as quickly as the partners
believed it should. The product was great. But something was wrong.
The partners decided that the problem was that they were trying to
run the U.S. operation (with market opportunities ten times the size
of Canada's) from Toronto.

They had had this conversation before. One of them had to run
the New York office. They couldn't both go. Peter, the engineer, had
to stay and run the manufacturing.

There was another element that influenced that decision. Peter
Munk's struggle to keep Clairtone in production and growing was
obsessive and all-consuming—so much so that he had very little time
for his marriage and family life. For Linda, it became too much. There
were other, intensely personal reasons apart from business, but all of
them added up to Linda's decision to leave Peter and make a new life
for herself. She took Anthony with her and moved to Spain. Peter was
committed to Canada and to making money to support his family.

David Gilmour and his wife, Anna, moved to New York on July
1, 1963. Gilmour took with him an "assault force" of twelve men
from head office. Their task—to crack the American market wide
open, and do it fast.

The assault force also had new technological weaponry: the world's first totally transistorized (no tubes) stereo and hi-fi consoles. And, by the end of 1963, they had produced Clairtone's beyond-state-of-the-art revolutionary stereo called Project G. In early 1964 it would hit the market with a tremendous impact, making its debut at the National Furniture Show in Chicago.

Project G had spherical speakers at each end of a highly polished wooden cabinet. These speakers were rotatable, so that the sound could be projected through a complete 360-degree field. The innovative sound system was still remarkable in 1995, when it was featured in the *Pop in Orbit* exhibition at the Design Exchange in Toronto. The curator, Rachel Gotlieb, wrote:

> The Project G stereo embodies the paradigm of futurism. Designed in 1964 by Hugh Spencer of Toronto's Clairtone Sound Corporation, its rich rosewood cabinet and sensual, metallic globe speakers appear so "un-Canadian" that *Time* magazine proclaimed, "The unit comes not from Mars but from Canada."
>
> Why does this hi-fi look the way it does? Certainly it is a product of its time. The spherical speakers articulate a kind of utopian futurism, a vision that sprang from the space race on one hand and the sexual revolution on the other.

The future looked bright indeed. In 1963 Clairtone sales were $8.9 million, producing an after-tax net profit of $300,000. However, the pressure for new capital was growing with every sale of a Clairtone product.

CHAPTER NINE

NOVA SCOTIA BECKONS

arly in 1964, Peter Munk and David Gilmour decided that Clairtone was large enough to manufacture their own electronic assemblies rather than buy them from American and Canadian suppliers. The savings (converted into profits) would be substantial. And to complete the circle, increase efficiency and lower costs, both the cabinet-making and the electronic manufacturing should be carried out under the same roof.

The facilities of the Middlesex Furniture Company of Strathroy, Ontario, were antiquated and overtaxed. The fast-growing Clairtone Sound Corporation needed a brand new, under-one-roof factory that would manufacture and assemble every component of every model of hi-fi stereo. *That* would cost $4 to $5 million. Like an inescapable black cloud, the shortage of working capital accompanied every expansion they undertook. The ever-increasing current requirements would come in at about $3 million plus or minus. Munk and Gilmour were looking at a $7- to $8-million package.

How in heaven's name could they put together that kind of money? The partners knew the rule—if you are driven to expand by market demand, don't even think about it unless you are in possession of bags of capital—and it was painfully apparent that it applied to them. At that point they had neither capital nor any prospect of finding it.

Enter I.W. "Pat" Samuel, a remarkable New Zealander whose life would be interlinked with most of the partners' future fortunes and misfortunes. Pat Samuel had already gone through a kaleidoscopic set of remarkable careers. A teenage wartime fighter pilot in the Royal New Zealand Air Force, he had survived enormous dangers—including volunteering to parachute into Hong Kong a full day ahead of the cessation of hostilities, to deal with the Japanese for the release of Allied prisoners of war. Postwar, Samuel had been a professional pearl diver, a sailor who went solo to the Fijis and points beyond. Finally, he arrived broke in Los Angeles. A skilled horseman and polo player, he became a professional at that sport, hobnobbing with the movers and shakers of the southern California scene.

Ever on the move, Samuel then went north to Vancouver, where, in short order, he became sales manager for a distributor of the rugged Swedish-made Volvo automobile, then general manager of Volvo Canada, eventually persuading Sweden to put together a Volvo assembly plant in Canada—with the encouragement and financial support of the government of the Province of Nova Scotia. It was Pat Samuel who put together the deal with the provincial government and built the new assembly plant, the first non–U.S. car manufacturer to set up shop in North America. As a result of all these activities, Samuel had developed powerful Nova Scotia connections.

In the spring of 1964, Pat Samuel made the first move toward Clairtone. He had been watching the very public progress of Munk and Gilmour. The incentives that Nova Scotia might offer, Samuel thought, would be attractive to the young partners, neither of whom he had met. Samuel telephoned to invite Munk to lunch. The younger man knew about the enviable success of the man on the phone, but didn't know then about his varied and adventurous background.

Samuel and Munk got along famously. They met socially several times during the following months, and learned all about each other's accomplishments, ambitions, successes, failures and needs. Back in Nova Scotia, he started talking up the Clairtone Sound Corporation as a prospect that the Nova Scotia industrial development agency, Industrial Estates Limited (IEL), might consider going after.

The highly regarded premier of Nova Scotia, Robert Stanfield, had set up and mandated IEL as a vehicle to bring manufacturing jobs to Nova Scotia. In those days provincial government subsidies and tax holidays were a novel concept—but Nova Scotia needed jobs, and IEL was an effective agent to get them. Pat Samuel brought Clairtone, a company that had the potential to produce several hundred jobs, to IEL's attention.

The opening telephone call, which Samuel had alerted Gilmour in New York to expect, came on a Tuesday in late August 1964. It was from an IEL director, Colonel J.C. McKeen, who had travelled to New York for the express purpose of opening the Clairtone door. McKeen was at the Drake Hotel. Lieutenant Gilmour, recently of the Governor General's Horse Guards, was properly respectful of a senior colonel and agreed to meet McKeen in his Drake suite that afternoon for tea.

McKeen laid out what Nova Scotia had to offer to induce Gilmour and Munk to make the move. IEL would provide working capital and build a plant. The government would come up with tax concessions and training grants. Back in his office after the McKeen session, Gilmour telephoned Munk in Toronto to give him the almost-too-good-to-be true proposal.

In New York four days later, Munk and Gilmour met with an IEL team. The partners were impressed by the Nova Scotians' ability and professionalism. Among those present were Frank Sobey, the IEL president and the head of the family-owned Sobey's stores; Harold Egan, IEL's finance and detail man; and IEL's general manager, Bob Manuge, a highly enthusiastic seller of the attributes of Nova Scotia and the agency. The Nova Scotians also extolled the virtues of their premier, Robert Stanfield, and his vision for his province.

Negotiations proceeded well, but slowly. Munk and Gilmour were sold, in principle, on the move to Nova Scotia, but the logistics involved in such a major relocation of equipment and people were horrendous.

The first news of a firm agreement being signed was in the form of a letter to Clairtone shareholders dated November 16. In contrast to Munk's usual expansive tone, this one was tersely worded. It told stockholders that an agreement was in place, under which IEL would underwrite $7,945,000 of Clairtone bonds, and the proceeds would be used to replace 1962 Series A bonds, build new and additional manufacturing facilities, provide much-needed working capital, broaden the scope of the company, and develop new interests.

What the last statement, about "scope" and "new interests," referred to would soon be disclosed.

In addition to the money, Munk had secured a three-year federal tax holiday for Clairtone because the new plant would be in a "designated area"—in need of special economic assistance—plus a further two-year tax break by way of accelerated depreciation rates on the new plant and equipment. There were other boons: a million dollars for "settling-in" costs; a 30-percent subsidy for out-moving rail shipments; a million dollars in federal grants for employee moving costs and the training of the local workers for whose benefit Clairtone was being moved to Nova Scotia, and the contribution of a large tract owned by IEL at Stellarton, ninety miles from Halifax. For his part, Munk had committed Clairtone to creating at least a thousand new jobs in two years. Immediate construction work would inject at least $3 million in payrolls in the first year as the move was gearing up.

David Ekmekjian, a well-known Toronto investment dealer who had handled many personal matters for Peter Munk back in the early 1960s, received a telephone call from Munk at the time the deal with IEL was signed. Ekmekjian recalls telling Munk there were bound to be logistical problems with the move.

While the Nova Scotia negotiations went on, Munk and Gilmour's pace of business activity continued virtually non-stop. Sales went to $9.6 million, up from $8.9 million in 1963. The giant American firm,

Wurlitzer, agreed to take a seven-model line of Clairtone stereos with the Wurlitzer name on them. There was a joint-venture deal with Ditchburn, the U.K. firm, to manufacture Clairtone products under licence and supply Europe. Dube Electric S.A. of Zurich became distributors of Clairtone. And at the Milan Triennale, Project G won a design award.

During this critical September–November period of 1964, the partners were also dealing with another Pat Samuel concept: Fiji. Munk and Gilmour had vaguely heard about the remote, romantic island in the South Pacific, but the peripatetic Samuel knew it well. In fact, many years before, the New Zealander had optioned some Fiji land, with a hotel on it fronting on a wide sand beach. In the middle of the Clairtone–IEL negotiations, Munk and Gilmour had dinner with Samuel and Mac Hogarth of the wealthy Gooderham family, who was a friend and Clairtone executive and director. As Munk remembers:

> Samuel said to me that the future is not in the Atlantic, but in the Pacific. We all knew how much money the E.P. Taylors and Chesler had put into Nassau and Grand Bahama Island right across from Miami and down. Samuel said, "The big money in the next ten years will be made catering not to the Europeans and the Americans on the Atlantic Ocean but to the Japanese and the Chinese and the Malaysians on the other side, in the Pacific." Samuel wanted to get us involved in Fiji. He had extended his option on some land two or three times; he'd paid, maybe, a thousand dollars to those poor Fijians. Now it was expiring and Samuel said, "I don't have the money. But I have the option and I promise you guys that with what is going to happen in the Pacific, somebody's going to make a fortune. With $240,000 I can exercise my option and buy a little hotel. It has sixteen rooms and the beach, and I promise you, with a bit of luck, we can get more land there

as time goes on. But at least we control the beach. Without that the land is worth nothing."

Gilmour, Hogarth and Munk liked the concept, but Munk felt that if he had one extra ounce of energy left, he wanted to put it into Clairtone, not Fiji. He didn't want to make an investment that required input. But Fiji was ten thousand miles away, and they had never seen it, so Samuel was able to convince him that the project would not divert any of his attention.

Munk, Gilmour and Mac Hogarth liked the idea enough to go to the Bank of Commerce and sign a promissory note. They deposited their Clairtone shares as collateral, then sent a Canadian lawyer with Samuel to check out the title and close the deal. It was under the British legal system, because Fiji was a British colony. So, in 1964, they ended up owning a beach and hotel in Fiji, and owing $240,000 severally. Munk says, "So I owed $80,000. So did Hogarth and Gilmour. And then I totally forgot about Fiji. I promise you, I forgot it like I'd forgotten whether I own an extra blue shirt or not. I totally forgot it."

THE STUDEBAKER
CAPER

While Munk and Gilmour were negotiating with IEL and the government of Nova Scotia, the man who had introduced them to Fiji and to the Maritime capital money scene, Pat Samuel, was busily putting together another of his inventive entrepreneurial adventures. Samuel had analysed the North American automobile market and had come up with a plan. He would go after franchises that would give him total North American rights to assemble, distribute and sell Japanese and European automobiles. The then little-known Japanese manufacturers would be his prime targets. With franchises in hand, he would establish coast-to-coast dealer networks in both the United States and Canada.

After much cross-continent wheeling and dealing, Samuel found his financial backers in Western Canada. They were led by Frank McMahon, the Vancouver industrialist who was, among other things, chairman of Westcoast Transmission Company. Samuel then headed for Japan, a place he knew well. In one whirlwind three-week visit at the end of February 1964, he negotiated letters of intent for North American franchises for the largest Japanese auto maker, Toyota Motors, and the third largest, Isuzu. His next target was Europe, but, after a visit to the major auto manufacturers there, he decided to concentrate on the Japanese products. However, letters of intent are not franchise and operating agreements. Samuel needed to incorporate, then go to Japan to make final arrangements.

A federal charter dated May 6, 1964, created Canadian Motor Industries Limited (CMI) with five million common shares as authorized capital. The directors were Frank McMahon and his brother, George; Pat Samuel; J.W. Sharp; W. B. (Bill) Pattison; and none other than Robert Macaulay, Q.C., whose Toronto firm had done the incorporation. CMI approached IEL concerning the possibility of locating its plant in Nova Scotia. As expected, IEL was enthusiastic.

Next, Samuel and Macaulay headed off to Japan. On July 15, 1964, after days of excruciating negotiation, they signed a deal with Isuzu for its four-door Bellett sedan for the U.S. (except California), Canada, and the U.K. Then Samuel and Macaulay zeroed in on the big target, Toyota, whose major control was in the hands of Mitsui, the huge international trading company. After more agonizing negotiations Toyota agreed to let CMI have assembly and distribution rights for Canada, the Caribbean and the South Pacific. Furthermore, Mitsui stated it was prepared to negotiate to put $250,000 into CMI.

Back in Canada, Samuel received federal government indications of approval and support from Simon Reisman, then deputy minister of Ottawa's Department of Industry. CMI was all set to go with its freshly signed agreements and franchises, which would in a few years be worth about one billion dollars. But in late August, Frank McMahon told Samuel he could continue only if a new backer was found, to share the risk and bring in more expertise. Understandably, Samuel was shocked and disappointed. To whom could he turn? To the high-flying Peter Munk, his good friend, of course. He, of all people, would see the potential, the incredible opportunity.

With his colleague John Davidson, Pat Samuel talked to Munk at Samuel's Bloor Street offices in Toronto. Munk and Gilmour were immediately taken with the plan. At the outset, when control of CMI was dangled like a multicarat diamond in front of him, Munk had to reach for it. His partner, David Gilmour, was with Munk 100 percent.

All they needed, as usual, was money. A million dollars would do it, according to Samuel.

Munk and Gilmour, who by now were on the best of terms with Bob Stanfield and IEL, asked if IEL would put up another million on top of the $7 million already pledged in exchange for Clairtone bonds, if CMI's facilities were located in Nova Scotia. There would also be the condition that the McMahon group would have to leave their money in and be represented on the board of directors. Munk knew that Pacific Rim influence and involvement would be significant.

The McMahon people accepted, in an agreement completed in September 1964. IEL, with Stanfield's approval, put up the additional money. Clairtone paid $1,037,350 for 251,000 common shares and 19,500 preferred shares of CMI, all out of treasury, which gave Clairtone control of CMI at 50.2 percent. The McMahon-led group put in $500,000, including their previous money, to receive 166,489 common and 9,750 preferred shares. Mitsui made a prudent, watching-brief investment of $250,000. Four Clairtone directors—Munk, Gilmour, Hogarth and Samuel—went to the CMI board to take effective control.

All this activity went on without any leak or public disclosure— until November 5, 1964. On that day Pat Samuel presided over a CMI press conference in the ballroom of the splendid new Inn on the Park hotel in northeast Metro Toronto. The directors of the new company were on display, as were models of never-before-seen-in-North-America Japanese automobiles, made by Toyota and Isuzu, which CMI had the exclusive right to assemble and market.

On March 15, 1965, Pat Samuel held yet another press conference, this time in Halifax, to announce that CMI would construct an automobile plant at Point Edward, Nova Scotia, and in fifteen months begin production of Toyota automobiles, with a first-year target of ten thousand. Two hundred jobs would be created. Samuel mentioned the names of the directors, all of them important business people, and added "Peter Munk, president of Clairtone Sound Corporation, has already made his mark—with his colleagues, David Gilmour and G.M. Hogarth—on the economic life of the Maritimes, and on the hi-fi listening habits of the continent."

Munk and Gilmour's names were mentioned, but it was still not publicly known that Clairtone was in control of the new company. Their control of CMI and its $1 million financing by IEL were not made public until April 3, 1965, in the *Financial Post*. As a result of that disclosure, Peter Munk made elaborate preparations for the Clairtone annual meeting, scheduled for April 25 in Toronto. It was his responsibility to explain to the shareholders, and indeed to his bankers, the CIBC, the reasoning that had led him to mastermind the CMI acquisition. He also had to explain the benefits of moving the Clairtone operation, lock, stock and barrel, to Nova Scotia.

At that time Peter Munk saw no perils ahead; he believed that he could safely widen his Clairtone focus to embrace the complex demands of a completely different enterprise. In typically persuasive terms, Munk's annual report described an opportunity that had arisen in 1964 that gave Clairtone "a stake in an industry which traditionally captures the largest percentage of consumer spending, a company which will also be the only domestically owned producer of passenger and subsequently commercial vehicles in Canada."

Munk then described the uniquely valuable asset that CMI had acquired:

Canadian Motor Industries Limited is fortunate to have manufacturing rights and the exclusive distributing franchises of Toyota Motor Company, Japan's largest, and the Isuzu Motor Co., Japan's oldest and third-largest car manufacturer. These companies dominate some fifty per cent of Japan's automobile industry. Their growth rate is unmatched by any automobile producer in the Western world.

What Munk was not yet prepared to disclose to the Clairtone

shareholders was that he and Samuel were also in negotiations to buy Studebaker, which, though still one of the "Big Four" of North American automakers, was in deep trouble. The company was losing some $30 million each quarter. Its sales had shrunk so badly that management had moved their manufacturing operation from South Bend, Indiana, to Hamilton, Ontario. When that move was complete Studebaker stopped producing new models because of the cost. The next step to be considered was whether to shut down car production. Studebaker, however, had a legal liability to its eleven hundred dealers, and would have to pay them in the range of $40 million if the car production was cut off.

Why was CMI interested in buying Studebaker? Peter Munk explains:

> Samuel's and Macaulay's ploy was a brilliant idea that they cooked up with Gordon Grundy, Studebaker's president, before they took it down to the chairman of Studebaker in South Bend. They said, "We are going to take on that legal liability at no cost to you. So we are going to save you $40 million. But you, in turn, have to give us your assets—which were worth about $300 million—for $1 million."

The Studebaker people in South Bend liked the CMI idea, and by July 7 the basics of the proposal had been submitted to the Royal Bank and CIBC. The two banks stipulated that they would come to the table only if IEL was there as a party. Peter Munk then took the fourteen-page proposal and its twenty pages of financial analyses to Premier Stanfield on July 9. He received the required approval.

The plan was for the Studebaker cars to be produced in Hamilton while the Japanese vehicles would be put together in Nova Scotia. The manufacturing plant in Hamilton would be slowly phased out while the new range of small Japanese cars, with the Studebaker name and marque, was introduced to the Western world. In one move the

Japanese would get top distribution and service facilities throughout North America, and Studebaker would not have to invest in new models. The projected sales were, as might be expected, highly promising. In 1966 Studebaker would have sales of $44.6 million and CMI would come in at $15.6 million. Combined sales would produce a substantial profit.

All sorts of wild promotional schemes were considered to introduce the new small cars to the Studebaker dealers internationally:

> Samuel got as far as hiring the *Queen Elizabeth*—which, at that time, was the largest passenger ship—for that fall because by then the Japanese had produced the first six models in the new Studebaker line. Pat Samuel, who was president, was going to bring out to the *Queen Elizabeth* all of Studebaker's eleven hundred dealers from North America, plus the Europeans, at this display of these magnificent low-cost Japanese cars.

Finally, more conservative heads ruled and it was decided to bring the throng of dealers to the Green Briar Golf and Recreational Facility in Virginia—if, in fact, the Studebaker deal was to close.

By this time Peter Munk was focusing on plans to get Studebaker back on its feet.

> The Studebaker plan was the embodiment of the best that marketing, logic and common sense in business could put together to get the best reception for these unknown cars with funny names: the Japanese engines, the Japanese creative genius, the Canadian–U.S. auto trade agreement, the unused facilities, and enormous docking facilities in Nova Scotia, where hundreds of millions of dollars were invested but sat totally unused in Sydney harbour. An unparalleled, instant coast-to-coast distribution and warranty system was in place.

The Studebaker–CMI proposition was possibly the most brilliant business combination I had ever been exposed to in my life. Nothing, nothing was in size and scope any better.

Financing still had to be resolved. This would have to come from IEL. The amount it would have to produce in cash and guarantees would be double that originally anticipated. Samuel and Munk pitched Bob Stanfield himself for $5.5 million, which would have been a bargain price for Nova Scotia to gain access to the Studebaker network.

The Canadians were in South Bend for the last of the negotiating meetings on Thursday, August 12. Among those present were Peter Munk, Pat Samuel, Bob Macaulay and the Westerners Bill Pattison and John Davidson. Nova Scotia and IEL were represented by their lawyer, William Mingo, and Harold Egan. Finally everything was ready for the closing, including the 100-page-plus agreement that the lawyers had been working on. The signing of the agreement was set for 2 p.m. on Sunday in the boardroom of the opulent Studebaker headquarters.

On Saturday evening David Gilmour arrived direct from France with a thoroughly thought-out position on what Munk was about to sign. Peter Munk vividly recalls what happened next:

> Gilmour arrived at four or five o'clock in the afternoon, still on European time. I went over the whole deal with him because I had done all the negotiating and he wasn't that familiar with the whole thing. We talked in his hotel room, and he was exhausted and just wanted to take a nap, and then order dinner. I told him that everything had been done, and that we sign tomorrow. I said, "I hope you realize that this is perhaps the most important moment of our lives. To go from Clairtone, making a handful of hi-fi sets, in 1958, and now, in 1964, to be doing this Studebaker deal, that's not a bad six years!" David was very tired, very jet-lagged, and he said,

"Peter, I think that this is a brilliant move, but I just hope you understand what it means." I said, "Of course. It's going to make us the biggest industrialists in Canada, and eventually maybe in the world." And David replied, "And it's also going to make you the slave of every fourth-rate car dealer you have to suck up to when they're signing up an order for the next model—which I have done for six years of selling Clairtone sets. It's not my idea of a good way to spend the rest of my life. This CMI deal is not going to be easy. You thought it was tough going from dealer to dealer for Clairtone every single summer, signing for the new models, competing against Admiral and RCA and so on. Try doing it with car dealers ... Clairtone has only six hundred dealers; Studebaker has eleven hundred. So it ain't for me, Peter. I'm well off. Why should I waste my life? We're on top of the heap. I'm young, and there's no way I want to do this for the next five years. You've got my backing if you want to go through with it, but you're on your own, kid. It's your decision, but it's also your pain."

With that David pulled the covers up over him. He went to sleep, and I sat there by myself and I felt awful. And I decided David was right. The next morning we had a breakfast meeting. I went down and I told the guys that I didn't want to do the deal. I apologized to the Studebaker people. I told them it was entirely my fault. I just could not cope with the pension fund and other liabilities. I was very sorry, I had changed my mind. And we left that afternoon.

It was time for Peter Munk to refocus on Clairtone and its ongoing move to Stellarton, Nova Scotia. The Studebaker dream was over, but the steadfast, unique partnership of Peter Munk and David Gilmour was very much alive and well.

CHAPTER ELEVEN

OUT OF CLAIRTONE

Back in Nova Scotia, the deal between Clairtone and IEL was signed in November 1964. Peter Munk, as engineer, chairman, chief executive and administrator, had been working his heart out in Toronto, Halifax and Stellarton. Buildings had to be completed, equipment installed, new employees hired and trained, the Toronto workers and their families moved to Nova Scotia; through it all the banks and financial houses had to be kept happy.

One of the first orders of business was to set up a temporary plant at Stellarton, where electronic chassis would be manufactured. General Instruments' contract to build them was to expire in mid-1965; they wanted a five-year extension, but Munk wouldn't give it. Clairtone therefore had to get the temporary plant finished and the chassis in production before General's contract expired. By May 1965 production had started, with 100 employees in place.

At the beginning of June it was announced that construction would begin on the main Clairtone factory, to be built with 270,000 square feet of space at a forty-acre IEL industrial park site, also at Stellarton. The main plant construction got under way immediately after the announcement.

Sales in the fall of 1965 were first rate, bolstered by the excellent advertising series with the theme "Listen to Sinatra on Clairtone—

Sinatra Does." By the time Christmas 1965 arrived, however, more working capital was needed again. Munk negotiated $3 million from IEL, but the money came with two conditions.

The first condition was that IEL would not be asked to invest further in CMI. That term, which would eventually seal the doom of Clairtone's and Munk's control of CMI and the enormously valuable Toyota and Isuzu franchises. Munk had walked away from the Studebaker deal leaving major expenditures for legal and other costs on the table to be picked up by CMI. On the other hand, the $5-million-plus commitment that Stanfield had approved for CMI hadn't been used.

The second condition attached to the next $3 million IEL advance was that Clairtone must get into the production of colour television sets. Peter Munk has consistently said that he was always opposed to putting Clairtone into the manufacture and sale of colour TV sets, and that the only reason he went that route was that Harold Egan, IEL's financial manager, told him it was either colour TV and its jobs for Nova Scotians or no $3 million. Be that as it may, the decision was taken to enter the colour TV market. The urgently needed $3 million went to Clairtone.

In response to Harold Egan's condition when it was first broached in early November 1965, Munk and his technical team produced a fourteen-page business plan for the manufacture of colour TVs. Munk had done market research showing a demand for 170,000 colour TV sets in Canada in 1968 and 5.3 million that year in the U.S. He expected Clairtone would be able to get a profitable share of both markets. The company would require $2 million, $1.5 million in working capital and the rest for new manufacturing equipment. He finished off his business plan with words he knew Egan wanted to see before he would produce the $3 million:

Your support of this program would not only provide substantially increased employment in our Nova Scotia plant but would also form the basis for a strong and prosperous company which would more than justify the confidence you have placed in us to date.

The proposal satisfied Egan, but he stipulated that there had to be a new supplementary agreement. For the first time IEL would buy first preference shares, which were a purchase of equity, not a loan. The thin end of the wedge was being inserted by IEL into the Munk/Gilmour control of Clairtone. In early March 1966, IEL purchased 300,000 first preference shares with a par value of $10 per share. One million dollars of the proceeds would be applied against the bonds held by IEL maturing in 1966 and 1967, $450,000 was for TV manufacturing equipment, and $1.55 million was for working capital.

Another stipulation was that IEL was entitled to two of the seats on the board of directors. Frank Sobey and Harold Egan would fill those two positions. This new penetration of IEL into the corporate structure in exchange for further substantial advances was a clear indicator to Munk and Gilmour that Clairtone was trapped. The company was so deeply indebted to the government of Nova Scotia and IEL, and its equity was so involved, that it could no longer go to the public markets to raise money, or for that matter to the nation's banks. Nova Scotia was now Clairtone's exclusive source of funds, and they could be made available or withheld at the whim of a provincial cabinet minister or bureaucrat.

At the same time, Munk's struggle to keep Clairtone's control of CMI, with its enormously valuable Toyota and Isuzu franchises, was in the process of being lost. IEL had refused money to Clairtone for CMI purposes. However, there was an understanding that IEL would put in more money if Mitsui increased its investment.

Munk, Macaulay and Ziggy Hahn went to Tokyo and worked out a deal, but it was a deal that clearly demonstrated the strength of Mitsui against Clairtone's pathetic weakness. Mitsui would lend

$1 million to CMI against a promissory note due September 30, 1967. The note was convertible into 910,000 common and 20,000 preference shares of CMI. Clairtone's 19,500 preference shares of CMI would be cancelled. Mitsui would have full voting control to elect the entire board of directors. Mitsui would guarantee the repayment of Clairtone's $216,666 cash advances, but the $1 million invested by Clairtone in CMI shares was lost—written down to $1. If Mitsui converted its loan to shares (which it promptly did) Clairtone's control position went to Mitsui, with only 18 percent left with Clairtone.

The operative agreement was signed on March 31, 1966. The Japanese were in control. Pat Samuel resigned from CMI as president on July 27, 1966. He was gone, and CMI was out of Clairtone's hands.

But Pat Samuel was not out of Munk's life. Not by any means.

Nor was Linda Munk. She and Anthony were back under Peter's roof. As he put it "Things didn't work out well for her in Europe. She came back in 1966 and we were reunited in the summer. Then in 1967 Nina, our second child, was born."

Munk, having taken his Japanese bath, decided to make the June 21 opening of Clairtone's magnificent new Stellarton plant a public-relations spectacle. To do that he had to bring hundreds of people from all over the U.S. and Canada to Stellarton, ninety miles from Halifax. To Frank Sobey's horror, Peter Munk did two extravagant things. In May he bought for $115,000 a ten-passenger Lockheed Learstar aircraft, which immediately began daily "milk runs" from Stellarton to Toronto and New York. The Learstar and chartered planes would fly opening-day guests into Halifax and Stellarton.

But it was the cost of the special Clairtone train that really got Sobey's unhappy attention. It left Toronto packed with hundreds of special guests, dealers, dignitaries and celebrities destined for Nova Scotia. More passengers were picked up in Montreal, and the Clairtone train arrived in Stellarton in good time for a tour of the new plant and the opening ceremonies.

There were about a thousand guests on hand that June day. Some four hundred of them were from all over North America while the rest were Nova Scotians. The young federal cabinet minister John Turner flew in to deliver some inspiring words before Premier Stanfield symbolically engaged the plant's power switch. Within a few seconds a fully finished Clairtone stereo set rolled off the production line to the delight of all present.

The main speech of the day was delivered by Peter Munk, who was at the top of his form. In his conclusion he made a pledge that Bob Stanfield would remember.

> Let me, then, on this occasion offer a pledge to the Premier. A pledge he can hold in trust for and on behalf of the people of this region. Sir, we shall not let you down! We shall be at the forefront of your industrial revolution. We shall be in the vanguard of your drive to place Nova Scotia in the mainstream of Canada's economic life.

With the new factory up and running Munk knew he had to find an electronic expert and administrator, an executive he could rely on, to run this sprawling state-of-the-art plant at Stellarton. Peter Munk had other personal goals, other objectives than running a plant with its day-to-day labour problems, technical difficulties and all of the details associated with a 1,000-unit-per-day factory. Munk preferred to create strategies, persuade, sell, and build corporate values. And, above all, to think and conceptualize.

To fill this newly conceived post of executive vice-president in charge of operations, Munk sought out an old Dutch-born friend, Dan Van Eedenburg, who was then in the upper echelons of the huge Philips Electronics empire in Holland and had once been president of Philips in Canada. Munk tracked Van Eedenburg down by telephone in Portugal, where he was vacationing, and talked him into coming to Toronto to discuss the virtues of taking over the job of running the

Stellarton operation. As a result Van Eedenburg left Philips to join Clairtone, as of November 1, 1966.

By this time the Stellarton plant was operating twenty-four hours a day. Clairtone had 1,250 employees and 2,135 shareholders of record. In the final quarter of 1966, sales were an incredible $8.7 million, and for the full year were $15.5 million, up almost 40 percent from 1965. What was exceptionally satisfying for Munk and Gilmour, and for their shareholders and Bob Stanfield as well, was that the net profit for 1966 was $601,000. Their success was capped in the spring of 1966 by Clairtone winning its second Canadian Design Council Award of Excellence.

The sparkling new plant was turning out Clairtone's superb stereo and high-fidelity sets and its newly engineered and designed colour TVs. In time to hit the fall and Christmas buying season, a massive, costly advertising campaign was launched to promote the Project G2 stereo and the colour TV line. Unfortunately, despite the advertising, the expected heavy market demand for TV sets never appeared. Clairtone began its 1967 operation with a staggering $5.9 million of inventory, most of it in the form of TV sets that dealers wouldn't buy.

There were also labour troubles at the plant. The United Steelworkers of America and a local union, the certified bargaining agents for Clairtone employees, were challenged by the International Brotherhood of Electrical Workers, creating an atmosphere of tension and dissatisfaction. Then Munk had to fire his very recently hired friend Van Eedenburg, whose rigid, highly disciplined European management style just didn't work in Nova Scotia.

The New York investment firm W.E. Hutton and Company, represented on the Clairtone board by James Hutton and Clifford Brokaw, offered to raise new capital. In May 1967, Clifford Brokaw, executive vice-president of Hutton, put together a $2.5-million U.S. underwriting of Clairtone debentures with the prospect of more money in the fall. Significantly, the Hutton prospectus stated that the proceeds would be used to finance "an increase in inventories of components and finished products." Those were code words for the unsold colour TV sets sitting in the Clairtone warehouse.

The Hutton prospectus showed a disturbing Clairtone loss for the first quarter of 1967 at $201,000 on sales of $3.6 million. Losses, caused entirely by the introduction of the high-cost colour television line, were increasing at a far faster rate than sales. The loss in the same period of the prior year was $78,000 on sales of $1.8 million. Clairtone needed at least another $2 million on top of the Hutton money if the company was to be profitable in 1967, and the money had to be in place by the end of June, in time for the big production runs for the fall season. Clairtone's new colour TV component suppliers were looking for either cash or payment in thirty days maximum. Two million dollars, in cash, was an absolute necessity for Clairtone if it was to stay alive.

Egan committed IEL to the extra $2 million, but by mid-July there was still no money out of IEL. There was now no way to buy the parts and material for fall production and marketing, causing potential chaos in manufacturing schedules.

The money-problem scenario had begun to develop in the spring of 1967 when Robert Stanfield decided to contest the leadership of the federal Progressive Conservative Party. The convention was scheduled for Maple Leaf Gardens in Toronto that fall. Stanfield wanted Ike Smith, then the provincial finance minister, to be interim premier until the Nova Scotia Tories held a convention to choose Stanfield's successor. At the outset, Smith said no. But by July 17, he gave in. Stanfield announced his candidacy on July 19.

With Stanfield out of the Nova Scotia power structure, and Ike Smith as interim premier, Clairtone's position in the province changed. Smith now held direct power over IEL and over the desperately needed $2 million for Clairtone. And Ike Smith, for personal reasons, intensely disliked Peter Munk.

Back in 1965, shortly after the Clairtone–Nova Scotia deal had been signed, IEL was still aggressively looking for new industry for the province, sending public-relations and sales teams to select American cities. Frank Sobey asked Munk to take part in IEL's beer-and-lobster luncheon for San Francisco businessmen at one of the city's best hotels.

Peter Munk was pleased to accept, and he wowed the San Francisco crowd with the story of Clairtone's and his own astonishing achievements, which had been topped off by the marvellous financing programs of the government of Nova Scotia, a great place to do business.

Munk then had to sit through a speech by the diminutive Nova Scotia finance minister, Ike Smith. In the irritated Munk's opinion, Smith's address to the sophisticated San Francisco crowd was dull and flat, and after the luncheon Munk said so to Sobey. Sobey replied that if he had a complaint he should tell Smith, not him. Which is exactly what the arrogant young Peter Munk did, telling Ike Smith in direct terms what he thought of the Nova Scotian's speaking ability. It was a confrontation that would have dire consequences for Peter Munk and Clairtone in the summer of 1967. In Toronto, on or about July 21, 1967, Frank Sobey called, asking Munk to meet him and Egan at Stellarton on July 25.

Munk complied. At the meeting, the messengers gave him the news from Premier Smith: Clairtone could have its $2 million, but only on one condition. As dictated by Smith, the condition was that Munk and Gilmour had to surrender management and voting control of the company to IEL. Peter Munk emerged from the Stellarton meeting in a state of shock. Everything he and Gilmour had achieved in their meteoric Clairtone success was gone. Clairtone was no longer theirs.

This time Munk could not negotiate his way out of trouble, or reduce the stark, negative impact of the decision. At the Clairtone board meeting of August 27, 1967, in Halifax, Munk and Gilmour had to accept the terms of the Smith edict. The motion, transferring control of management from them to IEL was duly moved and passed. As part of the deal, IEL made a loan of $165,000 to Munk and Gilmour, which would come back to haunt them when they had to sell shares of Clairtone to repay it.

While Smith was getting ready to pull the rug out from under Munk and Gilmour, they realized that the only way to escape the dreaded governmental control was to sell the company to a large U.S. retailer. They were already in serious negotiations with Singer Corporation, the sewing machine giant that had started down the diversification path. The New York–headquartered Singer had 1,800 outlets around the world where Clairtone stereos and TVs made with the Singer brand name were already being sold. The first area of interest on both sides was, therefore, the marketing of Clairtone's products. The second area of interest was a possible Singer takeover of Clairtone. The board of Clairtone had given approval to Munk to carry out negotiations authorizing him to deal with Singer in the range of $16 to $18 a share.

Mac Hogarth, who had been a director and early investor in Clairtone (and a partner in Fiji when it was first bought) remembers what happened in the Singer negotiations. Singer asked Munk and Gilmour to state how much they thought their shares were worth. If they were 10 percent below Singer's estimate, Singer would buy. If they were 10 percent too high, they would negotiate. If they were more than 10 percent high, they wouldn't hear from Singer again. Munk and Gilmour decided that they wanted $17 a share for their Clairtone stock. As a result they never heard from Singer again, missing a golden opportunity to put two or three million dollars in their pockets.

However, if the Singer deal had been agreed to in principle, there is a high likelihood that Singer would have backed off or renegotiated when it learned of the operating results for the half-year ended June 30, 1967. Clairtone had lost $799,000 on sales of $7.1 million.

What had Munk and Gilmour done wrong to wind up in this catastrophic situation? They, and Clairtone, were effectively in the hands of the man who was now the premier of Nova Scotia. Ike Smith stripped Munk and Gilmour of their creation and then, in short order, fired both of them. The partners would be terminated, not for any wrongdoing, theft, fraud or incompetence, but because they had been lured into the spider's web by promises of a plant and capital and, in the eyes of the government officials, had become a liability.

Matters moved rapidly after the Munk–Gilmour surrender of control of Clairtone. An extraordinary general shareholders' meeting was held in Toronto on October 17, 1967, to approve and enact the necessary corporate changes that gave IEL control of Clairtone. IEL had already started a search for a chief executive officer to replace Munk. Next, a board meeting was held on December 12 in Halifax. The board struck a committee to review applications received for Munk's job as chief executive officer. Peter Munk was humiliated and furious, but he kept his feelings hidden. He told the board to expect the company to make a substantial loss in its 1967 operations. The deliberate long delay in approving the $2-million advance had killed Clairtone's ability to create product for sale in the fall/Christmas season of 1967 and was taking its murderous toll. They lost their most valuable asset: floor space in the key department stores in Canada and the United States. The extent of that toll became known on March 11, 1968, when McDonald, Currie, the company's accountants, produced their 1967 audit. Sales had come in at a record level, $17.6 million, but the net loss for the year was appalling—$6.7 million.

Ike Smith's team had already chosen Peter Munk's successor. At a closed board meeting at the end of January, an American executive by the name of J.W. Mangels from the Winchester Division of Olin Mathieson was chosen as managing director and chief executive officer, to start on February 4, 1968.

At the request of Frank Sobey, Munk and Gilmour stayed with the Clairtone ship as directors even though Mangels had moved in on top of them. They had no doubt that Clairtone could survive with the Nova Scotia government behind it—but clearly not in the high-end electronics home-furnishings industry. The organization they had created was in deep trouble, but they were prepared to stay. However, Mangels proved too much for Munk and Gilmour. So far as they were concerned, he was a typical know-it-all American. By March 1968

Munk had had more than enough of him. Returning from Europe after a short skiing holiday he found that Mangels had moved into his office. The papers and documents of Peter Munk, both personal and business, were stacked on a desk in a small office several doors down the executive corridor.

Munk was finished at Clairtone. The formal action of the Smith-controlled IEL board of directors was taken at a meeting at Stellarton on August 6, 1968. Munk was offered an eighteen-month contract as management and engineering consultant for the company at $27,000 a year. The contract, which he accepted, was to begin on August 1, 1968. It included a clause precluding him from entering into any type of activity that would be in competition with the company. David Gilmour was offered a similar contract (but at $24,000 a year) as a design, advertising and merchandising consultant. He accepted.

Peter Munk and David Gilmour were gone from Clairtone. They were "fired" at 12:15 p.m. on August 6, 1968, just ten years and six days after the incorporation of Clairtone Sound Corporation.

During that summer of defeat Munk retreated to his island in Georgian Bay, where he concentrated on thinking through what had caused the debacle and making strategic plans for the immediate future.

CHAPTER TWELVE

CROSSROADS

The year 1968 was a crossroads in Peter Munk's life. He spent the summer on his island in Georgian Bay. His fertile mind was busy putting together two elaborate schemes. One was a sophisticated international securitized mortgage-financing plan. The other was an off-the-wall development project in Fiji.

Fortunately, before he was dismissed from Clairtone, a New York investment group had bought all of Gilmour's Clairtone shares and all but five of Munk's remaining shares. (He retained the five to stay temporarily qualified as a director.) After repaying the $165,000 loan from IEL, Peter Munk was left with working funds of about $150,000 to get his business life reorganized. His goal was to find an entrepreneurial path that would take him back to the top of the business world.

Munk was not, however, about to embark on any new project without David Gilmour. In late July he flew to New York to meet with his former partner, then working with an investment house. He told Gilmour what was on his mind, and asked if he would join him as a partner once again. Gilmour accepted with enthusiasm. In August they sorted out a new equal arrangement, which provided, among other things, that Gilmour would remain in New York until he was required full time in Toronto.

In August Munk left his island and began his rise out of the

Clairtone ruins. The farm and residence, Greystone, at Terra Cotta, northwest of Toronto, was sold to raise funds, and he and his family moved into the city in November to an apartment at 1 Chestnut Park in Rosedale. "We moved into the apartment," he recalls, "because I needed the capital and I could only pay rent."

He incorporated himself as Peter Munk Associates Limited, and rented a small suite of offices above an art gallery in an old house at 25 Prince Arthur Avenue. He could handle the rent at $150 a month. But he had to guard and conserve his diminishing grubstake.

The first strategic scheme, securitized mortgages, had enormous potential. Under Canada's National Housing Act (NHA), the government guaranteed approved builders' mortgages that paid an interest rate in the range of 8.5 to 9 percent. Munk recognized that European investors were highly attracted to securities that carried a Canadian government guarantee. Furthermore, the European market indicated that those investors would be prepared to buy in at a return equal or close to 6.5 percent, more in line with government bonds at the time. By offering lower-cost funds to Canadian builders, Munk could obtain the capitalized value of the 2-percent per annum cost differential, which amounted to 20 to 25 percent of the equity value of the projects financed under the arrangement. He could then offer part of that ownership interest to investors concerned with inflation as well as yield. It would be a unique, hybrid financial instrument, with a Canadian government guarantee of both principal and interest.

The complex international aspects of Munk's NHA mortgage scheme required the input of an expert legal mind. Munk chose Howard L. Beck of the fast-rising Toronto law firm of Davies, Ward and Beck. Thus began an association that has seen Beck at Munk's right hand in nearly every deal Munk has negotiated since then—with or without success.

This memorandum to file made by Beck dated November 18, 1968, after a visit by Munk and his advisers, accountant David

Perlmutter and Ziggy Hahn, explains the Munk scheme in short form. The meeting was to

> ... discuss a number of aspects of the proposal of Mr. Munk to form a vehicle which would offer N.H.A. mortgages to European nationals for investment. In short, Mr. Munk's idea is to sell interests in N.H.A. mortgages which are guaranteed by the Government of Canada to European investors at a rate of return equal to 6.5%. In addition, the European investor would obtain a portion of the equity of the Canadian borrower which for the first $20,000,000 raised in Europe would be approximately 20% of the borrower's equity position.

Munk says, "I thought this was one of the most brilliant single concepts I ever developed."

On September 5, 1968, Munk met with David Gilmour to sort out the responsibilities each man was to assume in relation to their new partnership. Gilmour would head off to London, Australia and Hong Kong to pursue possible interest in the mortgage security plan and Munk's development idea for their Fiji lands. Similarly, Peter Munk would fly to Geneva in pursuit of European money and support for the mortgage scheme.

Through his many connections Munk had arranged a Geneva meeting with Roberto Gancia, a man who was to become a lifelong friend and confidant. Gancia was a wealthy thirty-six-year-old Swiss/Italian, who was unhappy in the family business (which produced, among other things, Asti Spumanti) but was well connected internationally, even in a South American partnership with the Bronfman family. Gancia immediately agreed to become a full participant and adviser. There followed six months of intense work by Munk, Gilmour and several associates to market the mortgage plan to international investors. A final prospectus was drawn up for the new company, to be called Swiss–Canadian Investments and a push began to find a European underwriter.

Peter Munk explains the interrelationship between the Swiss–Canadian proposal and the Fiji development project:

> I said to David, "Whichever gets financed first, we'll go with. An idea is good only if it's financeable. I'm going to work my guts out in both of them, but within eighteen months, I've got to have a job, I've got to work and not just promote. So whatever comes first, the other will get thrown out."
>
> Fiji got financed first, because of Gilmour's contacts. So we dropped Swiss–Canadian and focused totally on the Fiji proposal.
>
> The concept of securitized mortgages, especially with government guarantees, was exciting, but it was just too difficult to get an underwriting. Also, Roberto Gancia was very rich, so for him the pressure was less.

Gilmour and Munk had spent a great deal of money on travelling and lawyers and accountants' fees for Swiss–Canadian. They had also prepared an elaborate land use and development plan for Fiji. But Munk had yet to make a deal that would produce a cash flow into his coffers. His total income as reported for the 1968 taxation year was $20,477.15.

Peter Munk was about to concentrate exclusively on Fiji.

CHAPTER THIRTEEN

OPTIONING FIJI

The acquisition six years earlier by Munk, Gilmour and Mac Hogarth of land and a termite-ridden hotel on a remote Pacific island they had never seen can only be explained by the word "faith." They had faith in their redoubtable friend and business colleague Pat Samuel, and in the inexpensive options he had purchased on two pieces of land on the beautiful island. The first option was on a rickety old hotel called the Beachcomber, which sat on a fourteen-acre parcel at Deuba, about thirty miles south of the capital city of Suva; the second was on a twelve-acre site with beach frontage, located close to Fiji's international airport at Nadi. Samuel could see that Fiji, with its warm climate, beautiful terrain and beaches, had enormous potential for tourism. However, buying options for a few hundred dollars was one thing. Coming up with $242,000 to exercise those options before they expired was quite another matter.

In 1962 Samuel had made his presentation to Munk, Gilmour and Mac Hogarth. Using his maps and an amateurish 8-millimetre film he had shot of the Beachcomber and the beaches of lush Fiji, Pat Samuel sold them the deal. Mac Hogarth put up the money for his quarter share (one-third of the option exercise price), out of his own Gooderham family inheritance. Munk and Gilmour came up with their two-thirds (for a quarter share each) with money borrowed from the CIBC against their personal promissory notes guaranteed by Clairtone shares. Samuel received his quarter share for no money in consideration for his bringing the deal to them.

Why did Gilmour and Munk go for the Fiji deal? Gilmour explains:

> We never invested separately during that whole period and we invested nothing outside Clairtone. But in this case we agreed we would because it seemed like a visionary thing the way Pat described it. Also, it had no carrying costs. There was no real estate tax in that country. And, too, it was so far away there was nothing to be done for a number of years. So here was a perfect investment that would not take us away from our focus. We took it, sight unseen.

Gilmour says that he and Munk invited Mac Hogarth to participate because "Mac was an old friend I'd known most of my life in Toronto. He had joined us at Clairtone as an executive. He was a warm, very fine man, and had independent wealth of his own. So when this opportunity arose, we just asked him to come in with us." And come in Hogarth did. Then, like Munk and Gilmour, he forgot about Fiji until 1968.

During the summer of 1968, Munk decided to research the potential growth of the Fiji area if tourist air traffic between North America and Australia increased. He needed numbers to justify the project not only to himself but also to potential investors. His idea was, after all, somewhat off-the-wall. It was to build a resort residential community with housing for purchase, hotels, recreational facilities including a championship golf course, and superb beach areas offering sailing and other marine activities such as scuba diving. He and David Gilmour had two months to sort out what they were going to do.

We reviewed the Fiji holding. Six years had gone by since we bought the option. Japan was coming up rapidly. Wealth was being generated. Tourism had increased rapidly in the Pacific. The Bahamas was already being bought by Germans, Americans and the English.

At their meeting in Toronto on September 5 the partners decided that Gilmour would visit London, Australia and Hong Kong, then, in October, Munk would fly to Fiji to meet Gilmour and Pat Samuel. Samuel would guide them and, influential man that he was, arrange introductions to the appropriate elected officials who governed the soon-to-be independent British colony. As soon as he saw their properties it was apparent to Munk that the Beachcomber parcel at Deuba had by far the best prospects for development. And although on most of Fiji only small pieces of land could be privately owned, the land abutting the Beachcomber—hundreds of acres of jungle, river, swamps and farm—was exempt from the restrictions and was in the hands of only a few owners. Within three weeks Munk and Gilmour had negotiated agreements to option all the available freehold land, 7,500 acres.

During that visit, the partners met with the prime minister of Fiji and his cabinet. They had to be told what the proposal was in principle that these two Canadian strangers and their New Zealand partner had in mind. Without the co-operation of the government there would be no exercising of options, no development, no jobs for Fijians, no tourism boost for the economy of the island.

With his Nova Scotia experience behind him, Munk knew what the prime minister and his politicians wanted to hear. He also knew that he wanted no government subsidies, no government interference, no government control except that which a municipal government might normally exercise in relation to land-use planning, engineering and the protection of the environment.

The prime minister, Ratu Sir Kamisese Mara, received the trio graciously and listened to their ideas intently. The proposal they sketched for him held much promise for the future economic growth of the island and the well-being of its people. Sir Kamisese Mara gave them his approval in principle and pledged his co-operation, provided that they consulted with him and his appropriate ministers on a regular basis.

Elated with their success, the three Fiji partners decided on the next step. It was to retain one of the world's foremost land-use planners to examine their vast tract and come up with a comprehensive, economically feasible plan for the phased development of the Beachcomber and Deuba lands and the area they had optioned.

Back at 25 Prince Arthur Avenue, Munk called a man he'd never met, Macklin Hancock, head of Project Planning Limited, whose national and international reputation as a land-use planner was growing rapidly. For E.P. Taylor, Hancock had designed the innovative new town, Don Mills, Ontario; and had planned Lyford Cay, the foremost development project in the Bahamas. Hancock and his team had also designed Expo 67 in Montreal, and were planning a waterfront project in Kuwait and other important work in the Middle East.

Macklin Hancock remembers that first meeting with Peter Munk in the little upstairs office at 25 Prince Arthur.

> Peter Munk said that he would like to build a resort development in Fiji. He hoped that it would help him recover some of his economic health. He was quite clear about that and he said that he didn't have much money. In fact he would have to borrow money to do this project. He said he could find $60,000 to work with but he didn't want me to spend all of it.

Macklin Hancock accepted the challenge. Munk would cover Hancock and his firm's expenses. If the project went ahead, Project Planning would be entitled to a percentage of the equity instead of an hourly rate fee.

Unfortunately, on his first visit to Fiji, Hancock and his colleague, Ron Thomson, found that the site had problems that Munk was unaware of. On the surface the soil looked like perfectly good development land, but the water was within a few inches of the surface. The land was in an estuary where the flatlands were good for rice growing, but posed a major problem for dwellings and permanent development. However, Hancock and Thomson also told Munk that the beautiful location was and could be utilized, provided that it could be engineered to make construction feasible. They envisaged a cut-and-fill operation to create waterways that would permit dredging. The land could then be raised above flood levels. Hancock recalls:

I think Peter was a little bit surprised that the land wasn't good enough on its own. But he was pleased when we told him what we could do to make it very attractive, especially for aquatic activities—boating and other things. I told Peter that we would have to devise a plan that would make the project economically profitable for him and for the government of Fiji.

Peter Munk worked closely with Macklin Hancock and his team in Toronto during the development of the plan for the Deuba property. Hancock says:

He gave his leadership all the way through the development of Fiji, Pacific Harbour as he called it. One thing about Peter Munk, when he takes something on, he gives it his full attention. He delegates a great deal, but he doesn't delegate top-level decision making.

Munk accompanied Hancock on his second visit to the site. This time talks with government officials occupied most of their time. Hancock presented his skilfully prepared maps and charts, and with a pointer took his audience through his proposals like a scholarly professor. Keeping the government informed and ensuring that the prime minister and his colleagues had a significant input was an essential role for Munk, and so was the urgent matter of finding the money. As Hancock recounts, "Munk persevered and persevered through thick and thin to get the money for Fiji. Of course it was by selling a site to American Airlines that he was able to keep the ball rolling."

The site Munk sold was for a hotel. American Airlines wanted to expand their business in the southwest Pacific. At that time aircraft could not fly the whole distance from Hawaii to Australia without refuelling. So Fiji would be an appropriate stop for the airline, and an exclusive airport and a hotel with the American Airlines name on it would be an incentive for people to go to Fiji—and to fly American Airlines.

The sale was a stroke of good luck, but it was only a small success in Munk's ongoing quest for money. Hancock says, "He told me much later that he had to go to as many as sixty different lending institutions and lenders to get the money for Fiji. It was not easy." That may be an exaggeration, but Munk certainly threw everything into the project. His target was to raise $4 million. That was the absolute minimum necessary before he could begin to arrange the construction contracts that would start the development and building of Pacific Harbour at Deuba.

One of the people Munk had approached was Irving Gould, who had made the initial arrangements for the MacNames financing of the capital-short Clairtone eight years before. Gould was a shrewd man with deep pockets and a lot of faith in Munk and Gilmour's ability.

After considerable wheeling and dealing, Peter Munk finally hammered out an agreement for Gould's funding and the creation of a new "public" company: Southern Pacific Properties Limited. It and the later corporations using the same name in various jurisdictions (e.g., Bahamas and Hong Kong) would also be known as SPP.

Southern Pacific Properties Limited was incorporated by Ontario letters patent, dated the 16th day of July 1969 as executed by the Honourable H. Les Rowntree of the cabinet of Premier John Robarts. It authorized 3 million no par value shares. The first nominal directors were Howard Beck, Harry Emerson and David Brown, all increasingly stellar members of the law firm of Davies, Ward & Beck.

The only indicator that linked the name Southern Pacific to that part of the globe was in the section that authorized shareholders' meetings to be held

> … at any place in Ontario or at the City of Sydney, Australia, or at the City of London, in the Administrative County of London, England, or at Suva, on Viti Levu Island, one of the Fiji Islands, or at the City of Honolulu, in the State of Hawaii, one of the United States of America.

The hunt for money for Fiji was on and had been for some time. Irving Gould's funds were used to keep the company afloat and pay the bills.

During the early months of 1969 two distractions took Peter Munk's focus away from the Fiji project and the Swiss-Canadian mortgage venture.

First, his marriage was over. His wife, Linda, left again, taking their children. Munk recalls:

> Linda left me again in January of '69. She took Nina and put Anthony in Le Rosey, the famous boarding school in Gstaad in Switzerland. I stayed alone at Chestnut Park. That was the final episode. We divorced after that. She later married a Swiss man and they had a son, Marc-David. She divorced him when Marc was one, and came back to Canada.

The second distraction was a lawsuit brought against Peter Munk by a London, Ontario, resident who alleged that as an insider Munk had benefited from his knowledge of Clairtone's financial situation when he sold personally held shares of the company in July 1967. In fact, Munk and Gilmour had prudently obtained advice from their lawyers to ensure that the sales would conform with Ontario's new insider-trading regulations. Then, being pressed by their stockbrokers to clear off their margin accounts, they sold.

The action against Munk had begun in February 1968. The demand was that Munk pay $10,500 for the one thousand Clairtone shares the plaintiff had bought for $10.50 each on July 13, 1967. Munk refused. The next legal gambit came over a year later in May of 1969, when the same man, John Adams, launched his Supreme Court motion.

If nothing else, the London lawyers for the plaintiff were creative in constructing this new claim, which received considerable attention in the press and in the Ontario legislature. The gossip was that Munk and Gilmour had made a fortune with their Clairtone shares before the company collapsed and had used the vast proceeds to buy a big chunk of Fiji and other South Pacific islands.

Peter Munk retained one of Canada's top litigation counsel, Charles Dubin (later Chief Justice of Ontario). Dubin sized up the situation—the litigation would take years, the financing of Fiji was paramount. By this time, Munk had negotiated a preliminary commitment from a brokerage firm, Cochran, Murray & Company of Toronto, to underwrite SPP. The firm had prepared and submitted to the Ontario Securities Commission for approval an elaborate prospectus for the public sale of SPP shares. Munk didn't want to jeopardize this process. Dubin advised that Munk settle out of court, despite the potential damage to Munk's reputation and the fact that Dubin believed the plaintiff had no case.

Peter Munk accepted Dubin's advice. Minutes of settlement were signed "without any admission of liability on the part of Mr. Munk" on June 20, 1969, with an unusual result. Munk maintained that the main payment should go to Clairtone, not to the plaintiff. Costs to the plaintiff and his solicitor were $3,500, while the payment to Clairtone was $21,393.50. To Munk's dismay, the settlement minutes, which were supposed to be confidential, were discovered by a diligent newspaper reporter. The resulting publicity left yet another Clairtone scar on Munk's reputation.

On July 31, 1969, Peter Munk's term as a director of Clairtone was finished. Clairtone, a beautiful dream that turned into a hideous nightmare, was a thing of the past. It would, however, remain in Peter Munk's memory, reminding him not to make the same mistakes again, and driving him to achieve new business successes that would ultimately restore his treasured reputation.

CHAPTER FOURTEEN

SLATER WALKER

Irving Gould was now chairman of SPP. His infusion of capital was to cover expenses until the $4 million necessary to realize the Fiji project and get construction under way had been raised.

Where would Peter Munk find that $4 million? The beginning of an answer had come while he was licking his Clairtone wounds on his Georgian Bay island in the summer of 1968, in the form of a simple, well-prepared prospectus for a share offering on a Bahamian island development. It was that document that gave Munk's imagination the impetus it needed to create the Fiji project.

A Georgian Bay island neighbour had left a copy of the Roberts Realty prospectus with Munk. The Roberts Realty stock promotion was a great success, with the shares going from two dollars to ten. As Munk tells it,

> I was desperate in those days, looking for what was I going
> to do next. Clairtone was over. I was all by myself on the
> island. I went through the Bahamian prospectus. It showed,
> on page 4, Macklin Hancock's plan for the island, drawing
> in a golf course and a couple of lakes, and on page 3 it
> showed how the island would be broken down into lots.
> Then it talked about selling the lots in Germany and

England and Tokyo and wherever else they were going to sell them.

When I woke up the next morning I remembered Fiji. This was what we had talked about with Pat Samuel six years ago. If they could plan a development and put out a prospectus with a nice drawing showing lakes and golf courses in the middle of a desert island without any fresh water, so could we.

Munk set about getting all the basic pieces assembled in a credible form.

By the time we went out to raise the money, we had Project Planning Associates working on the Master Plan, we had the Foundation Company of Canada for the civil engineering, we had American Airlines with landing rights, and a deal for our first hotel. We had the Fijian government. Believe me, I needed all that. Because when I first went down to Wood Gundy, the investment house, to raise the $4 million, they could hardly contain themselves laughing. They thought that Peter Munk must have lost his mind because of the setbacks. The last time they heard of me I was being fired from Clairtone and facing all the insider-trading publicity, and then suddenly I reappear as a resort developer in Fiji!

The only underwriting firm prepared to listen to Munk was Cochran, Murray. Mark Van Sittart, of Cochran, Murray, knew Munk very well: he was married to David Gilmour's sister, Shelagh. When his sister got married, Gilmour had asked Munk to put his new brother-in-law on the board of directors of Clairtone along with representatives of Nesbitt, Thomson and W.E. Hutton of New York.

Munk lined up his selling program, using the ever-dependable Gilmour in London.

I had the prospectus of Roberts Realty, so we knew where their sales office was in London. David was articulate, smart and elegant; he looked rich, and he talked rich. He went to the Roberts office and got all the sales information we needed. That was tremendously helpful to me back at Prince Arthur Avenue when I designed the sales program. With the Roberts information as a model I knew what to do: the prices, how to structure the lots, the size of the lots, plus of course Project Planning information about design, and information about the marketing from Gilmour. After the second time he was at the Roberts sales office he asked the salesman out for lunch and got out of him the commission structure, the overhead structure, the whole marketing approach. It only took us a week. We got the whole Roberts structure.

I was working with Cochran, Murray. It was very rough going. They could have raised $2 million. That would have been a wild gamble; but $4 million was the minimum. I could not do it for less. I could not take a chance, after what I'd gone through with Clairtone, to be short a million bucks. I just couldn't.

As always, David Gilmour was essential to Munk and the Fiji project.

He was doing his bit around the world and I was doing my bit at home. Without David, Fiji wouldn't have gone. My part was more the formulation and the strategy. David did the outside work; he was not a strategist. David sometimes heard more about the difficulties than I because I was more hard-edge to deal with. I was very pushy and very aggressive. It was very important to me. I had really thought about every aspect of Fiji, I knew it could be done, and I was very impatient.

Peter Munk had to have his underwriting, and as soon as possible. Howard Beck had filed the draft Cochran, Murray prospectus for SPP with the Ontario Securities Commission, hoping for an early approval. Without the OSC's imprimatur there would be no sale of SPP's shares to the public, and no money. OSC approval was critical. As Beck said:

> I was dealing with Ted Brown of the OSC, who was the person you had to deal with on filings. Ted said, "We won't issue a prospectus on real estate in Fiji unless you or someone from your office goes to Fiji and satisfies us as to title, and actually takes a look at the land and all the rest of it." I had gone with Peter to Fiji when we acquired the options on the property. We had a terrific lawyer in Fiji by the name of Arthur Leys. He was so good he could have practised in Toronto or New York or anywhere. A gentleman of the old school. Trained in the U.K. I gave the OSC an opinion based on Leys' opinion. The OSC cleared the file.

The financing for Munk and Gilmour's Fiji dream was set. All that remained was for Cochran, Murray to close the underwriting, then sell SPP shares to the public. Then disaster struck. Beck recalls:

> We thought we had an underwriting. Van Sittart was very friendly. We had gone through all the regulatory hoops at the Ontario Securities Commission. We were ready, then "bang" the market crashed in October 1969. It collapsed. It was impossible to sell any securities, and Cochran, Murray pulled the deal. It was a disaster.

Peter Munk was devastated. SPP and the Fiji project, into which he had poured almost every dollar, were on the verge of collapse. Gilmour, meanwhile, believing that they had been cleared for the big underwriting, had gone to London—and proved to be in the right place at the opportune moment. At a dinner at Lord White's (of Hanson Trust fame) he met Jim Slater, the head of Slater Walker Securities, then the pre-eminent British financier. "What are you doing these days?" Slater asked.

That was Gilmour's cue to tell Slater about the wonderful Fiji project. He explained SPP's holdings and plans for Fiji, and its strategic tourism and destination rest-and-recreation possibilities that underpinned his and Munk's enthusiasm and willingness to "bet the farm" on Fiji. The cool, articulate Gilmour was at his most convincing. He told Slater that the projected profit that SPP should reap by the time Phase 3 was completed (Phase 1 was 1,150 acres, 2 was 2,000 acres and 3 was 3,000 acres) was US$27 million. That final feather in the attractive, colourful lure caught Jim Slater, who had just returned from Australia and the Far East.

Slater wanted to send his managing director, Simon Pendock, to Toronto right away. The next day, Gilmour telephoned his partner in his Prince Arthur office and explained to an astonished Peter Munk who Jim Slater was. Pendock was in the Bahamas with Michael Wicher, the Nassau-based managing director of Slater Walker. Peter Munk, still reeling from the impact of the collapse of the Cochran, Murray underwriting, was overjoyed. He would get out the red carpet. He recalls:

> Slater Walker was at that time bigger than Hill Samuel in capitalization. I remember being quite nervous before I picked Pendock up at the airport. I took him to the Park Plaza. Then he came to our office, which was still above Albert White's Gallery. I mean, we still had not raised our capital.

Pendock was given a briefing on the numbers, cost projections, potential sales, and the attitude of the government of Fiji; and then there was a full-scale presentation by the master planners, Macklin

Hancock and his team. They showed him their plans and charts for the initial first phase of the Deuba development, then following through with Hancock's concepts for the following two phases. Munk says:

> In 1968 Project Planners were the top in land-use develop-
> ment. They told Pendock, "We think it's a highly suitable
> area for resort development." I had a market report of travel
> patterns in the Pacific, I had a copy of the *Economist's* study
> on excess wealth creation and luxury travel trends in the
> Pacific. I mean you could just tell that everything was moving
> up and they had to go somewhere. It was logical that
> Japanese and Hong Kong Chinese wanted to go somewhere
> where they could play golf.

Pendock liked what he heard and saw of the Fiji plans, and told Munk he was prepared to recommend it. He sent a team of lawyers to Toronto. Patrick Goodbody, who was Slater Walker's in-house attorney, and two junior English lawyers moved into the offices of one of their correspondent lawyers in Toronto to do a due diligence on Munk, Gilmour and the Fiji development. It took them two weeks and the result was quite satisfactory.

Pendock gave Munk a Slater Walker letter of commitment for $4 million on the condition Munk would not take his company public. Pendock's reason was that all of them would get more money for the first public issue of shares if they waited. Slater Walker intended to syndicate the deal privately to some big players. Then they would go public at prices three or four times as high as if they went to the market immediately.

It was time for Munk and Howard Beck to go to Fiji again to tie up loose ends. When Munk called Pendock in London to tell him about the trip, Pendock asked to go along. It was an eventful visit. With the assistance of his Fiji lawyer, Arthur Leys, Munk completed the purchase of the options on the 7,500 acres of land he needed. His option price was in the range of $100 per acre, about five times the presumed market value, but designed to make the owners of the land keen to sell. There were meetings with the prime minister and Peter Munk's ally Charles Stinson, the minister of tourism. And Simon Pendock liked what he saw and heard.

When Munk, Pendock and Beck arrived back in Toronto, Pendock had decided that there had to be another condition on Slater Walker's $4 million commitment. Irving Gould, the financier, had to be taken out. His position was incompatible with Slater Walker's. Pendock told Munk: "We don't want to play with Gould. We see Gilmour's role, we see Munk's role, we see our role, but Gould is out. And we're prepared to give him a profit."

Munk took Gould to Sutton Place for lunch and explained the situation. Gould's first response was to ask for a million dollars. "I almost vomited," Munk says. "I figured that was going to kill my deal." But it didn't. An arrangement was negotiated with Irving Gould to his satisfaction, and he was out, with a whopping profit.

By mid-November heads of agreement (as the British call them) were signed. Slater Walker required that an offshore company be set up in the Bahamas. It was duly incorporated as Southern Pacific Properties Limited.

Jim Slater's chance meeting with David Gilmour at a London dinner party had miraculously produced the financing that the partners and associates in the Fiji project absolutely had to find. The next steps to be taken as soon as possible were twofold: to get the contracts to begin construction; and to start selling lots and commercial parcels.

CHAPTER FIFTEEN

LAUNCHING PACIFIC HARBOUR

As soon as the Slater Walker deal was closed, Munk set his sights on marketing the Fiji lots and blocks of land. If Munk and Gilmour couldn't sell their project at Deuba, their shares and those of Slater Walker wouldn't be worth the paper they were printed on.

By the summer of 1969, under Munk's forceful supervision, the sales promotion of Pacific Harbour (the name assigned to their 7,500-acre Fiji dream) was being prepared, using models, plans and techniques similar to those that Roberts Realty used to market its Bahamian island lots. Roberts Realty had also indirectly delivered to Munk a very young British chartered accountant who was to become a mainstay in every one of the myriad business deals that Peter Munk was to orchestrate from that day on.

During the pre–Slater Walker period, when the Cochran, Murray underwriting was being processed, Howard Beck had warned Munk that the lawyers for Cochran, Murray were concerned that Munk had no experience in land development, let alone the building of a resort. And in Fiji, a faraway place that Munk and Gilmour had visited only once? Beck advised Munk to hire someone with credibility and experience in the resort development world to look after the finances. Munk didn't know of anyone, but Beck did. One of his clients was none other than Roberts Realty. Their accountants were Coopers & Lybrand, the same firm Munk had always used. Coopers had seconded to Roberts's Bahamian operation one of their junior people from England, William Birchall, and he set up the Roberts financial structure. According to Beck, Birchall had expertise in every phase of land sales and resort development in tropical climates. He would be perfect for Munk.

Munk asked Beck to invite Birchall to come up from the Bahamas. He arrived a week later. The young man made a positive impression on Munk.

> Birchall was a good accountant, and a very cautious one. He made sense and I liked him. We discussed the future and the risk he'd be taking. I said, "You know, with me you'll be a partner. I don't want you to come into this position unless you're comfortable." Of course, I told him the whole Clairtone story. He had to know. When we were finished, he told me, "I'm really excited!" I said, "Bill, so am I." I told him he was hired. The next day he flew back to the Bahamas.

The following day, before he dictated Birchall's hiring letter, Munk went through his file. There he found for the first time the young accountant's birth date. Munk was shocked. Birchall was only twenty-six!

> He was a virtual teenager! And I was going to make him into a chief financial officer for a multimillion-dollar company? It didn't make sense. I had enough handicaps. I called him and I said, "Bill, I'm sorry but I've changed my mind. I'm really sorry because you came all that way here to see me." As I was about to hang up, I said, "I wish you good luck with your life." And Bill said, "Please, Mr. Munk, can I ask you one question?" I said, "Of course." "Not that it will change your mind, but just for my own edification for the future when I

apply for other jobs, where did I go wrong?" I said: "You did nothing wrong. It's just that I was negligent in not checking your age when I called you. I can't see how we can go to the public market, raising millions of dollars and starting a major new enterprise with a kid who's twenty-six years old as chief financial officer. You're too young." "Is that the only thing?" he said. I said: "That's the only thing, I promise you." Then he asked, "Please, can I just come up once more and see you?" I said: "Yes, please come, but I've made up my mind." So the next weekend he came up with his wife, and by the time he left we had made a deal.

Birchall soon proved he was prepared to put the corporation's interests ahead of his own. Munk tells the story that, as his business interests flourished, he gave Birchall the responsibility of bonus recommendations for the people below him. On one occasion Munk wrote in a £50,000 bonus for Birchall and it went to the board committee for approval. It came back to Munk with the "£50,000" struck out and "£20,000" put in in Birchall's hand. When Munk challenged him on the change, Birchall replied: "If you don't mind, it's for you to decide for all the senior executives but when it comes to me, I know what I'm worth, and I'm not worth that much. The company really is not cash-flowing as it should and I don't think I should get extra money." Munk says, "He did that twice in a row."

Birchall, looking back now to those first days, recalls:

As soon as I joined Peter in Toronto, I started putting a budget to the process, with forecasts and the rest of it. Peter sat at my side for days while we questioned and reworked every assumption. It became quite clear to me that Peter is quite capable of doing a pro forma statement on the back of an envelope and being 90 percent correct. He's familiar and comfortable with a balance sheet, and that's why he has a lot of accountants still working for him. He's consistent, he's conservative in many respects, he understands and he can question. In our businesses we've taken on blue sky and turned it into cash flow. You can't do that without exacting qualities.

Birchall was taken on to bring his experience to the Fiji development. He says:

It wasn't until we had the funds in the company that we signed the construction contract, which was several million dollars, and went ahead with the deal. So Fiji was not one of these seat-of-the-pants operations. That was Peter's position, somewhat from common sense, but also as a reaction to Clairtone. Because he has permanent scars from Clairtone. He has to have control, and he has to know that he's funding something that's speculative from equity, and not from debt.

After Clairtone, Peter Munk would not do a deal unless he had control of the operation—even if he did not have the required 50-percent-plus shares. That was the situation with Fiji and it is the situation with his business ventures now, in the mid-1990s.

Birchall explains the Fiji control arrangements:

Control has always been achieved on an equitable basis. So far as initial SPP was concerned, when we got the original funding from Slater Walker, Peter and David probably had about 35 percent of the company. And, let's say, Slater Walker another 25. It was also understood that Slater Walker was going to sell off to other institutions like P & O and the rest. So the objective there was always going to be that Peter and David would not have a large-percentage shareholding but they would have control. I was responsible for preparing monthly management statements that were sent to all investors—Slater Walker and P & O and Jardine Matheson. They were done in very great detail. We ran it on a basis of total disclosure, of total communication and of consultation all the way down the line, to the point where they would ask us to please stop sending them all this stuff.

Birchall describes Munk's business principles: be as conservative with your finances as the good Lord can make you and do not be greedy; always share the pie; there's only one way you can ultimately go broke and that is by not being in a position to pay somebody to whom you owe money. So pay and don't owe.

When Birchall joined Peter Munk and David Gilmour, he was just in time for the first sales assault on the British market for the Fiji project. On February 22, 1970, the *Sunday Times* of London carried a breathlessly positive article. It did exactly what Munk and Gilmour wanted: it trumpeted the existence of the South Sea paradise of Fiji complete with a photograph of Munk, Gilmour, Simon Pendock and the huge Hancock-supervised scale model of the entire Pacific Harbour development. It was announced that the lots and commercial land of Pacific Hotels & Developments were available for option or purchase.

The next stop for Pacific Harbour's promoters was Australia. By the time they arrived they were able to inform the Sydney press that a number of celebrities had already signed for properties: Crown Prince Victor Emanuel of Savoy; Gunther Sachs—Brigitte Bardot's ex; the Prince of Liechtenstein; and none other than Peter Munk's old friend Roberto Gancia. Those names, together with the Queen's cousin, the Honourable Noel Cunningham-Reid, made up part of the growing list of star-studded names for Millionaires' Row.

At a press conference in Sydney before he left for Europe, Peter Munk said: "We believe the average man could buy into Pacific Harbour. But we do seem to be attracting our share of the world's privileged and titled. We aren't building this as a millionaires' playground, but that's the way it's turning out."

The Pacific Harbour project had also attracted two powerful investors: The ancient, solid British marine transportation firm Peninsular & Orient Steamship Co., the parent firm of P & O Lines Ltd., acquired an 11 percent interest in the Pacific Harbour project. The 120-year-old British-owned trading company Jardine, Matheson & Company, of Hong Kong, came in for 5.5 percent. Slater Walker's interest was now at 41 percent. The final block investor, at 5 percent, was an American by the name of James G. "Jungle Jim" Boswell, a Californian who owned an enormous cotton plantation in New South Wales, Australia. The remaining 37.5 percent was in the hands of Peter Munk and David Gilmour. It was understood by the investors that the Canadians were in control.

By May of 1970 construction of the services was under way. The golf course was taking shape. The dredging of the harbour was proceeding. Land sales were moving well. According to Peter Munk,

> the Germans bought because the British bought. And the Hong Kong guys bought because of the European demand. And then the Fijians started to buy because they saw these people from England and Germany and Australia and Hong Kong buying. They thought they were missing the biggest opportunity!

As the year 1971 opened, the Pacific Harbour project was booming. During 1971 Peter Munk spent an enormous amount of time in London and in airplanes between Canada, Britain and Fiji. Trips to Hong Kong, New Zealand and Australia were also crammed into his schedule. Except for his annual winter skiing trek to Switzerland, where he enjoyed an aggressive time on skis and the conviviality of his many international friends, Munk was totally focused on Pacific Harbour and Fiji. The Hancock-planned waterways, lakes, dredging, and road gradings were underway. The sewage-treatment plant site was under way, as was the construction of the centrepiece

Beachcomber Hotel, which was the American Airlines project. Landscaping was about to start. And, to Munk's great comfort, the airfield at Pacific Harbour was finished in November. He could now make that thirty-mile trip between Deuba and the international airport by air instead of by rough road.

He had arranged to have sample homes designed by international architects in collaboration with a local firm of architects, Larson, Holton, Maybin. Several samples were under construction and photographs of them found their way into the Pacific Harbour sales brochures.

As Munk had predicted in his initial research of Fiji tourism, the volume of tourists visiting and staying on the island was skyrocketing. The number staying for an average of 7.1 days was 110,042 for the year 1970, a 20-percent increase over 1969. The first six months of 1971 brought 67,643 visitors, up 44 percent over the previous year. The tourists' country of origin was of special interest to Munk and Gilmour and to their marketing manager, Leslie Berenyi, a long-time close friend of Munk's. Out of the 1970 visitors, there were 34,049 Australians, 19,070 New Zealanders, 31,257 Americans, 6,500 Britons and 5,574 Canadians. The optimistic Fiji Visitors Bureau was predicting 408,000 visitors for the year 1975.

The international airlines were increasing their services between Nadi International Airport and Europe, North America and Asia, with Qantas, American, BOAC and Canadian Pacific leading the way. Some 232 aircraft were landing at Nadi every week. The pace was quickening.

There was also good news concerning the road. Munk had been pressing Prime Minister Ratu Sir Kamisese Mara and his government to reconstruct the main coastal road between Nadi and Suva. Finally his efforts paid off. The World Bank came through with a US$11-million loan to finance the work.

In November 1971, Pacific Hotels and Developments Limited,

SPP, and Peter Munk gave up their ultra-modest office digs at 18 Hazelton Avenue in Toronto, where they had moved two years earlier. All of the files, maps, charts—everything but the furniture and office equipment—were boxed and shipped by air to elegant new corporate offices in St. George's House at one of London's most prestigious business locations, 15 Hanover Square, London W1. Peter Munk and David Gilmour had arrived once more on the first rung of the ladder to success, fortune and reputation, up from the devastating Clairtone debacle.

Munk decided that with the move to London he would separate his and Gilmour's activities on behalf of Pacific Harbour from the direct supply of services to the development company. As he told his shareholders, "a management company was formed under my chairmanship to provide management services to our group of companies." The key word was group. Corporations in the Munk supervisory group were Canadian, Bahamian, British and Fijian. Undoubtedly, there would be others to be formed as the needs of Munk and Gilmour's entrepreneurial activities might dictate.

An example of those activities was the opening in July of Pacific Harbour's North American sales headquarters in California. Munk said at the time: "We expect to commence operations in Hawaii and California during the first quarter of 1972, since federal approval to offer Pacific Harbour property to American citizens has recently been received."

In the U.K., Munk distanced himself and his key people from the time-consuming matter of selling Pacific Harbour building lots by turning it over to local experts. In October he engaged the leading London estate agents, Messrs. Knight, Frank and Rutley, to be principal sales agents for Pacific Harbour in Britain.

As to Fiji, Munk's strategy was to have islanders involved in the Pacific Harbour activities. It made good business and political sense to do so. He wanted the government and the people in Fiji on his side. So he created a new Fijian corporation, Pacific Hotels Estate

Management Company. To fill the post of managing director, he engaged Gerald Barrack, a Fijian-born executive.

During the summer of 1971—as he had done every year since 1958—Peter Munk spent a month on the still primitively outfitted Georgian Bay island where, with friends, he relaxed, played, sailed, fished and, as always, thought about the future. That focused corporate planning would crystallize in one of Peter Munk's best years ever, 1972.

CHAPTER SIXTEEN

MELANIE BOSANQUET

"Break a leg" is the actor's traditional good luck wish for a colleague who is about to step onstage: break a leg is what Peter Munk did in Switzerland in January 1972, when he went skiing with his beautiful new love, Melanie Bosanquet.

I met Melanie in Gstaad in early '68 after the Christmas season. Gilmour and I shared a whole house, and my friend George Huvos, the fashion photographer, was there. He naturally looked for pretty models. He found two girls who ran a very fancy boutique in the Palace Hotel. George didn't have a car and never had any money. So he asked if he could borrow my car. I said: "You can't borrow my car. I've got to go skiing." He said, "Well, let's go together. You wait for me for half an hour and in return you'll meet some good-looking chicks and then we'll go skiing." So we got dressed in our ski outfits and at nine o'clock that morning I drove Georgie to a chalet next to the Palace Hotel where the two girls were waiting for him. I waited in a room down the corridor while Georgie was getting them dressed in this Canadian–American ski outfit he was taking pictures of. While I waited I looked at the photographs on the dresser of her parents and her brother, and there was a picture of her dog, and her pony. I thought, she must be a good person if she goes from England to Switzerland for three months with pictures of the family, the dog and her horse. So I was quite impressed before I met her.

Then I met the two girls, Patsy Hayes and Melanie Bosanquet, and the four of us went skiing. Melanie skied well and we had fun. That night she and I went out to a bar and dancing at the Palace. She was nice and she was bright and good-looking. We had lunches and dinners and skied together after that in Gstaad.

One day a few months after we met she called me from England, just when I was trying to finance Fiji or Swiss– Canadian. She had some sort of problem with her old boyfriend. The next time I was in London seeing Jim Slater, I took her out for dinner. After that we met every time I went to England, which was once a month because of the Slater Walker deal.

Munk recalls that he couldn't go back to Gstaad because Linda had now moved there permanently with Nina and Anthony. Linda took over the family chalet and asked Munk not to go back to Gstaad, because it was "too small for two divorced people." So, for the first time, Peter went to Klosters for his skiing, and Melanie came with her parents from Lenzerheide, where they had a place and where the Bosanquet family had gone for thirty years. She had some cousins in Klosters.

She stayed with her cousins who are friends of Prince Charles. The next day I had lunch with Melanie and my son, Anthony, and my girlfriend from New York, who decided not to ski that day. Melanie and I went straight from the restaurant to the first hill.

We went down the mountain and, on practically the first turn, I fell and broke my leg. It was the first time I had an accident and I had been skiing since I was seven years old. Melanie organized everything—the first aid, the doctor, the ambulance. She kept me going on that hill. I had a compound fracture, so the bone went through the muscle and skin. It was very cold. I was starting to freeze. Melanie took some of her clothing off and covered me up because I was lying on the ground. I was shivering and in shock. Melanie stayed with me all the way to the hospital and for hours and hours later. I was operated on that night.

I had a nanny in my house to look after Nina, who was just three, and Anthony, who was ten. When the nanny found out that I had broken my leg, she called Linda in Gstaad and Leslie Berenyi, who was in Klosters with me, and explained what had happened. My cousin John was also in Klosters, so we had a big group, what with Melanie's cousins. And Linda came across that afternoon from Gstaad. And, of course, my New York girlfriend was there.

I've been told that at dinner with a bunch of people, my relatives and friends, at this long restaurant table, while I was being operated on, Linda said, with both my girlfriend and Melanie there, but out of earshot, "What is wrong with Peter? Why can't he go around and marry somebody like Melanie Bosanquet?" Linda didn't think very much of my girlfriend, who was a tall, blonde New York model, but Linda, of course, knew Melanie from the year when I still lived with Linda in Toronto and she liked Melanie very much. Four people reported back to me about this dinner where my first wife was present and my girlfriend sat there and Melanie sat there, with Linda voicing her views as to whom she thought I should marry.

Melanie stayed for another two or three days and visited

me at the hospital every day. I was in the hospital for two weeks. As soon as I got out with my leg in a cast I had to go see Jim Slater again in London. We were in our first year of operation in Fiji and doing really well. So I spent quite a bit of time in London and I took Melanie to cocktail parties and dinners. Then I said, "You've never been to my Georgian Bay island. Why don't you visit the real Canada?" She accepted and we made plans for her to come up to Georgian Bay in the summer. She came back again and spent another week with me in early fall. Coincidentally, it was the very same fall when Jim Slater came to Toronto and said, "You've got to move to England if you want a successful public float of SPP. That's where the big buyers of shares are." I called Melanie that night and said, "Guess what? I'm going to have to move to London. Why don't you go look for a house." She found this famous house on Maida Avenue—in Little Venice on the canal—which was super, and she and I moved in together in November of that year.

Leslie Berenyi, Munk's close friend since 1956, talked about Peter's skiing accident:

I was with him when he had his accident. And he lay on the snow with a broken leg—an open break—and he kept consoling the people who were trying to look after him. We delivered him to the White Cross Hospital in Chur, which is run by nuns. A couple of days later when I went down to see him, the chief nun said, "He keeps telephoning Australia, America. Can he pay for all that?" It had taken about two days for him to take charge. His hospital room became the social meeting place of doctors and ambulatory patients. The room was full. There was always plenty of red wine. He asked the nuns to bring him extra glasses. He was the conductor. He could not stop conducting.

It was Berenyi who was the key to Munk's purchase of the piece of land at Klosters where the chalet, Viti Levu, stands.

Peter was in the hospital with his broken leg. In Klosters it's very difficult to buy a piece of property on the sunny side. And one morning the ski instructor said to me, "Leslie, there is *the* piece of property for sale. But Peter is in the hospital, he can't do anything, it has to move right away." I jumped in the car, drove to Chur, went into the hospital and told Peter. I asked him, "What are we going to do?" He said, "Well, goddamn it! What are *you* doing?! Why are you here?! Why don't you go and buy it for me?" So I said, "You don't mind?" "No, you buy it. You like it, you buy it." So off I went and I bought the land. I walked around on it and it was really *the* spot in Klosters. I bought the land right then and there that morning. When Peter had the money to spend, we actually designed the house together, he and Melanie and I. Then came the architect and then came the hand-picked Swiss workmen who laid the proper Swiss-style slate floor and did proper wall painting. Step by step by step that house was not built, it was born. It was absolutely magnificent. Everybody thought Peter was an idiot because it was too high up. Peter said, "The higher I am the more difficult it is for people to come up unannounced."

Leslie Berenyi knows Peter Munk the businessman, as well as the private person, as thoroughly as any man. He says of Munk:

He's an absolutely zero-bullshit man. He inspires immense loyalty and he justifies this loyalty. He attracts people. In fact many of them at such low prices that later on they wonder why they did it.

He never stops. He's in perpetual motion. The ideas come continuously. He never questions whether or not it should be done but how. That's when the inspiration begins to radiate out of him.

There are some people who haven't learned that they're in the wrong slot, that they should make a career somewhere else. If such a person works for him, Peter won't shy away from this situation. He's not unkind, not rough. He will simply say, "You know, I'm concerned. You're a friend, but you are wasting your time here." And the person gets a marvellous letter of recommendation. This is the type of person Peter is.

I have seen him with really important people like Prince Charles. Peter never tries, he never pushes. Somehow the opposite occurs: they seek his company. Peter is not talking to the Prince of Wales. He is talking to a chap who skis well. For Peter, in those two or three months of the year at Klosters, anybody who can slide on the snow belongs there and he's a friend whether he's the Prince of Wales or a ski instructor.

While still in his hospital bed, Peter Munk was focusing on the next step of his plan, which he had hatched with Jim Slater, Simon Pendock and, of course, David Gilmour. Bill Birchall was at the number-crunching centre of the development of the plan. It was a scheme to take Pacific Properties and SPP public, using the increasing success of the Fiji asset. If they went public, much-needed funds for the development of Pacific Harbour would be raised, and their own share interests would have a substantial market value and liquidity.

Munk had to get moving. As soon as he was released from the hospital, equipped, of course, with crutches, he was back in London, putting together, with Slater and his colleagues, a blockbuster "go-public" scheme that they would soon drop on a surprised international financial world. The corporate vehicles would be Hong Kong companies with attention-getting Chinese names. The Hong Kong market was booming, and Jardine Matheson's involvement—with Slater's magic touch—were bound to attract investor interest.

Slater Walker had earlier purchased a Singapore-based pharmaceutical firm, Haw Par Brothers (Hong Kong) Limited, which was listed on the Hong Kong stock exchange—a fact that was all-important. Haw Par bought a controlling interest in King Fung, which would be the main vehicle for what was to follow for SPP.

Step two was the acceptance of an bid dated February 29, 1972, by Haw Par (Slater Walker) for King Fung Development Company Limited of Hong Kong, which, among other things, was also listed on the Hong Kong exchange and owned Regent's House in that city's Queen's Road.

Step three came on March 8, when a press release was made by Haw Par and approved by Peter Munk and Jim Slater, announcing that Haw Par had purchased 65 percent of King Fung. Haw Par then caused King Fung to purchase from the consortium of owners all of the shares of Southern Pacific Properties Limited (SPP) by an exchange of 14 King Fung shares for each SPP share. This resulted in the issue to the consortium led by Munk and Slater of 70 million new shares of King Fung.

The Haw Par offer price for each King Fung share was HK$2.50 per share, but as of March 8 the King Fung shares had climbed to HK$4.70. That put a value of some HK$377 million on the overall company, or C$67 million, which meant he had already surpassed the C$12 million market capitalization of Clairtone at its height in August 1967.

The transaction was described in the Hong Kong press as "the largest and most sophisticated move the colony had ever seen." All the publicity was concentrated on Jim Slater and Slater Walker. The financial editor of the *South China Morning Post* of Hong Kong concluded that "the move amounts to a reverse takeover which will give Southern

Pacific a share quote in Hong Kong." That was the Munk and Slater objective—to have their Pacific Harbour enterprise have a share quote on the Hong Kong exchange. With it would come the realization or conversion of the Fiji assets in the form of market shares, which could be sold for cash by their owners or by the company out of its treasury to raise new capital.

The final step was simple. King Fung's name was changed to the obvious: Southern Pacific Properties Limited.

In ballpark terms Peter Munk and David Gilmour's group, with a holding of 37.5 percent of the Fiji project, received 26.25 million shares of SPP Hong Kong. The paper value at the close of the market on March 8, 1972, was HK$123,375,500, or $22 million, compared with their holding in Clairtone of less than $2 million.

Having recovered sufficiently from his injuries to travel with crutches, Peter Munk was in Hong Kong for the final transaction, as was Simon Pendock. After all, it was Munk's Fiji project that was in the centre of the transaction. It was his deal, notwithstanding the advice and input from Slater, Pendock or anyone else. He had led the negotiators and made the decisions.

Munk and Pendock celebrated in Hong Kong during the evening of March 8 (Jim Slater was in England with influenza); and champagne corks were the order of day in London for Gilmour, Birchall and the entire SPP team.

Alongside the Haw Par story, the *Hong Kong Standard* of March 9, 1972, carried on the front page of its business section another column of interest. It contained a photo of a sleek, bushy-haired Peter Munk, and a headline, "SPP moves to HK for Fiji business." The story was in the past tense. SPP *had* moved to Hong Kong "for attracting property investment to the Fiji islands." Peter Munk said he was interested in attracting Japanese capital into Fiji; that SPP had already entered into arrangements with Japan's Nomura Real Estate Company that would lead to large-scale Japanese investment abroad.

Meanwhile, Peter Munk was being advised to sell some of his personal shares in the new SPP. The advice both shocked and delighted him. He was gun-shy about selling his personally owned shares after the Adams case and the new insider trading rules of the Ontario Securities Commission, but the new SPP was a Hong Kong company—not Canadian. He was in Hong Kong, not Ontario. And his shares were now worth millions.

Peter Munk tells the story. There is still amazement in his voice when he does so.

> When we went public in '72, the market went berserk. The shares just kept on going up. That's when I got frightened that the market was way ahead of the value. And I said to my partners, "I created this, I conceived this, but you know there's reality and then there are dreams. This is not reality." The company was worth US$20 million, but on the Hong Kong market SPP was worth $100 million! Our shares went from $2.50 to $6. Jardine's David Newbigging, one of my directors in SPP, gave a lunch for me. After lunch Newbigging, whom I adore, talked with me. He was a big shot, the *Taipan*. He shut the door and said, "You know, Peter, Jardine's going to have a fantastic year, because we sold much of our own SPP shares at a great profit, all because of your effort. Have you sold any shares?" I said, "Me? It's my company." He said, "I don't give a damn, Peter, whose company it is. You cannot afford not to sell. You're a rich man on paper—you must also have some in cash." I said, "I'm not a rich man, but I own a quarter of this company." He said, "Peter, I'm older than you are. I'm wiser than you are. Please. The market is boiling. The demand is enormous. The market is still open for another hour. Why don't you take two million dollars' worth of shares and put it in your bank?" I said, "You're crazy. How would that look?" He said, "How would it *look*? The Chinese don't care; they

need paper—the Chinese just buy and buy. The market is boiling over and out of SPP stock. You, in fact, would help to cool the frenzy."

He called in his company secretary while I was there and gave the instructions to sell some of my shares. Melanie and I were just talking about building a house in Switzerland but I would have had to borrow. I had bought this lovely piece of land at Klosters and I wanted to build a house there but I didn't have the excess cash. Now I had the money! It was near Christmas, the seventeenth or eighteenth of December, when I arrived in Klosters and I had the money in my bank! I said to Melanie, "This house is going to be called Viti Levu (the Fijian name for Fiji), because that money came entirely and totally from Fiji."

CHAPTER SEVENTEEN

TRAVELODGE AUSTRALIA

J ust after the Haw Par–King Fung deal was closed in March 1972, Peter Munk had already laid out a strategic objective for the new SPP. The shares of King Fung/SPP had become enormously overvalued. So unless some substance was added to the company, its shares were vulnerable to a correction in market price. Peter Munk's urgent goal was to increase the real asset base and underlying value of SPP of Hong Kong, so he had to buy assets that were undervalued with SPP's paper.

Munk's attention now focused on Travelodge Australia Ltd. (TAL), an Australian hotel chain, the largest in the region, that was in a tourist-related business somewhat like that of SPP. It owned and operated hotels across Australia, New Zealand, Fiji, and in many South Pacific islands and nations.

Travelodge expanded too fast. They were the biggest hotel operators in the Pacific and the fourth or fifth largest Australian company. They were expanding into New Guinea, into Tahiti, into Japan, and they just ran out of money. Their shares went down from $5 to the $1.50 range.

Travelodge was desperate for an infusion of new capital. Its shares were way below their underlying asset value, so it would be an ideal fit for SPP. There was, however, a major obstacle. Munk had decided that he would never participate in a corporate venture unless he had control. By the laws of Australia, a foreign person or corporation was prohibited from controlling a national- and international-scale Australian-based company of the magnitude of Travelodge. If Munk made an investment in an Australian corporation through his Hong Kong company, it could only be on a non-control basis—50 percent, but no more.

Alan Greenway, managing director of Travelodge, became Munk's biggest ally in solving this problem. Greenway needed the money badly, as well as investors the calibre of P & O, Slater and Jardine, and to him Munk was a necessary evil. He had wealthy international investors with him, and he had cash. And he seemed to be prepared to put his money in, even though, as Greenway knew, the laws in Australia were very clear: Munk could never get control of the company. Greenway could feel totally secure in his ongoing control despite having a single investor with 50 percent of the shares. All Greenway had to do was talk the government into allowing Munk to make the investment. With David Hoare, an Australian banker with Bankers' Trust whom Munk had retained as an adviser, Greenway flew to Canberra to meet with the prime minister and other politicians; approval was quickly granted. Munk says:

> Greenway, of course, thought I was the biggest sucker he
> could ever find. Who else would put up A$15 million in a
> non-control situation and pay a premium for his shares? So I
> got 50 percent but I had only one board membership out of
> twelve. Greenway himself had less than 1 percent of the
> shares, but he had a big country house and half a dozen ser-
> vants and chauffeurs at his disposal, as well as undisputed
> control—as chairman, managing director and CEO.

The Haw Par–King Fung/SPP transaction had been completed in Hong Kong during the first week in March 1972. The first public word of the bid for a 50-percent participation in Travelodge hit the Australian press only eleven weeks later. Peter Munk, his identity as yet undisclosed, was carrying out opening tactics of his strategic plan to assault and ultimately capture total control of Travelodge.

The *Melbourne Herald* carried the story on May 24, 1972, saying that "a Hong Kong-based listed public company is offering $1.53 a share for 50 percent of Travelodge Australia Ltd.'s capital. The offer is worth $14.65 million. The Hong Kong Company is Southern Pacific Properties Ltd. It trades under the name King Fung Development Co. Ltd. in Hong Kong and London. It is changing its name to Southern Pacific Properties." The extensive newspaper report then gave some reassuring news about the substance and prestige of the company making the offer: "Most of its shares are held by an international consortium including P & O, Slater Walker Securities of Britain, Jardine Matheson & Co. Ltd. of Hong Kong and J.G. Boswell Co. of California."

One of the board members of Travelodge Australia was Sir Charles Forté, the renowned London-based hotelier and entrepreneur. He had acquired a substantial shareholding in the company through his firm, Trust Houses Forté, and would be a valuable ally and connection for Peter Munk in the future.

The *Herald* further reported:

The chairman of SPP is Mr. Peter Munk, a Canadian. Directors include Lord Geddes, chairman of British Hotels Association, and Mr. H.T. Beazley, who are both directors of P and O; Mr. D.K. Newbigging, managing director of Jardine Matheson and Co. Ltd.; Mr. S.B. Pendock, formerly a director of Slater, Walker Securities of Britain; Mr. A.D. Leys, partner in the legal firm of Munro, Leys, Kermode and Co., Fiji; Mr. R.M. Grierson, managing director of Pacific Hotels and Developments Ltd., Fiji; and Mr. R. W. Jones, chairman of the Pacific Coast Stock Exchange, California.

Peter Munk was described in the Australian press as the "mystery man" who had flown into Sydney just in time for the closing of the Travelodge merger. "A merger is like a marriage," said Munk at the time. "I didn't want to propose and then be refused. I stayed in the background until I knew I would be accepted. I bought Travelodge's men, not the bricks and mortar. I wanted the management."

That was a principle that Peter Munk would adhere to in most of his future acquisitions. Of the Travelodge hotels he said: "Travelodge is going to run them. We are not hoteliers. They are." Before jetting off to Hong Kong on May 26, 1972, Peter Munk said a few other things designed to tell Australia what he had in mind. For example:

The Concorde is going to be a highway of steel into the southern Hemisphere—in tourist terms an underexplored area.

We don't regard Travelodge as Australian. It's a South Pacific company. We are going to provide money to build the hotels travellers need.

We don't worry too much about today. That's why these stories about half-full hotels in Australia don't disturb me. We are thinking about 10 years ahead, by which time nothing can stop Travelodge having filled the hotel vacuum in the South Pacific.

In early July 1972, just before Peter and Melanie went to their Georgian Bay island, the *Toronto Star* sent a staff writer to England to interview Peter Munk.

Frank Jones's piece appeared on July 11, 1972. His descriptions of Munk and his London scene provide a glimpse of the young entrepreneur and his surroundings at that time.

A black totem carving from the South Pacific frowns from

the mantelpiece, a huge map of the world's oceans fills one office wall, and exotic South Sea shells decorate the reception room ... Peter Munk, cherubic blond curls framing the face of a choir boy, sweeps around the futuristic glass and teak desk and is shaking hands and pouring coffee from a silver flask in one fluid motion.

A wad of airline stubs testify that he commutes to Australia on an almost regular basis as the firm's South Pacific interests expand. He made three journeys there in one recent month. A fat file of press clippings records that Munk has been interviewed everywhere from London to Hong Kong.

Even the three floors of offices, conjured up seemingly out of nowhere, and now complete with antique furniture, seem part of a movie set that might be cleared away, along with the sea shells and the totem, in the morning. But the air of unreality conceals some hard facts. Munk's firm has just taken control of the big Australian hotel chain, Travelodge Australia Ltd., a move which Munk says will give him control within three years of one-third of the hotel space in Australia, New Zealand and Fiji.

Control of Travelodge? Frank Jones must have misheard Peter Munk, since no one knew better than he that he did *not* have control of Travelodge—not with the government bar against foreign control, and with just one seat on the board of directors. It certainly appeared that Munk had abandoned his principle of control. But appearances can be deceiving.

Munk and Gilmour were enjoying their new success. On November 4, 1972, they celebrated the official opening of the flagship Beachcomber Hotel by the Honourable Senator Ratu Penaia K. Ganilau, CMG, CVO, DSO, OBE, minister for communications, works and tourism at the Hotel, Pacific Harbour, Deuba, Fiji.

The cover of the invitation to the opening is hand-painted in a native Fijian symbolic design in black, white and brown. Inside, on the left-hand page, is an artistically created map of all of the Fiji islands, the two most prominent being Viti Levu and Vanua Levu. On the right-hand page is a painting of a three-storey hotel, and below it the text of this special request to attend. Among the guests were Dr. and Mrs. Tibor Abranyi; Peter Munk was delighted to bring his mother, Katharina, and her husband from their home in Toronto to share in her son's new success.

The October 1972 issue of *Quest*, a Canadian magazine that was just getting into print, carried a profile of the forty-five-year-old Peter Munk, whose picture appeared, hair-over-ears, on the cover. The writer of the piece, John Gault, proved to be not only capable but prescient. He had spent a few days with Munk at his London home in June, just after the amazing Travelodge deal. In the closing paragraph Gault said:

> Munk is involved in a venture so vast, so daring and so entirely plausible that any day now he will be a superstar again— only this time much bigger. He loves Canada, and he loved being the darling of the smart set for those seven sunny years, and consciously or unconsciously what he's doing is getting ready for his comeback. He is going to make it so big that the Canadian Club will have no alternative but to ask him once again to address them. The Prime Minister will consider it an honour to have him to lunch, and the stories on the business pages will be headlined: "Hey, everybody, guess who's back, bigger than ever?"

INTO THE ABYSS

In his London offices in the spring of 1973, Peter Munk was carefully and apprehensively monitoring the activities of Travelodge Australia's management, in whom he had less and less confidence. Other than an article on April 1, 1973, in the *Sunday Times* of London, the Pacific Harbour project seemed to be proceeding smoothly without attracting much media attention. But for the avid skier Peter Munk, the year 1973 would be like traversing a new mountain plateau, then coming suddenly to an unforeseen, unavoidable drop into a steep-walled abyss, in which control and life are nearly lost.

Peter Munk's private life had changed considerably in the previous month. On January 14, 1972, a decree absolute had been granted in the divorce case of Linda and Peter Munk. Peter would continue to both support and care for Linda and the children, Anthony and Nina.

At the beginning of June 1973, Peter sent a message to his Toronto solicitor, Claude Thompson, urgently requesting a certified copy of the decree absolute. The reason for the urgency was that Peter Munk and Melanie Bosanquet had decided to marry. The required certificate was issued by the court and sent air mail to the groom-to-be. On Tuesday, June 26, 1973, in London, in the presence of her family and with David Gilmour and other associates of the groom in attendance, Melanie Bosanquet married Peter Munk. The newlyweds spent a few weeks at their Georgian Bay island retreat, then it was back to the business world and the fall social whirl of London. Life seemed to have opened out into a peaceful and prosperous new chapter.

Then on October 23, 1973, the Yom Kippur War began in the Middle East. The fighting between Israel and Egypt embroiled virtually all the Arab nations. As the Egyptians were furiously and effectively assaulted in the air and on the ground by Israeli forces, their Arab brethren, the oil-producing Arab countries, struck back. Led by Saudi Arabia, Kuwait and Iraq, they imposed an oil embargo on all nations that did business with, supplied weapons to or in any other way had an involvement with Israel.

The impact of the oil embargo was devastating for Munk and Gilmour's Fiji project, and for SPP's 50-percent interest in Travelodge Australia. As Munk recalls:

Every article you picked up implied that the world energy costs would be ten times greater. Everybody agreed that oil was going to be a scarce and expensive commodity, that the whole world would change. It changed the way people looked at travel. They always overreact!

My whole strategy in putting together Fiji and then New Zealand and then Travelodge and Tahiti was based on my belief that long-distance luxury travel would be a growing component in the world, that more and more people would be seeking exotic holidays. But every analyst said we were doomed. And we got hurt badly. You can't maintain thirty luxury hotels and forty resorts in places as far away as Fiji, Samoa, Cook Island, Tahiti, when people can no longer afford long-distance travel.

In Britain, property values collapsed. The secondary banking industry—the financial sector other than the major banks—was primarily funded by profits from the property boom, and the result was that nearly every secondary bank collapsed. And one of its leaders, Slater Walker, went with them. Munk says:

> My SPP shares lost their value: first 30 percent, then another 30 percent, then another 30 percent. We went from HK$5.40 down to 60 cents. Secondly, the mortgagors for our various hotels, if they had a chance, called back their debts. It was just like the property boom and bust in Canada later, in the eighties. Everybody was panicking. My main supports were all based in England. My cash flow became very precarious because land sales at Pacific Harbour simply came to a halt, but once you start building a hotel and it's three-quarters of the way finished you can't stop. We had big hotel projects at Narita, the new airport in Japan, and in Auckland at the harbour; and a major shopping centre in the middle of our Fiji development. We couldn't stop any of it.

Munk had to maintain offices in Germany, in England, in California, in Hong Kong, in Tokyo, even though there were no land sales in Fiji. There was enough money in the kitty for SPP to survive, but the cash wasn't flowing. The situation was awful. Munk had to raise money and the only way was to bring in equity. But every shareholder wanted to sell, even his major holders. (The exception was the enormous, old, cash-rich P & O.)

P & O began a takeover bid in early 1974 during discussions in Fiji between Peter Munk and Sandy Marshall, the CEO of P & O. Munk was in Fiji with Melanie. Birchall had arrived there ahead of Munk. Their objective was to cut spending down to the last possible penny. Marshall, whose chief financial officer was on the board, knew of SPP's financial plight. It was a perfect time for P & O to make a bid. After all, they were the oldest factors in the tourism industry and had an enormous presence in Australia. With their cruise and line ships, the hotels and resorts would have consolidated their position—forever. After painful negotiations with Marshall, Munk agreed in principle that P & O should buy the ailing company, although the price per share was not yet decided.

The next meeting took place in London, where Peter Munk met with P & O's representative on the SPP board, Clifford Nancarrow, and their finance director, Oliver Brooks.

> Nancarrow agreed to buy all the outstanding shares, about 70 percent, and we would run the hotel division for them. P & O wouldn't pay us a premium, nor would I sell for market price. So we agreed at the middle price of HK$1.80 and then we shook hands on it, at least I thought we did. That certainly was my impression, and Gilmour's and Birchall's, of the price we had agreed on. It was very important to us. I mean, this was our life.

Then came an unexpected roadblock. Someone on the main P & O board with Canadian connections, who had heard about Clairtone, questioned Munk's reputation and his integrity. Nancarrow was told to prepare a report on Munk; otherwise the deal would not go through. P & O would not allow Munk to run its hotel division if his reputation was in question. Nancarrow was embarrassed, but there it was. Peter Munk was shocked.

> Pat Samuel and David Gilmour and I decided to get a legal opinion from an independent and totally credible law firm in Toronto. We picked Bob Macaulay's firm because we knew him when he was involved with us in the CMI days and his firm was fully acceptable to the P & O board. He was an outside third party. He was not my lawyer. He was with the Thomson, Rogers law firm.

So we retained Macaulay to do a search and an opinion. I said, "Please be as thorough as possible. This is a major takeover. We're selling our whole company here and it's all hanging on my personal reputation. Do as detailed a report as possible. It has to be totally checkable because it's P & O."

Robert Macaulay produced what was asked for. His junior lawyer, Bruce Armstrong, carried out an intensive search in the files of the courts and of the lawyers who had performed for and against Munk and Gilmour in their Clairtone days. Under Macaulay's direction and supervision, Armstrong toiled long and hard. Then it was up to Macaulay to prepare the reporting letter. It was finished three weeks later.

Peter Munk was extremely pleased with Macaulay's sixteen-page report and in particular with its summation paragraph:

In short, as a result of our review of this matter, it is our opinion that any allegations of improper or wrongful conduct arising out of dealings in the shares of Clairtone Sound Corporation Limited on behalf of Mr. Peter Munk and Mr. David H. Gilmour are without foundation in fact or law.

A certified copy of the Macaulay letter was delivered to Clifford Nancarrow at the P & O offices as soon as the original was received at Munk and Gilmour's Hanover Square offices; the document was sufficient to allay any concerns of the P & O board of directors, who gave their approval of the bid.

In the intervening time the market had gone further down. SPP shares went down as well. As a result, the P & O offer, when finally received, was not at the HK$1.80 price Munk had agreed to, but was drastically lower, at HK$1.20.

Peter Munk would have none of it! He called the SPP board for a London meeting,where he convinced his directors to refuse the P & O bid. Their rejection brought a stinging letter from P & O saying no one had ever done that to P & O since its inception 150 years before and they could not be dealt with like that.

The shares continued to fall, especially after the bid's rejection. As a result, Munk was finally persuaded, by Gilmour and Birchall among others, that the only way to go for all of them was to accept the low P & O bid. A reluctant, proud Peter Munk called London to obtain an appointment to see the P & O chairman, Lord Inchcape. The meeting turned out to be one of the most difficult of Peter Munk's business life.

> I went into Oliver Brooks' office. He was their CFO and he sat on my board. Lord Inchcape came in. There were three of them, including Sandy Marshall, who was P & O's managing director. They sat there like British aristocrats. I told them the truth: "A group of my directors made me come back and tell you that it would be very nice if you could give us a face-save and make the price $1.30 or $1.40. The board's rejection of your offer was entirely my personal doing and did not repre-sent the board's collective view. It's only costing you an extra £400,000 or so, and then we take it and you get the company exactly the way you want it." And I'll never forget what Lord Inchcape said next after I made this highly apologetic and embarrassing pitch. He said in that fancy English accent, "We don't know what you're talking about, Mr. Munk. There is no offer on the table. I don't know what you're negotiating." I said, "I'm not negotiating, sir, I'm telling you that the bid you made a few weeks ago would now be recommended if you gave us a few cents more for face-saving." They knew that if they put it back at $1.30, I would have to say yes. Inchcape said, "Mr. Munk, there is no offer on the table. There is nothing to negotiate. You will go bankrupt, whether it's a year from now or fourteen months from now. Then we will talk to the receiv-

er and we will pick up your assets. We will pay nothing to the shareholders and you will face the wrath of your directors, which you well deserve, because you were pigheaded, Mr. Munk, and embarrassed P & O in public with your rejection of our offer. There is no offer, there is no $1.30, there is no $1.20, there is no $1.00. Your shares are today seventy-two cents. For the next year they'll be around that price and, as your cash dwindles, you will not be able to repay your bank loan or your first mortgage payments. We will be there to pick up the pieces—the hotel, the resort, the whole structure—for the debt only. We gave you a chance to come along gracefully. You could have had a great job with us." And I was thrown out. Melanie and I left that night for Fiji.

It was now up to Peter Munk to find a way for SPP to survive. The P & O bridge had been burnt. The situation was desperate.

At this crucial point Peter Munk had to start fighting Alan Greenway. South Pacific hotel occupancies were falling like rocks. Mortgage rates went through the roof. Munk had to oust Greenway and change the management of Travelodge, because he knew that it was going to go bankrupt if Greenway remained in charge. It meant moving to Australia with his key people, including Birchall and Samuel.

Munk talks about how difficult it was:

It was early '74 when we moved to Australia. We lived in a small, grubby apartment. We really had no money. We cut all executive salaries to the bone to husband our resources. We cut expense accounts and monitored travel costs to the penny. Bill Birchall stayed in Fiji. Pat Samuel was in Australia as my deputy chairman. It was very tough, but I'm good at those things. I react well under pressure.

Greenway asked why I was there, and I said, "Well, I'm moving here because I own 50 percent, I can't make any more cash flow from my Fiji land sales. There are no land sales in this new energy-short world, where all real estate values have collapsed. In fact, I can't even collect my receivables. So Travelodge's well-being is vital. When I bought my half interest in Travelodge you had a dividend program, and I depended on those dividends. Then you and your board cut off the dividends. You don't run the place properly, and I think you're going bust and I have to do something about it. I want to change the policies." He said, "Well, how do you do that with one board seat?" I said, "By increasing my board seats. Control should go with ownership. I own 50 percent!" And he got very mad. We had some dreadful, dreadful meetings. Violent confrontations. I had to go to make depositions to the police because he threatened me. He fought for his life, I guess, his lifestyle, his prestige, his position in the community. Alan Greenway was a big man in Australia. A local business hero. He was known and he was successful in Australia, chairman of the biggest hotel chain. And it was all Australian. Suddenly I threatened him when he thought he had an agreement, which he did. But, you know, agreements here, agreements there, they cannot cut across common sense or the fundamental principles of ownership. I offered to sell my shares if he could find a buyer. Anyone, any price. But the way they were going he just couldn't do it.

A little more than a year after he moved to Australia, he decided to buy out the minority shareholders in Travelodge so he would own 100 percent of the shares. It was the only way he could direct some of Travelodge's cash flow into SPP. Once he had his board's approval, he started building his case against Greenway, whom he had to dislodge before he could buy the whole company.

Munk knew from the board minutes that major mortgage payments were coming due and Travelodge had no money. Within eighteen months Travelodge was going to be bankrupt. Munk told the government that if Greenway remained in charge of Travelodge not only would they lose a major Australian asset that earned huge foreign revenues but they also would endanger the livelihood of four thousand Australians—in the middle of a major recession. He got in touch with every trade union that had a contract with Travelodge, warning them that the financial picture was bad. Through the labour unions, Munk got to the minister of tourism and the minister of finance of the Labour government. After all, he was a 50-percent shareholder of a very big Australian company and the unions believed that he could save their members' jobs—while Greenway would endanger them with his policy of rapid overseas growth.

> So I went to the union hall. I brought on these huge charts and I'm a good speaker. Plus, what I said was the truth. I said, "Listen, I have to have control, because I'm not going to put more money in unless I do, especially after the first two years when Greenway threw it all away." I had a photograph of Greenway opening a fancy hotel. I said, "Look at him. Every six months this guy goes somewhere and cuts ribbons. He gets his kicks from cutting ribbons with heads of state and celebrities. He doesn't care about taking on more mortgages because he thinks that the more hotels he has, the bigger a man he is. Well, you know, it's not a game of getting bigger for Alan Greenway. It's a game to make sure that we have the financial stability on which this company can grow and survive tough times that are coming."

The final step was that Munk out-manoeuvred Greenway by going to see Sir Charles Forté in London, even though Greenway was on Sir Charles's board in London. Munk's big break was that he realized that Charles Forté also thought that Greenway was incompetent.

Meeting Sir Charles was like meeting God in England. I never saw anything like the secretaries, the magnificent offices, and his hotels. I had to make a pitch against his own board member, Greenway, because Sir Charles had 10 percent of Travelodge. I said, "Sir Charles, this man is going to ruin us." And he had with him Kenneth Hall and Norman Jones, two old war comrades of his in their late sixties, distinguished people. And they believed me. They came down to Australia later and they saw that Greenway was ruining this company. I told Sir Charles that my people and I had a business plan: we would sell three hotels for parking lots, sell thirteen hotels overall and use the proceeds to reduce our mortgages; shrink the operation but make it financially healthy.

Seven months after his board gave its approval, Munk had control of the Travelodge board. After much politicking and persuasion of key board members Munk was satisfied he had a majority with him. Alan Greenway was gone. As Munk puts it:

I won. My new board fired him. Our taking control of Travelodge and the firing of Greenway was headline stuff in Australia. All the violence, the accusations. Greenway then disappeared.

Munk's policy was rationalization and not expansion. He set about slashing overhead expenses in Travelodge. They sold the dining-room silver. They sold off the corporate art collection. They liquidated the head office. And finally, they changed the name to Southern Pacific Hotel Corporation when they merged Travelodge Australia with SPP.

CHAPTER NINETEEN

EGYPT AND
KHASHOGGI

On Sunday, July 21, 1974, tucked at the end of a news report in Cairo's *Egyptian Gazette*, headlined "Work Begins on 760 Room $35m. Omar Khayyam Hotel," there was a paragraph that read:

> There is now in Egypt an English delegation considering choosing sites on the north coast and the Red Sea coast for joint projects of villages and camps with the Egyptian General Tourism and Hotels Organization.

There was indeed a delegation in Egypt but it was not English, it was Canadian—although with English overtones. It had origins in yet another London dinner party, at which the debonair David Gilmour had been introduced to Ashraf Marwan, the personal executive assistant to President Sadat of Egypt. Marwan asked what Gilmour did, in tones reminiscent of an earlier London dinner, when Jim Slater became fascinated by Gilmour, and the Canadian enthusiastically described the success that he and Munk were making in Fiji and the South Pacific with their tourist destination resort. The Egyptian was interested. "You know, that's what Egypt drastically requires during these dark ages of tourism. We have big ambitions and we need help."

He asked Gilmour whether he would like to come down to Cairo and meet some government people and look at the opportunities in Egypt. Gilmour went. He even paid his own way, because Munk refused to have cash-strapped SPP pay for Gilmour's pie-in-the-sky, far-fetched and far-afield trip.

Gilmour's role in the partnership continued to be as the point-man, "bird-dogging," and being out there finding new opportunities. As Gilmour understood Munk's job, it was to rationalize and digest, with Birchall, the propositions that Gilmour came up with, and what he saw now in Egypt was an opportunity, based on SPP's ability to create a resort that was a destination recreation facility—a place where tourists would stay for long periods. Munk also saw it as giving him access to Middle Eastern money—the only source for new investments in those difficult days in London.

In Cairo, Gilmour was welcomed into President Sadat's inner group of advisers, and taken to sites that they thought had the potential to attract tourists and visitors from all over the world. The Egyptians were impressed by SPP's international investors, the *crème de la crème* of the industry. They also liked that the company was Canadian and British, and not American. Finally, Gilmour was told, "You can take your pick. Any development will be a joint venture with the government. You choose the site."

Gilmour was convinced that Egypt was a place where business could be done. There seemed to be peace in the Middle East, and the government in Egypt clearly wanted to play catch-up. Sadat had kicked out the Russians and become friendly with the Saudis, who convinced him of the benefits of Western investments and know-how.

Gilmour flew back to London to tell Munk about his highly positive reception in Cairo. Gilmour says,

We had to design a presentation saying to Sadat's people, "Right, here's the philosophy. You put up the land, government. We'll put up the capital and give you our know-how and management. We'll show you how it cash flows. We'll take worthless land that you're not using now, and you'll have what you want: a destination resort, of which the government is a shareholder, that will bring jobs and foreign exchange, and will upgrade the Egyptian infrastructure."

There was only one firm to do the job, Macklin Hancock's. Hancock was in Toronto. He recalls:

I had a call from Peter Munk in Britain. He and David Gilmour had a large project in Egypt, to be called the "Pyramids Oasis" project. I said I'd be very interested in talking to them about it. I met Peter in his London office with David Gilmour. We had a wonderful reunion. Peter said, "Well, this is Fiji starting all over again."

Macklin Hancock and his associate, Ron Thomson, were soon off to Cairo with Gilmour to be introduced to Ashraf Marwan and to inspect the sites that the Sadat government was prepared to offer. This was the "English delegation" that the *Egyptian Gazette* had referred to. The Mediterranean coast, where Cleopatra had her summer palace, seemed to have ideal qualities. Munk and Gilmour, with their master planner, Hancock, could envision the Mediterranean's beaches and its waters drawing people from all over Europe. The parcel chosen was some twenty thousand acres at R'as El Hekma on the coast, where President Sadat's holiday villa stood. But it was the Pyramids Oasis site that would have first priority. This was a parcel proposed by an important member of the Egyptian government, with whom David Gilmour had been dealing.

Then General Zaki, who was in charge of the Egyptian tourist ministry, said, "I would like to have something really high profile. I think I can get you ten thousand acres just outside Cairo, near the Pyramids, where you can see the Pyramids, but the Pyramids can't see the project."

It was a sector of desert in the National Reserve at Giza. Development there would have a view of the Pyramids, the Nile Valley, the City of Cairo and, of course, the desert itself. The site includes a large desert plateau. On the northern tip of this plateau stand the Great Pyramids of Giza; bordering to the west is a broad flat valley extending northwest towards Alexandria; to the east, the land drops sharply towards the Nile Valley.

It was during this same summer that Munk and Gilmour first met the famous Saudi Arabian entrepreneur, the billionaire Adnan Khashoggi and his brother Essam. Adnan was to be part of Peter Munk and David Gilmour's corporate lives for many years to come. At the same London dinner party where Gilmour had met Sadat's executive assistant, Gilmour had asked Ashraf Marwan to suggest who might be able to finance a recreation development on the scale they were discussing. He was told to talk to a Saudi called Khashoggi. Everybody knew about Adnan Khashoggi. As Munk puts it:

In 1974, spring and summer, it was chaos in England. Everybody walked around with candles. The Wilson government, the secondary banking crisis, stock market collapse, property values nil, people committing suicide. The only people who had unlimited money were this new elite, these mysterious Arabs. Unless you knew an Arab, there was no money.

Back in London after his first Cairo trip, David Gilmour arranged contact with Adnan Khashoggi and his brother Essam. Contact was made through a Lebanese friend, Charles Riachy, who, as was the custom, would eventually be paid an appropriate fee.

Gilmour met the Khashoggis several times in London before a word of business was discussed. Eventually, Gilmour was allowed to make a business presentation that involved an invitation to invest not only in Egypt but also in SPP and its vast hotel holdings.

Before the Saudi billionaire would consider investing in SPP, he wanted to meet Peter Munk. Munk tells the story:

> The big thing for me was that I was Jewish. For the Arabs in those days the Jews were always the bogeyman. Gilmour organized an elegant dinner party. The host was a mutual friend, a banker, in the old town of Geneva. It was just a small dinner, eighteen or so people. Khashoggi told a story about his father: "You know, in my father's day we lived in the Bedouin desert. My father was a doctor. He had to go out on a call to a sick Bedouin sheik. The father rode across the desert to visit the sick man, and the sick man was cured. The son of the sheik gave the doctor a beautiful pot; it was absolutely magnificent. It had been hidden in the sand for centuries. My father brought it back to where we lived at that time, which was in Riyadh."
>
> In the usual fashion, everybody at the dinner table was paying attention to Adnan. Khashoggi said that his father realized the pot was extremely valuable and took it to his best friend, an old Jewish antique dealer in Jidda. It turned out that this piece was from the days when the Jews were wandering in the desert; it had been hidden, and passed from Bedouin to Bedouin. It's one of the original heritage pieces, and today it is in the Jerusalem Museum. Adnan's father's Jewish friend never forgot it, and they became closer friends.
>
> This whole story was designed by Adnan to make one person feel comfortable—and that was me, Peter Munk.

After dinner, Khashoggi invited Munk to go for a walk, just the two of them.

> We walked out towards the Lake of Geneva among all these bodyguards and cars; just the two of us. He said, "I really would like to be your partner. I checked you out, and please understand that we Arabs have nothing against Jews. They are our best friends. Just because some radicals have problems, that has nothing to do with us. If you're interested, I'm interested." I said, "Well, not only am I Jewish, I'm proud of being Jewish." And he said, "I have nothing but respect for that. I would never ask you to hide the fact that you're Jewish. I would only ask one thing of you. When we are in Saudi Arabia or Egypt together, don't flaunt the fact that you are Jewish. Please understand it's a delicate situation in those countries. Let me handle it. We'll go together; you will be my partner, the chairman of the company, the CEO; you call the shots, but just don't flaunt it." I said, "You've got a deal."
>
> That relationship never changed. He was generous, he was there when there was trouble, he was giving more than taking. He was what you expect a partner to be.

Khashoggi, however, wanted to invest in Egypt only. The partners nearly ended the negotiations by refusing to let Khashoggi sponsor just that one project. After all, the object of the exercise was to raise the cash needed for the survival of the main South Pacific/Australian operations until things could improve. Finally, Gilmour told him he could invest in Egypt only by investing in SPP. At the last minute, Khashoggi agreed to invest in the whole SPP group.

Bringing Adnan Khashoggi into SPP as a significant shareholder, involved much more than having the diminutive Arab take a walk by Lake Geneva with his new Jewish friend, Peter Munk. Munk badly needed Khashoggi's many millions of dollars in SPP's coffers, but deal-

ing with him and finalizing the actual share price on which his investment in a public company would have to be based was "probably the
most difficult negotiation I had in my life, because he couldn't understand how public corporations worked. He understood that Gilmour,
Birchall and I owned x million dollars in SPP shares, and his staff told
him what that was worth on paper or on the books. But he just could
not understand that he had to put up ten times as much as we had in
it, ten times x, but control was to stay with us," because that was how
public companies worked. Munk explained to him that it was not
money, but human effort and public trust, that would make his
investment grow, and Munk could not make that effort or generate
investor confidence if he did not have control.

Khashoggi had made his fortune mainly by collecting agent's
commissions from aircraft and arms manufacturers who sold their
products to Saudi Arabia. So Khashoggi's agenda was to sell more
Boeing airplanes or missiles to Saudi Arabia. Munk was concerned
about the potential repercussions: "If his king or the defence minister of Kuwait or Saudi Arabia leaned on him, and said, I'll give you
the contract for this jet or for these missiles, Adnan, but we know you
control this big hotel company in Australia because you've got this
large position in it, so would you just like to do me a favour and
make them put up two hotels here in my country?—SPP could have
gone bankrupt with Khashoggi in control. With us in control, he
could say, Well, Peter Munk will get us out of the problem. He will
build two hotels, sir, to get me the contract." Munk refused to put
himself and SPP in that position.

Finally, it was Munk's logic, his persistence and his goodwill that
convinced Khashoggi. As the years passed, "Adnan thanked us a
hundred times. He was able to say no to his own and other governments, because he had no control, he was just an investor in a public company and we could do what was right for him and for our
other shareholders. It was so logical. There was no way I would put
myself in any other position, not after Clairtone. No matter what

the consequences are, I don't give away control." It would take almost a year, until March 1976, to close the deal and bring Khashoggi's money into SPP.

The one remaining question was whether President Sadat would approve of SPP and the Pyramids Oasis project and give his consent to the complicated agreements necessary to get the imaginative development under way. Gilmour, the partner with the primary contacts, was negotiating and dealing with officials in Egypt, while Peter Munk and Bill Birchall were living in Sydney, dealing with Travelodge, and crunching the numbers. Munk, the engineer, was also working with Hancock and his staff on the development of the master plan for the Pyramids Oasis.

By the end of August 1974, it was time for Peter Munk to go to Egypt to meet President Sadat. As he recalls, "Here I was, this Jewish boy, going to Cairo. The Canadian ambassador kept saying, 'You mustn't come to Egypt. It's not safe!' But Adnan briefed me, and got me a special visa."

Peter Munk finally obtained his visa and, with Khashoggi and Gilmour, flew to Cairo armed with Hancock's plans and the preliminary corporate deal that Gilmour had worked out with Egypt's General Ahmed Zaki (El Sayed Ahmed Saky Abdul Hamed), the head of the Egyptian General Organization for Tourism and Hotels (EGOTH), the government body that was to be the "partner" of SPP. To isolate SPP's main Australian assets from any possible debacle in unstable Egypt, the program called for a fully separate subsidiary of SPP, to be called SPP (Middle East), and EGOTH to enter a joint venture in which the government would have its percentage of shares in return for the land.

This was a big deal for Egypt: a major new tourist project, with Saudi financing and Western expertise, and Sadat personally had to approve handing over land around the Pyramids to the largest-ever single foreign group to undertake development in the country. The transaction would be dealt with under a new Egyptian law, Law 43, the new foreign investment control law. Adnan Khashoggi had, of course, been given immediate access to Sadat. The president wanted to meet David Gilmour and Peter Munk and see the plans. An audience was arranged. Munk describes the scene:

> President Sadat sat in a chair that was almost like a throne, very Louis XV, gilded. Everybody had to be seated according to protocol. Then David said, "Sir, may we show you the drawings and models?" Sadat said, "Of course!" So we rolled out the drawings, set up the models, and the aides moved things out of the way. We had been told we had fifteen minutes, but fifteen minutes went, twenty minutes went, and Sadat asked more and more questions. His English was very good. Sadat kept on looking and asking questions, and within minutes he was down on his knees with us—Sadat, David and I. His staff people were flipping. We must have spent an hour. He kept on asking questions and making comments in Arabic to his aides and everybody got involved. In the picture David and I are on our knees explaining to him about the golf course, the private villas, the communication tower, the hotel, and so on. It was no great thing for him to get down on his knees with Peter Munk and David Gilmour—but it was enormous for us. We were little, almost failed hustlers from Fiji who couldn't make it in Canada. We weren't exactly a world-class act. And Sadat in that time was a hero of the Western world; he was like a king. And he was so big that he sent to our hotel—the very next day—pictures of the three of us poring over the plans on our knees together, to keep as a memento.

On September 22, 1974, amid appropriate ceremonies, the Government of Egypt and Southern Pacific Properties signed preliminary agreements to create a joint venture corporation that would build two resort/residential/commercial projects on the designated development sites. The value of the first project, Pyramids Oasis, was estimated at UK£170 million.

In basic corporate terms, what Munk and Gilmour had achieved was an arrangement whereby a new Egyptian joint stock company would be formed to finance and build the first phase, which was to be on the Pyramids plateau, a ten-thousand-acre site. SPP's subsidiary, Southern Pacific Properties (Middle East), would receive 60 percent of the new company's stock (to be used for financing and building) while 40 percent would be held by EGOTH in consideration for the lands to be conveyed to the new company called the Egyptian Tourist Development Company (ETDC). The authorized capital of ETDC was $3.4 million divided into 3,400 shares of $1,000 each.

In announcing the agreement to the press, General Zaki said that "the magnitude of this development will create opportunities for broad sectors of industry and the banking community—be they local, Middle Eastern or foreign—to participate in the growth of the Arab world." The deputy chairman of SPP (Middle East), David Gilmour, described the project as "a brand-new concept designed to give tourists a total environmental experience combining the unique attractions of the oldest civilization in the world with modern facilities in the traditional setting of Egyptian villages." The lofty objectives inherent in the statements by Zaki and Gilmour contained a challenge that, in the end, Munk, Gilmour and SPP could meet, but President Sadat and his government could not.

On the home front, the first child of the Peter Munk–Melanie Bosanquet union was born, a daughter they named Natalie.

CHAPTER TWENTY

THE NEVER-ENDING
SEARCH FOR CAPITAL

S PP barely survived through 1974 and 1975. It hung on because of the Egyptian deal, which was coming together, and because of the Japanese connection that Pat Samuel had developed during the better days of SPP/Travelodge.

By 1974 Samuel was chairman of SPP's Japanese subsidiary; Travelodge was building the Narita Hotel at the Narita Airport in partnership with the Mitsubishi Corporation, a major Japanese holding company. Samuel told Munk that the largest Japanese building firm, the Taisei Corporation, was very keen to get into Egypt and had heard that SPP had a big project there.

Koji Minami, chairman of Taisei, met with Munk a number of times in London and Tokyo. Minami wanted to win an Egyptian construction contract using Gilmour and Munk's contacts. Munk told him that SPP needed help at Pacific Harbour in Fiji, which was being developed to lure Japanese tourism. There was a deep lull in SPP's markets at that moment. Times were tough. Munk told Minami that if he could see his way to making a token investment in SPP (Fiji), then Munk would make sure that Taisei got special treatment for a construction contract in Egypt.

A group from Taisei went to Fiji to examine the site. They found a first-class management team and a great project that, like every other recreation development at the time, was dying for lack of money and tourists. Basing its decision on the group's report, Taisei agreed to become a fifty-fifty joint-venture partner in the second phase of Pacific Harbour, and to put $3.8 million directly into SPP. An additional $2 million, from a mortgage on the golf course and shopping centre, generated enough cash to keep SPP afloat. As Munk puts it: "It was just a fluke that we got the Egyptians and the Japanese. The Egyptians were superb; we flew them to Japan, and told them how important the Japanese were, and they agreed." And, of course, there was the anticipated Khashoggi money.

Nevertheless, the outlook for SPP was bleak. Still, P & O's financial projections—so clearly expressed by Lord Inchcape on the basis of the negative cash flow at the time—were wrong. They missed one vital factor: the human element, the contribution of entrepreneurs who can create wealth out of tools that no computer or accountant could ever recognize.

But it was the Pyramids project that was getting the publicity and most of Munk's attention. The contract that the Egyptian government had signed with SPP in September 1974 was conditional upon a series of approvals and clearances yet to be given by various arms of the Egyptian bureaucracy. The master plan, as developed by Macklin Hancock and Project Planning, envisaged a tourist city consisting of five hotels with 1,800 rooms, artificial lakes, a Robert Trent Jones, Jr., championship golf course, a convention centre and a commercial area. There would also be compounds of 5,800 villas and 5,100 apartment units. It would be a complete city with its own water supply, sewage treatment system, roads and electric power. The concept was so remarkable that it attracted worldwide attention as soon as it was announced. It also attracted the (negative) scrutiny of Egyptian environmentalists and archaeologists.

After the September 1974 signing, Munk and Gilmour carried on laborious negotiations with the Egyptians in order to reach the required next stage of approvals. On December 1, 1975, the *Egyptian*

Gazette of Cairo reported on a press conference held by EGOTH chairman, General Zaki, in which he stated that work on the Pyramids Oasis had begun. The chairman was somewhat premature on the time of the start, but the press conference gave him a chance to again announce the wonderful details of the project and to reap credit and publicity, both valuable commodities in the highly politicized labyrinth of Egyptian government.

Then, in April 1975, the Egyptian government announced the Sunnyland development near the Pyramids. For this $300-million commercial centre, the investor/promoter was Triad, the Luxembourg corporation owned by Adnan and Essam Khashoggi, with no involvement by Munk, Gilmour or SPP. Sunnyland would be located next to the ten-thousand-acre Pyramids Oasis block. Munk and Gilmour had structured a deal with Khashoggi in which he would use SPP (Middle East) as the planning and developing vehicle. Khashoggi would be the up-front developer and SPP would benefit from the publicity that he, as an internationalist Arab, would garner as a benefactor to Egypt.

In Hong Kong on May 28, 1975, his wavy red hair stylishly coiffed down over his ears, Peter Munk, the forty-seven-year-old chairman of the company, flanked by Bill Birchall and Simon Pendock, conducted the annual shareholders' meeting of SPP. Malcolm Surry, financial editor of the *Business News*, a supplement to Hong Kong's *South China Morning Post*, was present and summed up the challenge facing Munk and his partners:

> The previous Thursday, President Sadat of Egypt signed "Decree No. 77," which cleared the way for 10,000 acres of land near the Pyramids, and another 20,000 acres on the Mediterranean. With profits last year down from HK$25 million to HK$5.8 million, the accounts producing a HK$24 million writedown of property valuations and a HK$17.7 million provision for currency conversion losses, signs of a turnaround were being looked for.

The Fiji operation remained hard hit by the general world economic conditions.

Mr. Munk stressed the significance of the giant Taisei Corporation of Japan going into a joint venture with SPP to develop 6,000 acres of land in Fiji at a time when the company's fortunes were at a low ebb.

In Japan, where SPP is linked up with the Mitsubishi Corporation, a good deal depends on the hotel at the new Narita airport—but it is not yet open for traffic.

In Australia, where the group owns 55 percent of the Travelodge hotel/motel chain that employed over 5,000 people, Munk said that subsidiary had "survived a holocaust that completely neutralised other companies and wiped out some, but will find itself in a basically healthy position."

With Khashoggi now tied into SPP's Egyptian activities, and with the large amounts of money he could put on the table, SPP's financial future was looking more promising. The concept, scope and scale of Khashoggi's Sunnyland, however, fuelled the rising anti-development position that environmentalists, archaeologists and special interest groups had already taken against the "desecration" of the Pyramids. An Associated Press report from Cairo, which was carried around the world on December 16, 1975, contained this description of Sunnyland:

This plan calls for construction of a 500-foot-high "Golden Pyramid" made of glass and costing $300 million. Inside, a monorail will carry visitors up seven stories, viewing a different period of history at each stop.

It was the "Golden Pyramid" concept that would give the growing Egyptian anti-development forces one of their rallying cries.

Munk's efforts to persuade Khashoggi to become an SPP share-holder began shortly afterwards. In a memo to Bill Birchall dated June 5, 1975, Munk presented a rationale for "SPP Share Placement"—the selling of SPP shares to raise money. In typical Munk fashion he had focused on the problem of finding new funds and had come up with the solution. Now he had to "sell" his colleagues. In part this memo lays the groundwork for his later move to take control of Travelodge Australia Ltd. (TAL).

In it Munk spelled out his plan to have SPP expand its capital base by selling 40 million of its treasury shares to Adnan Khashoggi. With this cash in the kitty, he could take Travelodge private by buying out the minority shareholders.

The scope of Travelodge's operations was substantial by any defin-ition. TAL was in Australia, New Zealand, Fiji, Tahiti, New Guinea and Japan. In 1975 its system covered 78 hotels/motels ("units") pro-viding 6,783 rooms in six countries, of which 4,948 rooms were in Australia. Included in these figures were 3,222 rooms not wholly owned by TAL but by joint ventures in which TAL had interests rang-ing from 16 percent to 50 percent, and 4 franchised units (683 rooms), for which the company received a management fee.

A key element in Munk's strategy for TAL was contained in these two objectives set out in the financial plan:

The conversion of TAL to a private company, providing man-agement flexibility and the elimination of overheads associated with public company status.

The alteration to the structure of TAL's executive man-agement and board of directors to enable it to attain these objectives.

Munk planned to increase Travelodge's profitability by selling off many of the existing hotel and motel operations and cutting about half of head office operation costs—$4 million a year—and cutting

Travelodge's overhead costs of $6 million by two-thirds. From these moves Munk wrote that, "without increasing occupancy and improved hotel operating revenues, a constantly increasing dividend flow to SPP can be assumed." The dividend flow would come from Travelodge's increasing profits.

Peter Munk knew if he was to sell 40 million SPP shares to Khashoggi, he would have to have a solid financial plan for Travelodge Australia Limited. That plan became his priority and it was completed by Munk and Birchall in November 1975. By that time, through market purchases, Munk had also increased SPP's shareholdings in TAL from the original 54.8 percent of its issued share capital to 58 percent.

The cash flow summary of the financial plan foresaw an increase in TAL's cumulative cash surplus from A$646,000 in 1975 (actual) to A$17 million in 1980. As clearly set out in the financial plan, Munk's focused objective was to raise the required equity for SPP by showing the company in its most attractive light. He knew that Adnan Khashoggi would be lured by that $17-million surplus cash number. As indeed he ultimately was.

The driving factor behind Munk's creation of his plan for SPP Share Placement was the same monster that had plagued him in the Clairtone days: the lack of capital.

CHAPTER TWENTY-ONE

ONE HUNDRED PERCENT OF TRAVELODGE

S tage 1 construction of the Pyramids Oasis, which was to last for two years, was expected to commence sometime during the summer of 1976. Although the "City of the Pyramids," as it was sometimes being called, was to have a 300-bed hotel, the golf course by Robert Trent Jones, Jr., was still the centrepiece. It was to be in the form of the Egyptian cross, the Pharaonic "ankh" or key of life, to symbolize respect for the culture of the Pharaohs.

For Munk and Gilmour the ankh was an elusive symbol as they fought to get the necessary Egyptian government approvals so they could put a shovel in the sand to begin the work. Above all, they needed financing, a commitment of many millions of dollars. The only possible source of investment for a land development project in a country as politically unstable as Egypt was Saudi Arabia. This was particularly so after the Yom Kippur War.

Munk had three inflexible rules: first, capital had to come in as equity, because debt was unacceptable; second, he had to keep operational control of the enterprise, even if he and Gilmour had less than 50 percent of the voting shares; third, he would not risk the assets of SPP's Fiji development or of Travelodge for the Egyptian development. There would be no cross-pledging of these assets to support the financing of the SPP (Middle East) contract in Egypt.

The difficult Egyptian bureaucracy and the apparently corrupt methods of doing business in that society, combined with the elusiveness of the required Arab-sourced equity dollars, put the starting date of construction back again and again until the summer of 1976, almost two years after the signing of the first agreement in September 1974.

In April 1976 Peter Munk was upset by criticism of the Egyptian project that appeared in the Ottawa *Citizen*. An editorial in that paper called the Pyramids Oasis a "monstrosity" being built "in the shadow of the Pyramids" by "ripoff artists" and termed the project a "blot on our national record."

Munk was angry about the harm the newspaper had done to his reputation.

> They said we wanted to make money so badly that we were
> not stopped even by the most sacred heritage of mankind,
> which was the Egyptian people's pride in the land of the
> Pyramids. The fact is that Egypt missed out in one of the
> most exciting developments ever. The only way they could
> have done it was through us, with superb planning. They
> could have changed the whole Cairo landscape and established
> a coherent and superb infrastructure, from hotels to resorts to
> Pyramids, that could have earned a fortune in foreign
> exchange for them in perpetuity. It would have raised Egypt's
> ability to attract tourism and foreign exchange revenues by
> several notches. But that was not the perception here in
> Canada. There was great animosity.

Munk responded vehemently, with a letter that pointed out the inaccuracies, untruths and distortions in the piece. He was determined to defend his reputation in Canada against all comers, even though his life and business activities were now on continents other than North America. Little did he know that the Ottawa *Citizen* assault was just a precursor of the vilification that was to come from groups and individuals in Egypt and elsewhere who were violently against the project. This article and others were based on information that came from a lower-grade official in the Egyptian embassy in Ottawa. The official was enlisted by the project's enemies and fed lies to the gullible Canadian writers, who were not even told that the project was not only approved by the Egyptian government but that their tourism ministry was a full partner with the developers.

The financing breakthrough for Pyramids Oasis came in 1976 when Munk and Gilmour, after the protracted period of negotiation described in the previous chapter, finally wrestled Adnan and Essam Khashoggi and their Triad firm to the sands of Arab Egypt, convincing them that they could and should invest a large sum in SPP without getting control of the enterprise. At the end of February 1976, Adnan had capitulated. He said that, as an Arab, he realized he had a duty to assist his suffering brethren in Egypt. A substantial investment by him would ensure that Pyramids Oasis would be built.

On March 1, 1976, this message flashed across the world on the Exchange Telegraph tape: "... Triad buys stake in Southern Pacific Properties ... Triad Holding Corporation S.A. (THC) will subscribe 44,000,000 shares of SPP at a price of Hong Kong dollars 1.31 per share ... The proceeds, amount of approx. HK dollars 57m., will be used for the immediate commencement of the developments in Egypt ..." Translated roughly into other currencies HK\$57 million was reported as UK£5.7 million, or nearly US\$11.5 million.

This purchase meant that Khashoggi had acquired a 28 percent interest in SPP. His payment was the first tranche or advance of the US\$35 million required to complete the initial phase of Pyramids Oasis. Forty-four million shares had been sold to Triad, which diluted the interest of existing investors. As a result, the P & O stake was watered down from 34 percent to 23 percent. But P & O had approved the deal, welcoming the infusion of much-needed cash even though it meant the apparent end to Inchcape's plan to pick up SPP's post-bankruptcy assets.

By this time Munk had completed his arrangements with two firms to do the road, water and sewer servicing of Pyramids Oasis— the Bovis group of the U.K. and Taisei Kensetsu of Japan.

Peter Munk was confident that the presence of the "flying Bedouin" would attract other wealthy Arabs, especially the Saudi Arabians who were reaping unimaginable riches from the vast pools of oil beneath their desert sands. Munk therefore persuaded his colourful new partner to fly to Hong Kong in his plush private Boeing 727 to attend SPP's annual shareholders' meeting held on May 26, 1976. Munk knew that Khashoggi's presence would give SPP world wide press coverage. The annual meeting was chaired, as usual, by Peter Munk, but everyone's attention was on the moustached, cherubic Adnan Khashoggi.

The press carried gushing accounts of the event. The report of Malcolm Surry of the *South China Morning Post* said:

> Mr. Khashoggi is big in every sense of the word, a point not missed by the members of the banking fraternity who were busily pumping his hand at a lavish cocktail party turned on last night. His private jet, equipped with telex machines and all relevant business aids, will be lifting off today to a fresh business appointment, or a rest at one of the six apartments he maintains in various cities.

Having Adnan Khashoggi as a partner was clearly seen as a coup for Peter Munk and David Gilmour.

In late June, in London, Prince Nawaf Ben Abdel Aziz of Saudi Arabia bought a 15-percent interest in SPP (Middle East) for an investment of $5.5 million (£3 million) cash in their Egyptian project. Another would soon follow. Cairo's *Al Akhbar* newspaper reported on October 26, 1976, that

Prince Fawaz Ben Abdel Aziz and Mr. David Gilmour,
President of SPP (Middle East), exchanged documents regard-
ing the participation of the Prince with 10% of the company's
capital. Prince Fawaz is considered the second largest participant in the company. His brother, Prince Nawaf, has already
participated with 15% of the company's capital. This proves
the interest of Saudi Arabian businessmen in Development
Projects in Egypt.

Prince Fawaz's purchase, when combined with that of his brother,
produced a flow of at least $9.1 million into SPP's Egyptian sub-
sidiary. With the earlier Khashoggi money, which went into the parent SPP of Hong Kong, the total new money from Arab investments
in Munk and Gilmour's enterprises in 1976 was more than US$20
million. The infusion of money meant, among other things, that
Peter Munk could now focus on taking that which was rightfully his
(and SPP's): 100 percent ownership of Travelodge Australia.

At a meeting of the board of SPP, on May 27, 1976, Peter Munk
laid out his plan for the acquisition of all Travelodge minority interests. The plan gave a detailed forecast, in typical Munk–Birchall style,
of the extremely positive financial effect of the acquisition over the
next two years, and the repatriation of the TAL cash flow. The plan
also called for the outright sale of twenty-five TAL hotels, leaving
forty-nine to be managed, leased or owned by TAL, in line with
Munk's strategic position papers to Bill Birchall of two years earlier,
outlining the reasons for placing SPP equity.

The board unanimously approved the corporate plan and empow-
ered the executive committee to implement it. Armed with the
approval of SPP's board, Peter Munk was ready to begin his battle to
persuade the government of Australia to let a foreign corporation have
total ownership of Travelodge, and to acquire the minority shares that
would produce that 100-percent ownership.

A carefully crafted twelve-page brief created by Munk and Birchall, dated July 20, 1976, laid out TAL's financial woes starting with these alarming words: "Travelodge's present cash situation is such that its internal cash flow is insufficient to meet interest and loan repayments and working capital requirements." The brief was designed to convince the prime minister of Australia and his cabinet that it was in the national interest of the country and the unions to allow SPP to take 100 percent of the shares and complete control. The tenth page contained a paragraph that Peter Munk knew no right-thinking Australian politician could ignore:

> Currently Travelodge employs some 3,000 Australians whose present job security will be significantly enhanced if SPP is able to commit its total financial strength to reinforce Travelodge. Further, SPP's Fijian and Egyptian operations are managed by Australians and in Fiji, it has spent some A$20 million with Australian suppliers, contractors and professional consultants during the last five years.

Munk and his Australian deputy chairman, David Hoare (chairman of Bankers' Trust, Australia), used the strong brief and their own considerable powers of persuasion to gain the support of the unions, and finally, the assent of the government.

On the other hand, their offer to buy out the minority shareholders at the price of A$0.40 a share was hotly refused. Munk turned to the prestigious firm of Price Waterhouse for an evaluation of Travelodge's share price. It fortunately came in at the same A$0.40 per share. Nevertheless, shareholder resistance continued and forced Munk to extend the SPP offer for 90 percent of the minority shares from October 20 to December 12. By that last date the required number of acceptances had come in, as shareholders tired of the quarrel. The cash infusion from Khashoggi was more than enough to pay for the shares.

Travelodge was now ready for privatization and the execution of

Munk's rationalization plan for the beleaguered hotel enterprise. It was a done deal, thanks to the focused efforts of Peter Munk and the deep pockets of Adnan and Essam Khashoggi.

One of the things Adnan Khashoggi was famous for in those days was his fabulous parties. Peter Munk suggested to his new partner that, in the interests of SPP, Khashoggi might consider holding parties in Australia and New Zealand. Agreement was enthusiastic and immediate. The first party was in Auckland, New Zealand, on the evening of Thursday, November 18, 1976.

Adnan arrived in Auckland in his Boeing 727 with his companion, Laura Biancalini, while Essam Khashoggi flew in in his smaller DC9. Travelling with Adnan were Peter and Melanie Munk as well as David Gilmour and his London model friend, Jill Sweeny, all of whom were central to the Khashoggi bash at the Shoreline Cabaret, Takapuna. Two hundred guests drank Australian bubbly, ate splendidly, were entertained by a Maori concert party and danced to one of the best bands on the island.

For Melanie Munk this was one of the first trips after the birth of a daughter, Cheyne, on September 15, a child who, it is highly likely, was conceived in the Munk family's chalet, Viti Levu, in Klosters.

The Khashoggi party was repeated the following evening in Sydney, Australia. The host made sure that many important government people were on the invitation list. The relationship of the SPP leadership with the power people of the government of Australia was of the highest importance to Peter Munk, David Gilmour, Pat Samuel, Bill Birchall and, of course, the gracious Adnan Khashoggi.

To that end, meetings for Khashoggi and Peter Munk had been arranged for the following day with Sir William Pettingell, chairman of the Foreign Investment Review Board, and Michael Cranswick, the acting head of the foreign investment division of the Treasury. As always, the opportunity to favourably influence the course of events was seized by Peter Munk. The occasion of the Khashoggi party in Sydney was yet another chance for him to advance the interests of SPP and each of its principals.

CHAPTER TWENTY-TWO

TURMOIL IN EGYPT

Opposition to the Pyramids Oasis scheme was growing. The fact that foreigners rather than locals had been favoured with the development contracts was resented, and the realization that the project was an overwhelming commercial success didn't help. Allegations that the foreigners were making money out of Egyptian land led to charges that they were destroying antiquities.

Peter Munk and David Gilmour agreed that Gilmour would take care of Egypt while Munk concentrated on the South Pacific, but with the situation deteriorating, there was no way Munk could stay away from the Egyptian scene. He was in Cairo on February 2, 1977, to welcome His Royal Highness Prince Nawaf Ben Abdel Aziz to the city. The prince had come to take a look at the site of the project, in which he had a 15-percent interest. The Cairo newspaper *Al Ahram* reported on HRH's visit and noted that:

> On the same day the Company celebrated the first anniversary
> of start of work which had been devoted to the establishment
> of the Company and preliminary studies for the incipiency of
> the Pyramids Oasis Project as well as follow-up of the execu-
> tion of the various basis facilities to reach the jobsite ...

The start of work referred to was not the start of construction. Only a little earth moving had taken place in relation to certain planned roads and excavation for one proposed building. By mid-August some rough grading of a single street in Village 21 and grading of the initial section of the major arterial road had been completed. The excavation of the golf course lake was half finished. Earthwork for the most modern sewage system ever contemplated in Egypt had started.

There were drawings being prepared for all aspects of Pyramids Oasis. A September 19, 1977, progress report of the Egypt Tourist Development Company (EDTC) showed that all working drawings had been prepared for the water supply and sewage systems, arterial roads, local services, electricity, communications, solid waste disposal, the golf course and club house. But Pyramids Oasis was stuck in the sands of Egyptian politics and bureaucracy, despite Gilmour and Munk's efforts to get it moving.

In London that spring, Peter and Melanie Munk were visited by Marci McDonald of the *Financial Post* magazine. Her assignment was to do a cover story on Peter Munk. The article that appeared in the June 1977 edition didn't help the Pyramids Oasis development. Instead, headlined, "The Return of Peter Munk," it gave fuel to the fire of the opposition to the project. Parts in McDonald's well-crafted piece apparently offended and inflamed the left-wing, anti-development, anti-Sadat lobby in Egypt. Two sections of the profile dealt with Munk's work in Egypt. Apart from her description of the project as "one of the most grandiose development flings since the Pharaohs ..." it is a stretch to find anything offensive. On the other hand, a full platter of Munk braggadocio was served up: a dish that might not sit well on an Egyptian table, especially translated into florid Arabic by someone motivated to do harm. The statement that "Peter Munk was personally summoned to create this playground outside Cairo by Sadat ..."—the exaggeration of a writer carried away by Munk's enthusiasm—certainly embellishes the truth, and there was one paragraph in the McDonald article that might justly have been called inflammatory: "Munk said that he 'couldn't think of a bigger challenge than to tackle the Pyramids, I mean, to take a little water and a little shit and make an oasis of green where there's only been sand for 5,000 years, to create a golf course where every plane from Europe on its way to the Middle East or Africa has to pass over and look down on that green symbol of life, where you can see Arnold Palmer play golf with the Pyramids as a backdrop—wouldn't that turn you on? I mean …' Peter Munk pauses a moment for a disconcerting reflection—'… doesn't everybody think like that?'"

It was probably Munk's excremental imagery that was deemed offensive in Cairo.

At the May 25 meeting of the board of directors of SPP in Hong Kong, the chairman Peter Munk was in attendance, as were Pat Samuel and Bill Birchall. The financial and operational situation of the hotels was discussed and recommendations made. Peter Munk advised that Mr. Greenway, as a result of his termination, had initiated two legal actions, the first being a claim for compensation and the second being for an injunction to prevent SPP from acquiring his 16,000 shares in TAL. On the advice of SPP's lawyers, it was decided to let the matter run its full legal course.

Next, in the absence of David Gilmour, Munk gave a briefing on Egypt, where the situation was going from bad to worse. Peter Munk informed the meeting that the Egyptian public-sector partner, EGOTH, had been attempting to remove SPP from the joint venture on the basis that SPP did not have the financial capacity to carry out the projects. A meeting had been held with the minister of tourism at which SPP's case was presented and the minister advised by Munk that if any previous agreements with SPP were broken, SPP would request that the matter go to arbitration at the International Chamber in Paris. In order to protect its interest, Munk concluded, SPP (Middle East) had already retained senior British counsel to study its case and advise on its actions.

Notwithstanding Munk's warning, on May 2 the minister of tourism issued a decree that suspended ETDC's previous development approvals, and instructed that site sales should be halted. This action was taken despite the fact that as soon as land sales began, the elite of every Arab nation, and of Cairo itself, lined up. More than US$3 million was taken in in a matter of weeks.

After extensive, frantic negotiations conducted by Munk and Gilmour, the development approvals were reinstated and site sales were allowed to continue. Somehow, SPP and the project survived the next board meeting of the Egypt Tourist Development Company. Gilmour and Munk were both in attendance. The project would continue.

On June 28 Dr. Sahad Abdel Wahab, the new chairman of ETDC, and David Gilmour sat together at a cramped table below a photograph of Anwar Sadat at ETDC's Cairo offices. Seated between them were two representatives of the largest construction company in the Arab world, the Arab Contractors' Company, owned by Ahmed Osman Osman, the father of President Sadat's son-in-law. They were all there to sign a $5-million infrastructure contract for the first phase of development of the Pyramids Oasis project.

In the midst of the growing controversy in Egypt, Peter Munk decided to engage a public relations consultant to fight the escalating Cairo press and propaganda attacks mounted by factions that seemed determined to destroy the Pyramids Oasis development. Munk retained London-based writer David Wynne-Morgan, one of the leading British international journalists. Over the years, he had written about the Middle East for the *Sunday Times* of London and the *New York Times*. In 1962 he had been granted a series of interviews with then President Gamal Abdul Nasser, which resulted in the publication of his book on Nasser's life, *The President, or "El Rayess."* Substantial excerpts from the book had appeared in the *Sunday Times* and Cairo's *Al-Ahram* newspaper.

Munk found Wynne-Morgan in his paper-strewn cubbyhole office in London. He explained the nature of the crisis and offered to retain him as public relations manager for SPP's overall operations, with immediate concentration on the shambles in Egypt.

On July 22, 1977, Peter Munk sent this memorandum to the newest top-level member of the SPP team, David Wynne-Morgan, with a covering copy to Gilmour:

> I had a meeting last night with some of our banks and solicitors from Cairo who had informed me about a negative article on the Pyramids Oasis project in *Al-Akhbar*. This article apparently appeared on the 13th July and was repeated on the 14th July with a heading "Hands off the Pyramids."
>
> I understand that a lady doctor wrote the article and was inspired by General Zaki. At the same time, our Cairo friends had advised us in the strongest terms to—as soon as possible—make another release in the Egyptian and possibly Middle Eastern press along similar lines to the one featuring Dr. Wahab and David Gilmour signing the contract, but this time with a picture showing equipment actually working, in any part of the desert, as long as the Pyramids appear in the background.

The lady doctor Munk referred to was the prominent, outspoken Egyptian archaeologist Dr. Nemat Fouad. Her goal was to obliterate the project.

David Wynne-Morgan immediately began to implement Peter Munk's instructions. Articles explaining the benefits of the project soon appeared in newspapers and magazines in Cairo and elsewhere in the Middle East.

Munk and his SPP development team intended to get model villas built as quickly as approvals permitted. Four hundred and twenty-six lots were already being marketed, based on Project Planning for Phase I. By September 1977, 319 had been sold, mainly to wealthy Egyptians, Saudis and Kuwaitis at premium prices ranging between US$32,000 and $74,000. The villas were to be built by the buyer within three years of the lot purchase date at a cost of at least US$35,000.

The next meeting of the board of SPP was on October 3, 1977, in the Hotel Carillon in Paris. Munk assured everyone that the Egyptian minister of tourism's withdrawal of appropriate approvals had been rescinded and approvals reinstated so far as the villages offered for sale were concerned. Gilmour then advised the board that a parliamentary committee had been struck to investigate the project. It was recorded that later in the meeting,

> Mr. Gilmour summarized progress in Egypt and reported that visually there was a high degree of activity on site. However, we had had to face some problems with the Egyptian and—subsequently—the Kuwaiti press, because the original participants no longer involved in the project wished to serve their own interests by replacing SPP in ETDC and because of the vested interests of current operations already profitably installed on the site. Mr. Gilmour informed the Board that Mr. D. Wynne-Morgan, SPP's public relations adviser in London, went to Cairo and did an excellent job in neutralizing the campaign. Nevertheless, the adverse publicity had resulted in the formation of a Parliamentary Committee to investigate the Project.
>
> Mr. Gilmour said that SPP (ME) were bringing a lawsuit against the newspapers.

That parliamentary committee was indeed at work absorbing, listening to and believing every criticism of the foreigners—their lack of financial input, their desecration of antiquities and every other false or defamatory statement that the "anti" forces could conjure up. The pressure on Sadat to cancel the Pyramids Oasis project was intensifying.

SPP's lawsuit against Dr. Nemat Fouad and certain Cairo newspapers, which was later thrown out of court, was the first sign of desperation, a recognition that SPP (ME) was losing not only the battles but the war.

Another anti-Sadat and anti–foreign-investment furore erupted when the Egyptian president, the sponsor of SPP's developments, seized the initiative and travelled to Israel to meet Prime Minister Begin and his government and to deliver an address to the Knesset. A torrent of criticism poured on Sadat from the press in Cairo and the capital of every Arab country. The reaction against him was couched in terms of treason and apostasy. Bombings and riots occurred. Assassination threats were made against Sadat by the PLO.

Meanwhile, the press attacks against the Pyramids Oasis project were still growing in ferocity. In late October, David Wynne-Morgan and Anthony McLellan, the SPP (ME) commercial manager, spent three days in Kuwait talking with journalists, businessmen, and financial and banking officials concerning the advantages and benefits of the Pyramids Oasis development. In December, Wynne-Morgan made a tour of the United Arab Emirates for the same purpose. However, it seemed impossible to stop the tide of violent opposition that threatened to swamp the entire SPP initiative in Egypt.

In Peter Munk's "Chairman's Statement" in SPP's annual report for 1977 he commented that the SPP Group's cash flow, liquidity and asset base had all improved during the year. There was a continuing improvement in the Australian economy that was beneficial to the TAL hotel operation, but no such improvement was appearing in Fiji.

As for Cairo, he explained that the situation was difficult. The press attacks and the hostile parliamentary debates had undermined the international financial communities' confidence in the Project. Certainly Munk and Gilmour had grave concerns about their future in Egypt. But the Pyramids Oasis project was only a small part of the interests of the SPP Group. Peter Munk had so structured SPP (ME) that the failure of its Egyptian venture would not cause damage to the whole. Whether that structuring was viable might soon be put to the test by the actions of the government of Egypt.

CHAPTER TWENTY-THREE

A LUCKY MAN

Peter and Melanie Munk were somewhat removed from the fury of the Cairo storm, because they were mainly in Australia, where Peter was tending to the day-to-day operations of SPP's hotel holdings. The Fiji development and the Travelodge Australia holdings had to be managed, nurtured and made to grow for Southern Pacific Properties' shareholders, Jardine Matheson, P & O, Trust Houses Forté, Boswell, Triad (Khashoggi's holding) and others. Munk was also focusing on taking SPP private, and developing a proposal that would entice his friends, Adnan and Essam Khashoggi, to finance that transaction. The two Saudi royals, Prince Nawaf and his brother, had invested in the subsidiary, SPP (ME), not in the Hong Kong SPP. On the other hand, the Khashoggi money had gone into SPP, not into SPP (ME). The Egypt project was in an entirely separate corporate body, South Pacific Properties (Middle East), with no SPP guarantees.

Munk had started to negotiate with Khashoggi in 1977, trying to get the flying Bedouin to understand what it was that Munk wanted him to do. Out of all this, the name "Barrick" would emerge. Peter Munk usually avoids giving an answer when the question is put to him: "Where does the name 'Barrick' come from?" He knows the answer. It's just that the explanation is complicated.

Munk tried to explain the concept of privatizing SPP to Khashoggi:

I said to him, "Now, this part is the hotel business. Over here this is Egypt. This compartment is the SPP public company and what we're doing now is forming a new company, and this new company will buy the whole thing." I lost him. So Bill and I got this chart and we drew on it to explain. And he said, "Well, what company is that?" I said, "Sir, it doesn't matter what company it is. It is a new holding company. We are going to own it and we're going to borrow from the Hong Kong Bank and bid for the public shares, which means we're going to own all these SPP assets directly." He said, "But which company will do that?" I said, "A new company, any new company." He said, "Well, what do you mean?"

We also had a language problem. On top of that Adnan doesn't think in terms of corporate entities. So Birchall and I picked a corporate name for the holding company— Carrick—to put in the box on the corporate charts. For one year we negotiated with Khashoggi for Carrick. He thought it was a real entity. But there was no Carrick because, until we had the financing in place and were prepared to make a bid we didn't want to waste money on incorporating. When we finally did the deal, Adnan said, "Let's not form a new company. Let's use Carrick." Then we learned we couldn't incorporate Carrick because the goddamn name Carrick was gone. I blew my cork. I said to my lawyers "Get something—Arrick, Barrick, Sarrick, Darrick, I don't give a damn what it is."

The name Barrick was available.

By January 1978 Munk, at Klosters, had written a "Statement of Purpose for Carrick Investments." With variation and amendments, including the change of the name to Barrick, it was the basic deal to which Munk and Khashoggi agreed a few months later, when Barrick Investments Limited was incorporated, not in Hong Kong, as suggested by Munk's accountants, Coopers & Lybrand, but in the tax haven known as the Cayman Islands. The statement of purpose was the genesis of all of the corporations that bear the name Barrick: Barrick Investments Limited; Barrick Resources Limited; and American Barrick, now Barrick Gold Corporation.

Fundamentally, it was a plan to convert Southern Pacific Properties (SPP) from its public company status to a private holding company.

By June 1978, word was out that Adnan Khashoggi was about to buy out the Hong Kong–based Southern Pacific Properties. At the end of July, the deal was made public. The *Financial Times* of London reported that

> the takeover offer has the agreement of SPP's other major
> shareholders, the British hotel chain, Trust Houses Forté, the
> Peninsular and Oriental Steam Navigation Company (P & O)
> and J.G. Boswell and Co, which own a total of 29.4 per cent
> of the issued capital.
>
> Triad is to make the takeover through its wholly owned
> subsidiary, Barrick Investments Ltd. Barrick owns no other
> assets and has been set up for the purpose of acquiring SPP.

The offer was accepted on July 26, 1978.

In fact, Barrick, a private Cayman corporation, was not a "wholly owned" subsidiary. In the complex transactions structured by the Khashoggis and Munk's lawyer, the shares of SPP (38 percent) owned by Munk, Gilmour, Birchall and Triad (the Khashoggis) were bought by Barrick with its shares. The other SPP shareholders (62 percent) were bought out by Barrick for cash raised by loans from Triad ($6 million), Wardley's Bank ($10.75 million) and the merchant banking subsidiary of the Hong Kong Shanghai Bank.

The shares of Barrick Investments (now the owner of all SPP

shares) broke down as follows: 50 percent owned by Monex, a Liechtenstein holding company, and 50 percent by the Khashoggis' company, Triad. The Khashoggis owned 74 percent of Monex and the Munk team held 26 percent.

The agreement between the Barrick shareholders gave complete management control to Monex with no interference. Monex would be controlled by Munk, which meant that he had unimpeded control of Barrick and its subsidiary SPP. Provision was made for five directors of Monex—two from Triad, then Munk, Gilmour and an independent director to be selected by Munk. It was also agreed that the Munk group's share percentage holdings in Monex would be increased if certain performance objectives were reached.

In the publicity that resulted from the Barrick Investments transactions there was scarcely any mention to be found of the usually high-profile Peter Munk and his close friend and partner, David Gilmour. It was Adnan Khashoggi who was the star.

Meanwhile, SPP (ME) and its Egyptian venture had turned into a complete disaster. Dr. Nemat Fouad, the leading Egyptian intellectual and archaeology professor who opposed the Pyramids Oasis project, promised to "fight and fight again to the last breath in my body." She would also fight to the last dollar of the Sabri family, who owned the largest night club—the Black Tent—on the Pyramids Oasis property and whose survival was threatened by the project because it was on government land. Tent City's cash flow exceeded $1 million a week at that time. She and her followers believed that the development would irretrievably damage cultural treasures she claimed were buried beneath the sands. She wrote a series of critical articles in the newspaper *Al-Ahram*. They were so defamatory that Peter Munk decided to have SPP (ME) launch a libel suit against her, but the lawsuit simply became a rallying banner for Dr. Fouad's supporters.

The flood of anti-development editorials, commentaries, letters to editors, columns, and articles that followed reached its peak in May. The parliamentary committee hearing evidence and preparing its opinion on all the so-called improprieties carried out by SPP (ME) was in full flight. Its damning report against SPP (ME) would be delivered in June and would find the "foreign associate" guilty of every conceivable transgression.

Finally, Sadat had no choice. The political and press attacks were too much. On May 28, 1978, he ordered that the Pyramids Oasis development be terminated and that all contracts with SPP (ME) be cancelled. The official announcement quoted Sadat as saying that Egypt's historical heritage should be preserved and national feelings considered in planning future economic projects. The announcement also indicated that the government had decided to adopt the necessary measures to protect the interests of "subscribers and beneficiaries," which some interpreted as implying that investors would be paid back, at least partially. Munk and Gilmour had earlier decided that if the Egyptian government breached the contracts they would launch a massive lawsuit to recover their losses.

Peter Munk had been in Fiji for three days conducting a shopping centre meeting with his staff. Pat Samuel was there, as well as Bill Birchall and Melanie. On May 28 Munk, Melanie and Bill departed Fiji in a Learjet for Hong Kong and a full board meeting of SPP. It was a long flight: five hours to Sydney and another eight to Hong Kong. About an hour out of Fiji there was an urgent radio message from the air control tower at Nadi asking Munk to telephone Samuel as soon as possible. The plane landed at Norfolk Island, and Munk called Pat Samuel, who gave him the news that the Egypt project had been cancelled by Sadat.

Peter Munk's reaction was never made public.

I was relieved because Egypt was a cash flow drain. After four years, it was a morass. We had a separate holding company for Egypt and it was separately financed. Four million dollars had gone into our Egyptian holding company from the princes. From the cash flow, every month, we had to send over a quarter million to half a million dollars from what the princes had invested.

Those trips to Egypt were killers for me emotionally because there was such duplicity and dishonesty. It's one thing to fight Alan Greenway in Australia, with lawyers, or with votes in a boardroom. Whether it's Clairtone or Travelodge we know the rules, we know the laws, and we know how you win and how you lose, but one of our Egyptian executive directors was in the pay of the secret police and he stole documents from us. They forged. They changed letters. Everything was rumours, nothing was quite right. People you thought were your friends were your enemies and the laws could be changed depending on which Arab scholar interpreted it and who paid them. We couldn't operate like that. There were people shooting at our truck drivers from the Sahara city, from the squatters.

Munk and Gilmour wasted no time commencing legal proceedings against the government of Egypt for restitution, damages and costs. James McGee of the London law firm Erickson Morrison was retained to advise in the compensation negotiations with the Egyptian government. The Paris law firm of Coudert Frères was engaged to handle the arbitration complaint before the International Chamber of Commerce in that city. At SPP headquarters on Sloane Street in London, Tony McLellan was in charge of orchestrating the entire preparation and conduct of the claim, which was for US$17.5 million. In December 1978 Peter Munk and David Gilmour instructed Coudert Frères to file the claim for arbitration by the International Chamber of Commerce. It would take some twelve years, several appeals, enormous costs, and a great deal of persistence on the part of Munk, Gilmour, McLellan, and their lawyers and professional consultants before the matter was resolved to their entire satisfaction.

*

Distant from Canada as he might be, Peter Munk was still attracting the interest of the Canadian media. There was yet another interview-with-Munk article, this time with Dean Walker in the December 1978 issue of the Toronto-based magazine *Executive*. Munk talked about David Gilmour, about why the two of them were still equal and affectionate partners after their ordeals and achievements over more than twenty years. Were there no tensions, Walker wanted to know, over who should get the limelight? Munk replied:

> There never have been. That's one of the elementary cohesive factors in our relationship. There are things he does that I would not really like to do, and things I do that he would not like to.
>
> He wouldn't like to chair a stormy shareholders' meeting. He wouldn't like to stand there making a bid for a company while the shareholders scream. I don't mind that. He wouldn't like to fire somebody very senior; I don't mind. He has a superbly smooth and brilliant social sense, and he makes the right contacts with a great amount of ease. Those contacts often require a great amount of social input, which I would not like to provide.

Even Canadian television producers were interested in the carryings-on of the intriguing Munk. Adrienne Clarkson's *Fifth Estate* sent a crew to track him down, and during that interview the fifty-one-year-old entrepreneur revealed for the first time that he might very well return to Canada and get into the natural resource business.

The December 1978 volume of the world-renowned *Architectural Digest* had a complete pictorial spread and text on the Munks' London pied-à-terre on Cheyne Walk, a restored Queen Anne townhouse in Chelsea. The accompanying article by Elizabeth Dickson described the couple's elegant lifestyle, which would alter very little when the Cheyne Walk residence was replaced, but in Toronto not London:

The Munks have just flown from the other side of the world. The form is that Mrs. Munk telephones ahead, alerts her staff—and one of her homes is immediately brought to life. Today, everywhere the eye falls there are bowls of carefully arranged flowers: marguerites in one corner, lilies elsewhere, fresh pink roses in the unused guest room of the house.

"We are probably the world's fussiest people," continues Melanie Munk. "Just as well, since I travel with Peter Munk around the world, and he's a very precise husband. He expects his slippers out, whichever home we walk into. I'm hyperactive, he's hyperactive, our tastes agree—and so I make running our homes a full-time job. The secret lies in having a team you can trust, and preplanning everything. I learn to switch off and delegate. But even so, I find myself sometimes thinking about cushions for Switzerland when we're in Australia."

Peter Munk has the last word. "We had planned to be really contemporary in this house—rip out the ceilings and so on—before we discovered the place is a landmark, and we needed permission to move a moulding. Now I'm glad the house is the way it is—cosy, welcome, packed with objects we both love. All in all, I'm a very lucky man."

CHAPTER TWENTY-FOUR

BACK TO CANADA

During his annual skiing holiday at Klosters in 1979, Peter Munk made a decision that had been nagging at him for some time. Actually, he had made the choice years before—but the time had to be right. At the beginning of the new year he had made up his mind. Peter and Melanie Munk would return to Canada to live.

> When I married Melanie I said to her, "Darling, we may have a lovely house in London, and an English country place and a Swiss ski chalet, but our home is Toronto. That's where we're going to bring up our kids. If you marry me, just remember that." I wanted to be sure that my children weren't nomads. Georgian Bay and Toronto, that's where we belonged. There was never any doubt that I would come back, once the foundation was safe. I couldn't come back with all the negative publicity and with all the debts.
>
> So, I had to come back, but I had to be prepared for a couple of bad years. That meant that I had to come back to Canada with success behind me.

Peter Munk's return to Canada meant a significant change in the lives of his young English wife and their two little girls, Natalie and Cheyne, but they made the adjustment with ease.

His decision also meant that he was in effect announcing that the entire London head office of Barrick Investments Limited and its wholly owned Southern Pacific Properties would be shut down. Peter's partners, Gilmour and Birchall, would have to decide whether they wanted to move to Canada or reside elsewhere; senior employees, such as Tony McLellan, would have to choose between leaving the companies or moving along with them.

Munk knew he wanted his Toronto office to be located somewhere within range of the restaurants and hotels of the Avenue Road and Bloor area. He had not forgotten the ambience he enjoyed when he was struggling to finance the Fiji project, back in '68 and '69, from those cramped quarters above White's Art Gallery at 25 Prince Arthur, and then at 18 Hazelton, not far from the Park Plaza Hotel.

He settled on rental offices in a comfortable converted Victorian residence on Hazelton Avenue, the street his friend Dick Wookey created. The transfer of operations from Sloane Square to Hazelton Avenue could be done without a rush. Munk set himself up in Toronto quickly, but the day-to-day operations of SPP and its various subsidiaries remained in London for the rest of 1979. The target would be to complete the entire move by midsummer 1980.

Meanwhile, the continuing Egypt fiasco and the arbitration proceeding had to be managed. That was Tony McLellan's special fiefdom as, subject to Munk and Gilmour's directions (Gilmour was still the Egyptian point man), he managed fruitless settlement discussions whose chief object seemed to be a great expenditure of money and time. The negotiations were complex and made more tedious by the Egyptians' insistence that meetings be held in distant Cairo, to which city McLellan and SPP's British, French and American arbitration lawyers and experts had to travel. Finally, their patience exhausted by Egyptian officialdom, Munk and Gilmour directed that negotiations cease and arbitration proceedings begin (the Egyptians had delayed arbitration by refusing to recognize that they were bound by the jurisdiction of the International Chamber of Commerce in Paris, despite specific clauses to that effect in their signed agreement).

The years 1979 and 1980 were transitional ones for Peter Munk. SPP had been privatized and was now wholly owned by Barrick Investments Limited. The Australian hotel battles had subsided and the company was prospering. The team of Munk, Gilmour and Bill Birchall (whom they had made a 10-percent partner when they took SPP private and created Barrick Investments) had their own people in the senior positions at the now secured Southern Pacific Hotel Corporation (formerly Travelodge Ltd.) in Sydney. Now they had to deal only with the Khashoggis.

In Toronto, one of the people Munk re-established contact with was Gloria Collinson, an advertising and promotion expert who had been with Peter Munk and David Gilmour since the early 1960s. Beginning in 1962 as Munk's secretary, she had then become director of public relations and advertising for Clairtone. When that company left Toronto and Munk and Gilmour later departed Canada, Collinson set up her own business and worked with the partners on their Fiji project.

Gloria Collinson and her agency were waiting for Peter when he arrived back in Canada in the spring of 1979.

> He hasn't changed much over the years. He's mellowed, certainly; he was quite a firebrand as a young man; he is redheaded you know, and he just charged.
>
> We flew over and worked with him all the time that he was in England. Then when he was thinking it was time to come to Canada he had that building on Hazelton completely remade for his Horsham offices.
>
> I felt then that he had a very good opportunity to be the first newcomer Canadian prime minister and together we

started to plan the campaign. We planned a series of speeches for him …

One of the speeches was delivered to the Winnipeg Chamber of Commerce on May 16, 1979. The last paragraph of the text hints at a political leadership objective.

> Maybe it is not coincidence that the polls for this election rate the three men who aspire to be our next prime minister as low in leadership appeal. The other thing they have in common is an academic background. Our instincts must be telling us something. I am convinced that all of us—all Canadians— love Canada. A generation of new Canadians, many millions of whom fought their way here from tyrannies, from concentration camps, from government controls of all kinds to come and build this country along with those who came before them, care as much as those who have been here for hundreds of years about the traditional values of Canada that bind us together. But maybe the newcomers are more aware of how much they have to lose.

Unfortunately, as Collinson notes, "he kept referring to *men* all the way through. He never said a word about women. The audience was about half women, and they were getting angrier and angrier. At the reception afterward a group of women told me that, forget it, they would never vote for this man. It was terribly shocking to me. It was shocking to him. I think he decided that, no, this definitely was not the time for politics." His speech did, however, provide what Munk and Collinson were looking for from the press: nationwide coverage and publicity. The reaction from the women in the audience was not what Munk was expecting, but it was a highly instructive exercise.

Turning his back on politics, Peter Munk focused during 1979 and into 1980 on an advertising program in the American market

designed to bring visitors to the large number of hotels that had operated before as Travelodge; as of July 1979, Munk and Gilmour had
decided, their company would be called Southern Pacific Hotel
Corporation, a more suitable name for the anticipated international
tourist trade.

That winter Munk visited Australia, where he announced at a press
conference that his Southern Pacific Hotel Corporation had entered
into a franchise agreement with the world's largest hotel group,
Holiday Inns of Memphis, Tennessee. The news surprised Australians.
Asked whether he would change the names of any of his sixty-one
hotels to Holiday Inn, Munk was noncommittal, saying only that he
would assess the situation. What he really wanted was to increase the
value of his hotel holdings by hooking them into the huge Holiday
Inn booking and reservation system. Munk knew that he was not
going to keep the hotels forever. "My plan was to reinvest the cash
flow and, ultimately, the proceeds of any sale. The cash flow was very
strong then. We had about US$20 million a year coming from SPP
and Travelodge." But he was not certain what he would reinvest in.
One chapter of Munk's business career was ending, and a new one was
about to begin.

It was the ever-resourceful David Gilmour who came up with a buyer
for SPP.

> I got a phone call from an accountant who said, "I have a
> client who wants to buy SPP." I said it was not for sale. He
> asked, "Would you have lunch with me?" So we had an enjoy-
> able lunch at the Wentworth Hotel in Sydney, Australia. The
> chap said, "I've got this client who is coming from Malaysia.
> His name is Tan Sri Khoo Teck Puat. He's in love with
> Australia. This is the place he'd like to have for his family to
> come to, have a business involvement, have a strong presence.
> And I think I can get the Australian government to accept

that and allow the control and the company to pass to him."
So I told Peter about it, and he said, "Well, it's the wrong
time." I said, "Peter, there's never a good time. We're always
just getting in a bit too late, and selling too soon ... just jok-
ing." And so Peter listened and we agreed that we'd pursue it
further. Peter and Bill Birchall got very involved in the negotiations. The buyer wanted to write a personal cheque for the
company. So Barrick sold SPP for cash. We wound up with
cash, experience and a certain benchmark in achievement. It
gave us a chance to create Barrick Gold and Horsham, and
realize our final ambition, which was to form something
North American–oriented that would become the ultimate
success of our careers.

The proceeds of the $130-million sale (after the assumption of all
debts by the purchaser) went to the owner, Barrick Investments
Limited, a Cayman corporation. Out of that substantial sum a divi-
dend went to Triad and to Munk and his partners. That left more than
$100 million to provide Barrick with an investment base. By this time
Munk had decided to buy into natural resources in Canada and North
America and, in particular, into oil and gas.

Having headquarters in Toronto, Munk needed to incorporate a
Canadian company as a vehicle through which to channel funds from
Barrick Investments to buy oil and gas assets. But corporate compli-
cations arose around the issue when it came to foreigners taking control of Canadian assets; the Foreign Investment Review Act, and
FIRA, the federal agency set up to enforce the legislation, required
that control of a corporation be in the hands of Canadian residents.
Since David Gilmour didn't want to return to Canada, he was a non-
resident. Birchall did join Munk in Canada and was a resident, but
he was also British and was concerned about keeping his tax flexibility open. Munk adds, "And of course, Khashoggi was never
Canadian. So we formed Horsham Securities Limited and all the vot-

ing shares were transferred to me. As the only Canadian resident in the group I had effective control over the company and that's how we got the dispensation from Ottawa. And that's how Horsham financed Barrick Resources."

Horsham Securities, with a modest initial capital of C$1 million, was a Canadian vehicle to do business in Canada. The only two resident Canadian shareholders were Munk and Birchall, and they had the only two voting shares. This arrangement satisfied FIRA. Everybody else had non-voting shares. When Birchall left Canada a few years later, his Horsham voting shares reverted to non-voting status. The only person then with voting shares was Peter Munk. Birchall explains:

> Barrick Resources was started up a year or so later, to do some (unsuccessful) oil and gas exploration deals. Barrick Investments, the Khashoggis and ourselves were loaning money into Horsham Securities to invest in Barrick by way of debt. We didn't have an economic difference in the shareholdings, but he had the voting share control and the money was going into this Canadian vehicle. What happened over the years is that, probably, 25 million dollars went from Barrick Investments through Horsham Securities into Barrick Resources.

Peter Munk was indeed back in Canada, with a new family, a new fortune, and the focused goal of making his mark in his adopted country. The words that John Gault had written in 1972 were about to come true:

> He is going to make it so big that the Canadian Club will have no alternative but to ask him once again to address them. The Prime Minister will consider it an honour to have him to lunch, and the stories on the business pages will be headlined: "Hey, everybody, guess who's back, bigger than ever?"

CHAPTER TWENTY-FIVE

HORSHAM'S VIKING

Horsham Securities Limited was created in 1980, the holding company through which Munk would channel funds from the cash-rich Cayman-based Barrick Investments. So far as Munk was concerned he had to have personal voting control of Horsham for two reasons. First, he had to comply with the Canadian-residency requirement of FIRA. Second, it had been a principle with him since Clairtone that he would never be part of a deal or a corporation where he did not have both management and executive control.

That did not mean that Munk had to have more than 50 percent of the equity in a company; it did mean that either by agreement (as with the Khashoggis in Barrick Investments), or by the device of owning voting shares or multiple vote shares, he could maintain voting share control of a corporation even though his equity holding was far less than 50 percent.

The Horsham name had two connections to Munk's private life. The first was that the Bosanquet family estate, where Melanie was raised, was near Horsham in Sussex. The second was that when they owned the beautiful Cheyne Walk pied-à-terre in London, the Munks also leased a country house with a most English name, Floodgates, which was close to the Bosanquets' estate. Its address: Dial Post, Horsham, Sussex.

The back-in-Canada chairman and CEO of Horsham, Peter Munk, was keen to buy into the oil and gas industry. He had $100 million of Barrick Investments' money burning a hole in his pocket, and he just had to get going. After looking at countless deals in Canada and the United States, Munk and his team found the ideal candidate. Viking Petroleum, an Oklahoma producer, met all his requirements: it had producing wells; it was cash short; and it had experienced, capable management. Since none of Munk's Horsham group knew anything about the oil and gas business, they had to buy a company run by experts who were already in place and had a great track record.

Munk says: "Viking met all the parameters. I'm very cautious, I learn from experience, and I don't make many investments. Viking met all our criteria, and we liked it."

Milton Mackenzie, Viking's founder, and his partners had been born and raised in the oil patches of Texas and Oklahoma. They had built their little $1-million company into a $100-million exploration and production firm. Mackenzie wanted Viking to continue to grow so he had hired a well-known and respected oil man, Swede Nelson, the president of Chevron International, to run Viking. Nelson came to the company with a first-class reputation. He was one of the inducements that led Munk to buy; when he was looking at Viking as a possible investment, he was told by Bob Forman, then president of E.F. Hutton, the major oil and gas fundraiser on Wall Street, "If you people come in with equity and you team up Swede Nelson's reputation with the local presence of Mackenzie, we will raise for you as much money as you can drill." Barrick had an unlimited offshore influx of funds, and not a dollar of debt. It seemed the ideal situation.

To do the Viking deal Munk had Barrick Investments funnel $60 million into Viking for a 55 percent interest in the company. A little later he incorporated Barrick Resources in Canada and brought in two outside investors to bolster his board, Norman Short, the head man at

Guardian Capital, and Joe Rotman. Short was an experienced and much-respected financial expert and president of fund managers Guardian Growth of Toronto. Rotman was a Toronto entrepreneur who had been, among other things, a trader of tankers of raw crude oil, and an oil exploration investor. Neither Short nor Rotman was an investor in Viking. Munk had all his ducks in a row. Everything looked perfect.

> So I made a deal with Milt Mackenzie, we put up our money—$60 million—and Swede took over as president. And it was an unmitigated, total, complete and irredeemable disaster. It was one of the biggest, the swiftest and, possibly because of that, the least painful of my disasters.

Munk clearly controlled Viking, but his problem was that he couldn't control Swede Nelson. Birchall and Munk had a command structure set up to control how each and every drilling or purchase allocation was meant to be handled. Everything had to be approved by all the Tulsa partners and then they had to go to Birchall. But Nelson just rode roughshod over everyone. He made commitments for tens of millions of dollars with no follow-up. Munk moved Tony McLellan, one of his top people who had been with him for ten years in London and then Toronto, down to Oklahoma; he had his best financial people try to deal with the problem. But it was too late. Nelson was out of control. Every time Munk thought the cash flow was stabilized, he would find another batch of unauthorized Nelson commitments for millions of dollars each. Viking's drillers threatened to sue for payment and Munk's American partners were going to take legal action against his group. He says, "We were being threatened with lawsuits from everywhere."

To his great regret, Munk had introduced Swede Nelson to Khashoggi at a Viking board meeting in Nassau, where the Khashoggis had two of their yachts and two of their planes.

Those two yachts were so big they were like half of the islands. And they had a huge villa where Adnan and Essam met the Viking Oil people. Of course, Swede Nelson spoke Arabic because he was in Saudi with Amoco for nine years, and the Khashoggis loved him. Swede told them, "Peter Munk and Birchall are nothing but administrators. I now finally know where the big money comes from." He told Khashoggi, "I'm not after the little ten-million-dollar programs. We're after the billion-dollar stuff." Adnan said, "You know, if you perform and I mobilize my Arab friends behind you, you'll have anything you want." Nelson spent thirty-six hours with the Khashoggis, and he went insane. In those days you'd turn on the television set and they'd be talking about Arab billionaires and Adnan Khashoggi, the richest Arab. Swede told Adnan, "I, Nelson, am looking after the big stuff," and I didn't know what to say. I wanted to give encouragement, but the man was going crazy. I thought we'd given him a real carrot, I mean, what else do you offer a big-shot manager? He had always worked for salary, so I wanted him to feel that he could be a principal and be worth ten million dollars and twenty million dollars. But Nelson was too much.

So far as Birchall is concerned:

The whole thing was just a shambles. Thank God it was, in hindsight, because if we hadn't got out we would have spent the next ten years trying to develop Viking and borrowing more and more money. There's no way in the world that Munk would have had the focus to create Barrick Gold. So luckily we had a quick death rather than a slow strangulation.

Munk's assessment of the Viking interlude is that it was something nobody could have predicted.

When I reviewed all of this a year and a half later with Birchall and Gilmour and Khashoggi, I said, "You know, we never lost so much money quicker. And we're smart guys, where did we go wrong?" I went through every single thing I'd done in Viking and actually had a full review. We found nothing wrong with our decision-making process. We'd do absolutely the whole thing over again. And yet we totally screwed up in eighteen months. We lost a big bundle of money. We had our tax losses and some other leftovers, and eventually we got part of our money back.

In the end Munk just walked away from Viking Oil and turned his focus—and that of Barrick Resources—to gold.

CHAPTER TWENTY-SIX

THE MOVE TO GOLD

Peter Munk's time at Klosters—time for reflection and review—had by 1983 become central to his life, including his business operations. (Georgian Bay had played a similar role in the 1960s. When others were spending weekends socializing and partying, he was on his own or with someone he was close to.) "At Klosters I have made some of the most important business decisions of my life. Because when I'm there I can see the forest, not just the trees." His move from oil to gold was decided there, and his first Trizec deal was conceived there. It was at Klosters that he first made contact with Tony Novelly of Clark Oil, and later he did the Horsham deal to acquire Clark.

I certainly now believe that Klosters is a very important part of why I'm maybe a bit different from other executives, because there I have a vantage point. I go at Christmas and come back at Easter; I have a little office, but I don't work that hard. I like to ski for four or five hours. So when I get up in the morning, I get all my reports and the news. My secretary in Toronto, Sheila Fennessy, summarizes whatever has happened during the previous day and it's on my fax. So I get production reports, financial information, phone calls, clippings, whatever is important. I have breakfast at eight in the morning and my Swiss secretary brings in all the faxes. I have my coffee and I go through it all, and I give her dictation or instructions and reply to the faxes. Then I leave to go up the mountain for skiing at nine or nine-thirty.

Then, when Sheila Fennessy in Toronto gets into the office, and Greg Wilkins comes in or Birchall or Bob Smith comes in at eight o'clock or nine in the morning, Toronto time—which is two or three in the afternoon in Klosters— they have everything in front of them, my comments on faxes sent to me when they left their offices the day before.

When I get back from skiing at three or three-thirty, it's nine-thirty in the morning or eight-thirty in the morning in St. Louis, and six-thirty in Nevada. My Klosters secretary gives me the press clippings and faxes from that morning, and I return my phone calls and reply to queries. I work until six, which is noon in Toronto. At six I go to town, read my papers and have coffee with people in the village. I come back and do another hour on the phone if I have to. Melanie and I go out for dinner, and when we come back I might have a fax on my machine about the phone calls or anything else that happened in the afternoon. If it's urgent I can call back, but 90 percent of the time I put it on my breakfast table and I handle it the following morning.

That's my life in Switzerland. I don't have to use a car. I spend four or five hours on the mountain with my guide or my wife or my friends or my family. I love the mountains. I love the challenge of skiing—I'm a bad athlete but I love it. It's the best thing you can do with five of your kids and your wife and your friends and have fun all day. Klosters is the ideal lifestyle for me, just like in the summer I think my Georgian Bay island keeps my sanity and keeps my mind and my focus, enables me to live with the pressures. I've had big pressures. Clairtone, the hotel days, then Egypt. The Viking disaster. Those were very heavy times in my life.

I've often made big initial strategic decisions on my own. I've had lovely partners like Gilmour and Birchall, but somehow I still feel they look to me as the person responsible for coming up with the strategic initiatives. When the proverbial hits the fan I have to come up with the right response, and for that you need your mental stability when the pressure is the greatest. With the things I've done, I've had to be tough, because otherwise you can be destroyed. Being out in the fresh air and doing physical things and being removed from business environments has helped me enormously in coping.

At Horsham headquarters on Hazelton Avenue, Peter Munk was beginning to focus on something about which he really knew very little—gold mines.

Bill Birchall was on Munk's wavelength about gold. In 1981 and '82 he had spent time in Australia, where he looked at some gold mines, and he claims that he learned how to do a profit-and-loss of a gold mine on the back of an envelope. Peter Munk's criteria for gold mines were all related to their potential. He and Birchall considered South Africa, and they looked at gold mining businesses in North America. They found only two sizable publicly quoted gold mining companies, Campbell Red Lake and Homestake Mining. Both had large market capitalizations in the range of a billion dollars and enormously high share price–earnings ratios.

Munk and Birchall wondered why, if the price of gold was not going crazy, would a gold mining operation have such a high price–earnings ratio? The answer was very simple. There was a scarcity of major gold producers. There was a plethora of gold exploration firms in those days, but an institutional fund manager wouldn't invest in an exploration company, and if he wanted a share in a gold mining company, he had a choice of two: Campbell Red Lake or Homestake.

It seemed that there were very few good investment opportunities in mines already producing gold. Munk and Birchall did, however, find a role model: Echo Bay, a new North American gold mining company in operation in the Northwest Territories. It had good reserves, and its management intended to acquire additional production facilities: it also had institutional investors, because the mine was in production creating gold bars. So Echo Bay became the initial model for Barrick Gold.

Munk's first step was to switch Barrick Resources Corporation away from its disastrous oil-and-gas foray and make it the corporate vehicle for his gold quest. Horsham Securities Limited (still owned by Munk, Gilmour, Birchall and the Khashoggis) controlled 62 percent of Barrick Resources, the shares of which were listed on the Toronto Stock Exchange in mid-May 1983. With David Gilmour lending a diplomatic hand, Munk had enlarged the stable of investors in Barrick Resources to include not only Adnan Khashoggi, Prince Nawaf, Joe Rotman and Norman Short, but also Kamal Adham, a former financial adviser to the Saudi Royal family. Another new investor was the youthful American entrepreneur Tony Novelly, whom Munk had met through the Khashoggis. He was a high-flying member of the super-rich club. He owned and ran one of America's largest private companies, Apex Oil, an independent refinery and trading business with an annual turnover of US$20 billion.

Barrick Resources' first gold mine was about to be acquired. It was the Renabie mine near Wawa, Ontario. The deal was that Barrick would merge with Sungate Resources of Vancouver, which owned a 100-percent interest in the Renabie mine. The merged corporation would be known as Barrick Resources Limited. When the merger was completed in September 1983, Cullaton Lake Gold Mines of Toronto bought, from the merged company, a 50-percent interest in the Renabie gold mine.

Campbell Resources Inc. of Toronto, which held a 21-percent interest in Cullaton Lake, had agreed to manage the Renabie mine until January 1, 1989. The plan was to increase Renabie production in two years to about 60,000 ounces of gold per year.

Renabie required about $15 million for the rehabilitation of its mine and ore-processing equipment. How did Barrick and Campbell raise that kind of money? It was Ned Goodman, one of Canada's leading financiers, who had the answer. "Ned Goodman is as bright as anybody at devising things," says Birchall. "He invented a gold royalty interest scheme which we then publicly offered. By a miracle we sold it, and raised the $15 million. It was the Barrick–Cullaton Gold Trust. When that was done we had $15 million and a half-interest in a gold mine that was going to be rehabilitated."

With that series of transactions closed, Peter Munk and Barrick Resources were in the gold mining business with all the leverage for the raising of capital that the magical lustre of gold can excite in the minds of potential investors. Peter Munk's aim was clear: he was not in the gold exploration business—he was in the market only for gold-producing companies already in operation and located in North America. His next move was, however, slightly out of line with that stated policy. In September, as the Renabie merger was being completed, he signed a joint venture deal in which Barrick Resources, with a 23-percent interest, and three other companies financed a stake in a potential gold mine in the farthest northern reaches of the United States, at Valdez Creek in Alaska. Valdez Creek began to produce gold in August 1984.

In the fall of 1983 there was an article of interest to the Peter Munk family in Zena Cherry's social column in the *Globe and Mail*. On October 6, 1983, her opening two paragraphs were these:

> Mr. and Mrs. David Bosanquet of Horsham, Sussex, are in
> Toronto from England for the Canadian launch of Mr.
> Bosanquet's new book, *Escape through China: Survival after the
> Fall of Hong Kong*.

They are staying with their son-in-law and daughter, Peter and Melanie Munk. Mr. Munk is chairman of Barrick Investments.

Cherry, the doyenne of Toronto society chitchat, provided a few details about Melanie's distinguished father, who had one more coincidental link with Peter Munk. One of his significant investors in SPP was Jardine Matheson, and

> author David Bosanquet was a director of Jardine Matheson and after the war served in China, Singapore and Malaysia. He now has his own companies which distribute to and supply interior decorators all over Europe. He was formerly High Sheriff of Sussex and is now Deputy Lieutenant of Sussex.

David Bosanquet's book is a gripping, suspense-filled story, written skillfully. Regrettably, it was the only book that Melanie's father was to write.

> In [the Bosanquets'] honour, the Munks had cocktails on Tuesday at their grey stone Rosedale mansion. In keeping with the subject, the party theme invitations and hors d'oeuvres were, of course, Chinese.
>   Guests included Leslie Berenyi, Mrs. Conrad M. Black, Janusc Dukszta, Adrian Wordsworth Edwards, Prudence Emery, Barry Haywood, Janet James, David Perlmutter and Shelagh Van Sittart.
>   Chairmen with their wives included James R. Connacher, Daly Gordon Securities Ltd.; W. Lawrence Heisey, Harlequin Enterprises Ltd.; John A.C. Hilliker, The Permanent; Paul G. Opler, Canadian Foundation Co.; and Gurston I. Rosenfeld, Guardian Capital.

At the end of 1983, Munk began to investigate a Canadian mining company as a prospect for acquisition, along with its management professionals. An article in the *Wall Street Journal* reported:

> Camflo Mines Ltd. and its affiliated companies are looking for partners as Camflo tries to ease its heavy debt load.
>
> Brian Meikle, operations vice president, said cutting the company debt is Camflo's top priority. At Dec. 31, debt was $81.2 million (Canadian), while shareholder equity was negative. William Robertson, secretary, said debt remains at about $80 million. To conserve cash, the gold-mining company is farming out some of its oil and gas interests, cutting exploration and actively seeking partners for two affiliates' projects. Camflo also would be willing to sell its 90% interest in La Luz Mines Ltd., which mines coal in Ohio, and would consider an equity issue if its stock price improved.

Obviously, Camflo was in serious trouble. Munk knew, however, that its gold mine was a top-quality, low-cost producer and that Camflo had an excellent mining team running the operation.

CHAPTER TWENTY-SEVEN

CAMFLO

Munk's strategic thinking shifted into high gear. As his investigation and research progressed, he became convinced that even with its mountain of debt Camflo would bring new credibility to Barrick Resources. The key factor was that Camflo was producing gold in significant quantities, and had acknowledged and reputable management under Bob Smith, whereas the Renabie production was only 16,000 ounces in 1984. Munk needed gold production against which he could obtain major financing. As the *Globe and Mail* noted:

> Toronto-based Camflo owns a 40 per cent interest in the Malartic Hygrade gold mine in Quebec—equipped with a 1,250-ton-a-day mill—and carries out mineral and oil and gas exploration. Its 1983 revenue of $33.1-million consisted of $23.4-million from bullion and $9.7-million from oil and gas.
>
> The Malartic mine is a low-cost producer.
>
> The major drawback of Camflo is its debt burden, a legacy of its failed venture in coal mining, which resulted in huge writeoffs in 1981 when its Ohio mines were sold.

Camflo's unstated debt burden was over $100 million, with the Royal Bank holding almost all of it.

Until he began his Camflo research, Munk had never heard of Bob Fasken, who controlled Camflo Mines through his family's company, Bob-Clare Investments Limited, which owned a 22-percent share holding of Camflo. When Munk approached Fasken to discuss a possible acquisition or merger, he discovered that Fasken was not about to talk to Peter Munk, whom he doubted would have the credibility—let alone the financial strength—to take on his C$100-million debt load.

> I had to see Fasken, but he wouldn't see me. Didn't return my phone calls. So I went to my friend Norman Short, of Guardian Capital, who was on my board, and knew Fasken. He then put me in touch with Gurston Rosenfeld, and Rosenfeld said the only way to get to Fasken was to go to a director of Camflo, Max Goldhar.
>
> So then Gurston took me to Goldhar. I told them both that I wanted to buy the two companies. Goldhar says, "You know, there's a $100-million-dollar debt. You haven't got $100 million." I said, "No, but I can raise it." And he said, "Well, that's a new approach. But it's for you to satisfy the Royal Bank better than Fasken."

Munk convinced him that he could handle the debt load, and retained Max Goldhar as a consultant. In a few days the elusive Fasken agreed to talk with Munk. Courteously, he made it clear to Munk and Goldhar that they would have to deal with the "workout" department of the Royal Bank in Montreal. The workout department's function is to collect on debt accounts that have "gone bad" or defaulted.

Munk was prepared to put up $30 million and undertake to pay off the Royal Bank's remaining $70 million in a year. He would get the $30 million from a private placement.

So Fasken pushed us back to the Royal Bank and its workout department which was organized or run by John Clark. He was one of three people in the workout department. Very tough. But as the bank told me afterward, they only put the hard, tough-as-nails people in that department, who deal with you like dirt, because you're not a client anymore, you're a *defaulted* client. I heard a conference-call conversation of Bill Birchall and Stephen Dattels, one of our key executives then. They were talking with the Royal Bank workout department people in Montreal. I had just happened to walk into their office. And these bankers were talking to my guys with such a lack of respect, I said to Dattels, "Hang up! Who is talking to you? Who would dare to talk to us like this?" Dattels says, "It's so-and-so in the Royal Bank workout department in Montreal." I said, "But we're not in default. They can't talk to us like that." He said, "Well, that's the workout department." And I told him, "You just tell him to go and shove it. Unless they learn manners then they're not going to get their money back." The Royal Bank wouldn't play. I mean, we had no credibility then, even though I had the solution. I was prepared to accept the debt, and put money into the company. I couldn't understand his attitude. It went on for almost a year.

Even Munk's own board was difficult to deal with in the Camflo matter. They didn't like his idea of taking over a $100-million debt.

And then when I finally got done I couldn't sell it to my own board! Without Gilmour and Birchall, who support me even when they think I'm making a mistake—and they did—I think I couldn't have gotten it through. I heard the arguments, "Why would we do this? This is a sick company. It's got geothermal and coal. The Faskens couldn't make it go,

Bob Smith couldn't make it go, the family couldn't make it go. They were into the bank for over a hundred million."

That whole summer of '84 was like pulling teeth, as Munk tells it. Nobody wanted to do it. The Royal Bank, Fasken, Munk's company, his management, and his board were all either dubious, or dead against it. But to him it was obvious that it was the right thing to do.

I saw the strategic benefit and it really was a turning point for me to be able to execute the gold strategy that I knew was the correct strategy. I thought initially that I didn't need the mine management—I could give it over to Ned Goodman and his New York Stock Exchange–listed mining company called Campbell Resources. But if I had to worry about management I could not focus on strategy, so I realized that I had to have in-house management who were part and parcel of us. And the only ones I could find that had any credibility and competence were Camflo. But my board was concerned about balance sheets and values and debts, rather than seeing the strategy. It didn't matter to me whether I paid ten million dollars more or ten million dollars less—if that was all that was in it why did we all hustle around and work to make the deal? The big picture was vital, and we had the Prudential-based gold royalty trust; we had done the Barrick–Cullaton Gold Trust for Renabie. The whole concept worked well. We wanted be able to raise $200 million through another trust and buy more gold mines—but we had to have the management and the credibility.

It really was a very, very tough time. Camflo was one of the toughest takeovers. And then we had to do a private placement as part of the deal. The bank didn't believe we could raise $30 million. So I had to do the door knocking, I had to keep Fasken in place, and above all I had to get my board in place with me. Then I had to look after Barrick's oil and gas people who saw that this was the writing on the wall.

The last thing Bob Fasken wanted to do was sell out to me. He had a private jet and had a good time with it. Nobody wants to give up a company that they're living off. His two or three sons were with him in the company. It was a family bonanza for him, and Camflo was also his company. Who wants to sell out? And he was a fishing buddy with the big shots in the Royal Bank. But the hundred million was *his* debt.

Peter Munk himself never went to Montreal to visit the workout department. Instead he sent as emissaries Joe Rotman and Howard Beck. Norman Short made a phone call to the right man at the Royal. Munk was putting on all the pressure he could generate.

I had to use the help of Joe Rotman, who had credibility with the Royal Bank. Then, with the workout department already discussing our proposal, Camflo defaulted; there was no hope unless gold went to $500 or $1,000 an ounce. And even though I was prepared to put $30 million cash into it, I, Peter Munk, was not credible. They liked Fasken better with a hundred-million-dollar debt than Munk with only a seventy-million-dollar debt, even if Fasken was bust and I paid off thirty million to start. Now how that perverted thinking came into being I'm not sure, but my reputation was at stake. I'd been away thirteen years and who knows what they thought— maybe Munk is a crook, or who knows? Joe Rotman was a good friend of Brian Gregson, who was the head of Royal Bank's commercial lending. And Joe and Howard flew to Montreal together to tell him that I'm trustworthy, I'm honest, I'm able, and that they shouldn't worry about me. That was an indicator of changed attitude, that people like Joe Rotman and Howard Beck were prepared to speak for me.

Norman Short, who was Guardian Capital, a major multimillion-dollar pension fund manager, made a phone call to the Royal and said he'd known me for twenty years, he was on my board, he was an investor and Peter Munk's a good guy. The problem was that the workout guys at the Royal didn't want to do the deal either. They eventually did it, but it took me a year. And then I got sick.

Munk's acceptability problems with the Toronto financial establishment continued.

For the three years before 1984 there was the oil business and Viking and Khashoggi, and people were just turning their backs on me. Old friends would invite me down to Bay Street for lunch in their boardroom, but at the last minute they'd have to cancel because one of their colleagues would find out that they had invited Peter Munk. That actually happened to me. I had just arrived back in Canada and this guy said, "Wow, you're back! Fantastic. I'll get my directors. Come down and I'll give you a boardroom lunch." And I was excited. I told him, "The financial community will understand what I've done in Australia. They'll understand that this Clairtone thing was years ago. Since then I've successfully built companies ten times the size of Clairtone, just not in Toronto." Then they cancelled, saying that the host got sick. And then they said, "You know, when he's better we'll reschedule." It was very tough.

The initial face-to-face approach to John Clark of the Royal Bank was made by Bill Birchall, Steve Dattels (then head of Barrick's corporate finance group) and Gary Last (then a Barrick oil-oriented executive) in November 1983. Their proposition was dismissed out of hand. The two were back again in Montreal on January 13, 1984, for a meeting

with Clark and Bob Fasken. Their new Barrick proposal was also totally inadequate, according to Clark, but they were back again in a
month with an offer at $21.8 million. The Royal was finding out that,
if nothing else, Peter Munk was persistent.

John Clark recalls how it looked from the Royal's point of view.

We could tell that these guys were just salivating over the
prospect of acquiring Camflo. Remember, we were in the
Bank's workout group; we weren't interested in being Mr.
Nice Guy.

We finally got them to the twenty-seven-million-dollar
level, which we felt pretty good about. And we had reached an
agreement with Fasken on his side, and that was concluded on
another Friday—Friday, April 13, 1984.

Now, here's where the fun starts. Part of this deal involved
a confidentiality agreement. We didn't mind them doing due
diligence but, you know, from a technical standpoint that's as
far as it would go. But they went back and they started to
rework the numbers and they thought maybe they'd better
talk to their friends over at Sun Life. They were the largest
institutional investor, apparently, in the proposed Camflo
deal and it would be essential to get them on side somehow.
The Sun Life people looked at it and said this is ridiculous,
you've offered far too much. The Bank has taken you guys to
the cleaners.

So, they came back to us on April 19, and said they
couldn't go forward with the deal. We were absolutely
shocked. They were supposed to put up $250,000 as earnest
money, which they didn't. And they said Sun Life wouldn't
support it. And we said, "Well, you had no business talking
to Sun Life. You've violated the confidentiality agreement."
So on May 2, 1984, we told Bill Birchall that Barrick's
revised proposal was not acceptable. We said, "We dealt in

good faith, we had a deal, and if you're not prepared to honour it then we'll see you later, but we don't want to see you later. All bets are off, the deal is finished." And they tried to get us on again. But I've always gone on the basis that principle is more important than expediency and, you know, we had a deal.

It was tough for us to turn our backs on a twenty-seven-million-dollar deal, but the principle was more important. They came back with another, much lower offer and we said that's it. If you don't want to go forward we're not interested in any further discussions. And so we closed the file.

On May 7, Clark had a telephone call from Max Goldhar, the Toronto accountant and Camflo director Munk had retained. Clark recalls:

We'd had a number of dealings with Max. He was a tough customer but we got along all right. He had a good reputation with the bank and I guess Bill Birchall or somebody asked him to see if he could get this thing on the rails again. I said, "Max, I'm not interested, I'm sorry. They've broken their deal and I'm not interested." And he said, "Look, John, I've got a cheque for $250,000 and I'd like to come down and see you." And I said, "Well, Max, you know, if you really want to, fine. But don't bring those other fellows."

We met on May 7. He came in and said, "I've got the cheque right here." And he put it on the desk.

I said, "Max, I hope you didn't bring those other fellows." And he said, "Well, they're not too far away if we can get something going here." By the end of the day I had the cheque. It was agreed that we would resume negotiations, and seven days later on May 14th the heads of agreement were signed.

At this critical moment the seemingly indestructible Peter Munk became seriously ill for the first time in his life.

> I had to have an operation. They had taken a polyp out of me earlier, then they called back and told me they had just a tiny suspicion that it was possibly malignant, and they'd feel more comfortable if they removed the bowel five centimetres each way. I said, "Jesus, now that's some suspicion." There was nothing there but they cut a piece off anyway. It was the only operation I had in my life other than my broken leg. I really was in bad shape for a few days. It was right in the middle of the final deal with the Royal Bank on Camflo in 1984. I was in the intensive care unit for the last things I had to sign for the Camflo deal. Bill Birchall had to bring the documents into the North York General Hospital. They told him, "You can't go into intensive care!" Bill said, "I'm afraid I have to. I'll put on a white coat." I was strapped to forty-four tubes. He snuck in and I signed.

Basically, the deal was that Barrick would pay $30 million up front and pay off the Royal Bank's balance within a year.

After months of effort, Peter Munk had finally got the deal worked out with Fasken and the Royal Bank, and the Barrick board approved it. At that point, Fasken's board said no. According to Munk,

> in the end, the bid was conditional on Fasken's board approving. But they rejected it.
>
> The Camflo board member who turned my offer down was Bob Smith, whom I had never met, and he was against it because he thought that Fasken and Bob-Clare got too sweet a deal. Bill L'Heureux—who is now with Trizec and at that time was a partner of Jim Tory's—was on the board of Camflo, and he came up to my house in the middle of the night and gave me the rundown of what was happening on the Camflo

board. He said, "I'm totally on your side, Peter. I want this to happen. It's the right thing for Camflo. It's the right thing for you. But we got a problem with Bob Smith!" We decided how to sort out the Bob Smith matter, and Bob's been the most valuable member of my Barrick team ever since.

The whole deal almost came apart at the last minute. And Peter Munk had no idea of the crisis that almost blew his Camflo merger out of the water until he received a letter from John Clark a decade later. He was certain Munk knew nothing about the events behind the scenes at Camflo.

There was a Camflo board approval session in the morning of July 13, 1984, followed by a Barrick meeting. Then the main players, Munk, Gilmour, Fasken, Clark, Birchall and others, went to the Four Seasons Hotel for a convivial lunch. Neither John Clark nor any of his workout department colleagues had ever seen or met Peter Munk before that day. After that they went back to the offices of Davies, Ward & Beck at the CIBC building, where the lawyers were toiling over the final documentation. At about 3:30 p.m., Clark went into the closing room. As he tells it,

> there was all this furious activity, and somebody said, "Where's Bob Fasken?" And I said, "I don't know. Do you need him?" And they said, "Well, of course we need him. He's got stuff to sign here." And I said, "Well, I had lunch with him. He seemed to be in good humour then. Let's see if we can track him down."
>
> We called his office. I had him on the speakerphone and I said, "Bob, you're supposed to be over here signing documents." And he said, "I'm not signing any documents. I think I've been screwed here, I didn't get a good deal." I said, "Bob, for God's sake, you never said a word about it at lunch." "Well," he said, "that was social. I didn't sleep last night and I got to thinking

about this and I think I've been hosed." I said, "Bob, we have
to have your signature, we had an agreement." "Yeah," he said,
"but there's two or three things that have got to change."

Bob Fasken was serious. He was not about to sign any documents.
And if he refused to sign, the closing, and the deal, would collapse.

Clark immediately went to the Camflo offices in the Royal Bank
south tower. Fasken was in his office, a bottle of Scotch on the desk,
tie askew. Clark says,

> What I sensed was that this was a very proud man, who'd
> built up the company and done very well, and it was all slip-
> ping away. He wasn't going to be left with a lot compared to
> what he formerly had, but I think he came out with some
> pretty fair cash, or shares of Barrick. But he really was feeling
> emotional about it.

Fasken insisted he wanted the deal to be post-reviewed by Clark's
boss before he would sign. Clark said,

> "Bob, you and I are going to make the deal today or there's no
> deal. You want the deal reviewed. That's a hell of a position to
> put my boss who's your best friend in." And he sat back and
> he looked at me and he said, "Yeah, I guess you're right." We
> shook hands, and he said, "I guess I better go over and sign."
> So, anyway, he went over, he signed and we all met some-
> where later for dinner.

Peter Munk had no knowledge of that episode. If John Clark had
failed to persuade Bob Fasken to sign on that fateful night, the Camflo
deal would have collapsed, Bob Smith would not have become an
integral part of the Munk team and, quite possibly, a mine called
Goldstrike would never have become the Barrick motherlode.

CHAPTER TWENTY-EIGHT

GOLDEN DEALS

At the end of October 1984 Peter Munk was intensely focused on paying down the Camflo obligation to the Royal Bank within a year. It would not be done easily.

One reason Munk had wanted to buy Camflo in the first place was to make the Prudential Bache deal work. This was a deal that would finance a partnership between Barrick and a new Prudential company called the Gold Corporation of America. Munk formed a partnership with Prudential to float in the U.S., under the Gold Corporation of America (with the Security Exchange Commission's approval), a gold royalty trust or a pool trust. People would give Prudential their money and they would give it to Barrick to buy gold-producing mines; the investors then would get ownership of part of the mine and a future return based on the price of gold.

If gold was flat, they would receive a 3-percent return. If gold went up from $300 to $350, they would get a 5-percent return. If gold went from $350 to $400, they would get 10 percent. If gold went from $400 to $450, they got 15 percent. As Munk saw it, it was not only a great opportunity for leverage, but it also gave him the money to buy gold mines. When gold was at a low price he paid a very low interest and a low price for a mine. But if gold went up to, say, $600 an ounce and Barrick was making a fortune, Barrick would have to pay huge returns—which they would not mind at all. Everyone would win!

From the investors' point of view it was a novel and attractive liquid instrument. It was to be listed on the American stock exchange, and underwritten by Prudential Bache, who would get a guaranteed return. If gold went up, their yield would go up. Sales were good and, as intended, that money was used to retire the Camflo debt to the Royal Bank, since the first mine to be acquired under the new structure was the Camflo mine in Quebec.

But Munk ran into a problem. Prudential Bache, instead of raising $200 million, which is what they wanted, were not able to raise more than $60 million, because of what Munk called "a Wall Street macho" thing between E.F. Hutton, Prudential Bache and Merrill Lynch. They wanted to put their names on a $500-million prospectus. He begged them to make it $200 million. The demand was there. If they couldn't sell what they put on the prospectus (the $500 million) that would mean to a buyer that he must have bought something wrong. Munk recalls:

Camflo was vital because of its gold-producing asset base. Then Prudential went to market and made this fatal, stupid error. I knew it was an error to put a $500 million tag on the prospectus. It was all greed and Wall Street nonsense.

When Prudential Bache underwrote a deal for anything involving more than $100 million, the Prudential board for the parent company in New Jersey had to approve it as well. When the proposal went up to the board, Munk was in Paris pitching an Arab prince for another $4 million he had to raise for the Camflo deal. He received a phone call at midnight from Barrick's lawyer in New York saying that the Prudential Bache offer was being withdrawn. Without that offer, everything could have collapsed. Munk would only take on the Camflo debt if Prudential Bache was raising the money. And he knew that even US$50 million would be enough to repay all the debt, but that he had to have more if he did not want to risk all the assets of Barrick. After years of work putting the entire package together, and with the time it had taken to acquire the Camflo mine and do the Prudential Bache deal and get the SEC clearance—Munk had been under a lot of pressure, but he had done it. And now the Prudential board had turned it down!

Munk went to see George Ball, the Prudential Bache president, to explain.

> I thought the world had come to an end. I thought, "I'm going to kill myself." Ball told me that there was a Canadian director on the Prudential board who said, "Five hundred million U.S. dollars! What Canadian company is behind it?" They told him, "Barrick," and he said, "Barrick? Noranda, yes, Placer yes, but Barrick? It's a penny stock with Peter Munk who went bust in electronics." And you know who the director was? Dick Thompson, chairman of the TD Bank, who is my friend. But being on the Prudential board, he felt it was his duty to be cautious when it came to a half-billion dollars exposure for a minor Canadian company. But, of course, I wasn't allowed to call Dick. Ball said, "It's a board matter. We're not supposed to tell you who said what but that's what happened." But because Dick was not quite sure himself of where Peter Munk stood or what Barrick was, the board agreed to postpone the final decision by three weeks while they appointed a committee of three people headed by their Canadian lawyer, Purdy Crawford, to look into the situation.

At that time Purdy Crawford was still a senior member of the Toronto law firm of Borden, Elliott. Prudential also appointed two others, one American and one Canadian. Their job was to check out Peter Munk from top to bottom.

Purdy did his homework. His firm represented Prudential in Canada, and he was a senior partner. He spoke to Howard Beck, Jim Tory, the Ontario Securities Commission and many, many other people who had done business with Peter Munk.

Apparently Crawford's report was very detailed and made it clear that Munk had done nothing wrong and Barrick was of substance. Prudential gave Barrick their approval. Munk says: "Purdy Crawford, whom I did not know at that time, saved my life. He could have gone the opposite way."

As an aside, Purdy Crawford had come into Munk's life earlier when he represented Charles Riachy, a Lebanese who gave them access to Anwar Sadat. Riachy was in the first meeting with the Egyptian president, when they got on their hands and knees to look at plans.

> I had a lawsuit, which I don't very often have. I've won every lawsuit so far in my life, and usually people who go after me lose. We had an agreement with an Arab agent by the name of Charles Riachy—he was initially Gilmour's Lebanese friend and he had the connection with Khashoggi. When we sold the hotels Charles Riachy was entitled to a fee. Instead of getting the $11 million we proposed, he thought it should be $13 million. So we had a fight over $2 million. Riachy threatened to sue me and then he threw the book at me. And he hired a Canadian law firm to sue me in the Canadian courts to put pressure on me in my home town to pay the extra $2 million out of Barrick. The law firm he hired was Purdy Crawford's. This lawsuit, of course, was eventually settled. Charles Riachy's a friend of mine. But Purdy was retained in the middle of this thing when he was supposed to give a report to Prudential, and I thought, God, here's a lawsuit against me, the same guy who is doing this report. But Crawford was magnificent; he was way above the fray. He saved my life.

Munk got his money on December 31, 1984 (he was skiing on the mountains of Klosters). From the proceeds the Gold Company of America advanced to Barrick US$40 million (C$53 million) against Barrick's commitment to deliver to the Gold Company of America each year a number of ounces of gold that varied with the price of gold. For example, in 1984 the price was US$365, against which Barrick delivered 8,767 ounces.

That package produced C$53 million, which was used to pay the Royal Bank debt. In January 1985, Munk sold the Camflo energy holdings for $32 million. With the initial private placement of $30 million made before the finalization of the Camflo merger, the total of $114 million was more than enough to take out the Royal Bank debt. It was a remarkable achievement by any standard, starting with Peter Munk's practically door-to-door effort for the private placement; he claims to have approached at least fifty potential investors to raise that key first $30 million. Without it there would have been no Camflo merger.

There was another hitch in mid-January. Bill Birchall and Jerry Garbutt, who at that time was chief financial officer, informed Munk that they were on the verge of having to repay the Prudential Bache money. There was a technical hitch under an obscure U.S. law that stipulated that if a big-enough proportion of the money sought in the prospectus was not achieved, the investors had another chance to withdraw. By the middle of January the situation was critical. But the scheme survived. If it hadn't, Barrick would have defaulted on its obligation to the Royal Bank. But the funds came in and Barrick repaid the money to the Royal.

Then Barrick had a fight with the Royal Bank because they thought that out of the money raised by the Gold Corporation of America, $74 million should have gone to them. Garbutt's view was that Barrick only had to pay part of it to the bank. The Royal then accused Barrick of dishonesty. Munk says:

A year later, in 1986, Brian Gregson, one of the top people of the Royal, came from Montreal and gave a beautiful lunch at the Royal Bank dining room. There were all the big shots from the Royal Bank. Gregson said. "We're giving you this lunch in the most prestigious of the boardrooms in the Royal Bank to tell you how wrong we were and how right you were. And we're here to tell you that we at the bank don't very often apologize, but we apologize." Because of that, the Royal Bank remains our favourite Canadian banking institution. Two years later, we went to them for the largest gold loan ever done in the world, 1,050,000 ounces. We sold the gold for US$450 million. It was because of that single action, the lunch and apology. It was a very gentlemanly thing for them to do.

After the Camflo deal had closed, Munk next looked at changing Camflo management personnel. Fasken was advising him to get rid of Bob Smith. Munk recalls:

I trusted Fasken. He became a good friend. He said, "You've got to get rid of this guy, Bob Smith. He's burnt out. You've got to put in John Charles." So John became my new guy but the real gold nugget was Smith, whom we considered phasing out, but thank goodness didn't.

One of the Bob Smith factors that Munk had to consider was the Camflo board's vote on the Barrick merger. Bob Smith was against the deal, but it was approved by the board, notwithstanding his negative vote and that of geologist Dr. Brian Meikle with him. In the end Munk did not terminate either Bob Smith, his "gold nugget," or Meikle. Munk needed a tried-and-true gold mining operator in his search for producing mines with potential for increased production and reserves. And Bob Smith was it.

The Mercur mine in Utah was Munk's next acquisition target, and Bob Smith was front and centre in the decision to go for it. Mercur was owned by Texaco, but had originally been developed by the mining arm of Getty Oil Company. With permission from Texaco White Plains' senior executive, Peter Bijur (later Texaco's chairman and CEO), Munk sent his newly acquired Camflo team of mining engineers to do a two-day appraisal of Mercur. Bob Smith, the chief, took two of his Camflo geologists with him, Brian Meikle, a McGill graduate, and Alan Hill, a former Noranda mine manager.

Smith and his team liked what they saw. Mercur was producing 70,000 ounces a year, but Smith reported that production could be increased dramatically, that the base cost per ounce could be lowered just as dramatically, and that he could run the mine much more efficiently.

On Smith's advice, Munk put in a bid. When it turned out to be close to but lower than Exxon's, who came in at about $60 million, Munk withdrew. But then Exxon backed off and departed. Munk lowballed with a bid of US$31 million with a sweetener: Texaco would get half of any proceeds should gold go over US$385 an ounce, topping out at US$9 million. Texaco took Munk's offer.

The next step was to finance the deal. Munk's recent feat of paying off the Royal's $100-million Camflo debt gave him new credibility. The Continental Bank Company gave Munk an equity loan of US$31 million. With the funds already in hand, Barrick closed the Mercur deal in June 1985.

Smith and his team immediately went to work installing new high-tech equipment with the financial assistance of the Bank of America. A $10-million state-of-the-art autoclave unit was the major piece. When it was installed, processing went from 3,000 tons per day to 5,000 tons; morale among the workers took off, the cost of recovering the gold out of the ground was down from US$285 to US$199 per ounce. And Smith introduced his revolutionary college education program for all the Mercur staff, together with the Barrick profit-sharing plan. Production and productivity went through the roof.

In February 1985 Peter Munk had announced his strategic goal for Barrick Resources: in three years its mines would be producing 300,000 ounces of gold a year. In 1984 the production was 34,000 ounces.

As 1985 closed out, Peter Munk was beginning to maximize the leverage that only ownership of the gold reserves of producing mines could bring. He borrowed (at 2-percent interest) 77,000 ounces of gold against Mercur's reserves. He then sold that bullion on the open market for US$25 million. Those funds were used to pay off the total short-term debt to the Bank of America, leaving only $8 million in long-term debt for the Mercur acquisition.

Munk's involvement in pioneering gold-backed financings was emerging.

Peter Munk (left) and his lifelong friend Erwin Schaeffer. This photograph, a gift from Schaeffer for Munk's sixtieth birthday, is one of Munk's most treasured possessions.

Gabriel Munk's seventy-fifth birthday party in Budapest in
November 1935. These were happier times, when the family still retained the
wealth it would lose during the Second World War. Grandfather Gabriel, seated
at the head of the table, paid dearly to buy safe passage out of Hungary for Peter
and the other members of the Munk family.

The entire Munk clan gathered for Peter's bar mitzvah in
November 1940. Peter is seated at the centre of the photograph. His grandfather
Gabriel is directly behind him.

This photograph, taken in neutral Switzerland in 1945, shows
(from left to right): Hedy Munk; Gabriel and his wife, Irma; Peter's father, Louis,
holding baby Paul; Peter's step-mother, Olga; Peter; and, in front, Hedy's sister,
Steffi Gross, and Olga's son John.

Young Peter Munk's first experience with the news media. This *Evening Telegram*
article celebrated the cultural diversity of U of T's 1948 engineering class.

Nova Scotia premier Robert Stanfield, Frank Sobey, president of IEL, and Munk inspect a model of Clairtone's new plant at Stellarton.

Munk and Gilmour grimly look on at the press conference following the
shareholders' meeting that gave IEL control of Clairtone.

Newspaper headlines, annual reports and advertisements chart the meteoric rise
and fall of the Clairtone Sound Corporation.

Munk shares a laugh with Ratu Sir Kamisese Mara, the prime
minister of Fiji, and Essam Khashoggi (far left) at the Beachcomber Hotel, the
focal point of the Pacific Harbour project.

Munk addresses the 1976 annual general meeting of Southern Pacific
Properties. To Munk's right sit Bill Birchall and Clifford Nancarrow. Birchall has
been one of Munk's top advisers for almost the last three decades.

٧٧٠مليون دولار لأضخم مشروع سياحى فى مصر
على هضبة الاهرام ورأس الحكمـــة

بيدا مع مطلع اليوم الاول من عام ١٩٧٦ تنفيذ اكبر مشروع سياحى ا
بلادنا حتى الآن .

يتضمن المشروع انشاء مجموعة قرى سياحية على هضبة الاهرام ورأس الحك
على مساحة ٤٠ الف فدان تضم ٢٠ الف سرير وتتكلف ٧٠٠ مليون دولار
بيدا المشروع بتنفيذ الجانب الخاص بهضبة الاهرام الذى سيشمل اقا
فندقين عملاقين ومجموعة فيلات تحيط بكل فيلا حـديقة وحمام سبــا،
خاص بالاضافة الى اكبر قاعة للاحتفالات فى العالم تتسع لعشرة الاف شخه
وقاعات اخرى للمؤتمرات الدولية وملعب للجولف وقطع ارض معدة للبناء .

وقع عقد الاتفاقية فى ١٢ ديسمبر الماضى احمد زكى رئيس مؤسس

This clipping from *Al-Akhbar*, the major Egyptian daily, shows
how, with the Pyramids Oasis project, Munk and Gilmour's presence began to
be felt beyond the English-speaking world.

Munk and Gilmour with the Egyptian president, Anwar Sadat, at centre.
Sadat was so interested in the Pyramids Oasis project that he even got down on his
hands and knees at this same meeting to review the building plans.

Munk's persistence and Gilmour's charm eventually paid off
with Adnan Khashoggi. In the mid-seventies they were able to interest him in
investing in their Southern Pacific Properties.

Peter and Melanie Munk enjoy a quiet moment at Klosters with their friend Prince Charles. The Munks have a coterie of rich and powerful friends.

Munk and Bob Smith, the man who encouraged Munk to go after Goldstrike and then helped develop it into one of the most profitable gold mines in the world.

Munk in his trademark brown fedora. On his right is his legal eagle, Howard Beck.

J.M. CARISSE PHOTO

Munk addresses the audience at the Prime Ministers' Night, held
at the National Archives Building in Ottawa in 1994. Munk, who once wanted to
be prime minister himself, had Horsham sponsor at the event.

A. MUNRO / TORONTO STAR

Munk receives congratulations from Robert Prichard, the University of Toronto's
president, after being awarded an honorary doctorate for his contributions to
business, philanthropy and education.

Peter and Melanie Munk on top of the world.

Munk and Melanie, centre, enjoy some private time with four of their five children (from left to right): Cheyne, Nina, Natalie and Anthony. Marc-David is missing.

Munk celebrates Barrick's listing on the New York Stock Exchange
in February 1987 with Bill Birchall, centre, and David Domijan, vice president of
the Exchange. Munk bought 100 shares for each of his five children, the first
transfer ever on the NYSE of Barrick stock.

Barrick's International Advisory Board is made up of some of the
most influential businessmen and politicians in North and South America and
Europe. Standing, from left to right, are Howard Baker, Andronico Luksic, Vernon
Jordan, Karl Otto Pöhl, Bob Smith and José Rohm. Seated are George Bush,
Brian Mulroney and Peter Munk.

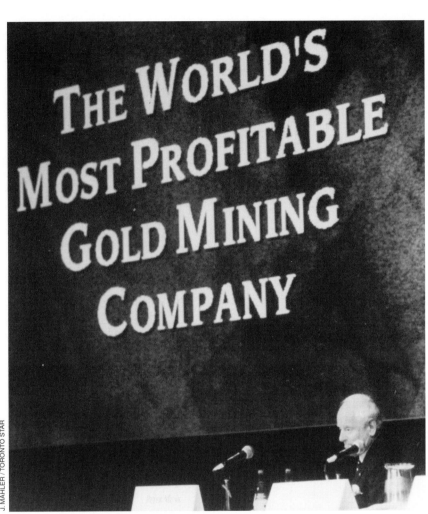

The backdrop says it all at Barrick's annual general meeting in 1995.

CHAPTER TWENTY-NINE

AMERICAN BARRICK

Peter Munk admits that he ultimately depends on advisers to screen deals before they are finalized.

But with something critical and big, like going private, like changing your ten-year program, like buying the hotels or buying out Khashoggi or going out of petroleum and into gold, all those strategic ideas are mine. I usually come back from Klosters with written proposals. I write and then at night I rewrite, because I get very excited so I write badly and I have to rewrite it ten times. Then I circulate my concept, my proposition, to the five or six people I need to convince. Then I bring them together and I give them my arguments. I don't take any of those major steps unless I convince my colleagues and have their full concurrence. If I can't convince them, and if they argue their opposition well, I abandon my plan.

There are several examples of Peter Munk's use of this technique. His move on the London-based Consolidated Goldfields (Consgold) is a case in point.

In the summer of 1986 Munk decided to go after Consgold, the largest gold company outside South Africa and at the time one of the blue-chip firms of the London Stock Exchange. Consgold had two gold mining properties in North America that Munk wanted to acquire, Mesquite in Nevada and Chimney in California, but he had to make his play against Consgold itself in order to give himself some leverage whereby he could wedge out of Consgold those two target mines.

Before he could make his Consgold move, Munk had to obtain the support of his board. He wrote a five-page memorandum which he distributed to them. That was followed by meetings and telephone board meetings. In the end he convinced his people and his directors, and the run at Consgold began.

The first action was the open-market purchase by Barrick of 4.9 percent of Consgold. Rudolf Agnew, the CEO of Consgold, perceived the potential of a Munk takeover bid, and was threatened because he thought that was what it was. Agnew made immediate contact with Munk. The two men met on January 13, and discussed the promising possibilities of Consgold's two mines in North America—Mesquite and Chimney.

At that time, the Oppenheimer family of South Africa were the largest single shareholders of Consgold, with about 30 percent of its stock. Under British law Munk couldn't talk to or deal with the Oppenheimers. It would disqualify Barrick from bidding as a "concert party" bid. A stand-alone takeover bid would require some £1.8 billion, and as Munk says:

> With a bid of that magnitude a mistake would be fatal, and I could not take a chance. At the last minute, we had advances from the Oppenheimers through third parties for me to go to South Africa and talk. I was afraid to compromise our legal position and didn't accept. And by that time I had promised Rudolf Agnew that I would not engage in a dialogue with the Oppenheimers.

He had made that commitment because Agnew, in return, promised to explore the possibility of Munk's taking Consgold's two American gold mines, and that was Munk's main interest. He didn't want Consgold's big U.S. holding, Newmont Mining, nor did he want any of their South African interests. He wanted only Mesquite and Chimney. Agnew promised that if Munk stepped back, he would explore the opportunity to sell them to Barrick for Barrick shares.

That, to me, was a very great promise. In the middle of this Consgold turmoil, which lasted almost a year, we made several million pounds on the transaction because, as we kept buying, the attendant publicity suddenly focused on Consgold as a takeover target. In fact, the Oppenheimers themselves then subsequently made a bid for more Consgold stock.

The move on Consgold promised to give Munk much-needed mines, which "I would get later on by buying Goldstrike, but at that time I needed the next step." A week after Munk met with Agnew, Bill Birchall received word that Hill Samuel was interested in buying all or any part of Barrick's 5-percent shareholdings in Consgold. That useful information was of great comfort to Peter Munk, whose Consgold play had driven the market value of Barrick's 4.9-percent holding up by over $10 million and rising. That would mean a tidy profit on an investment made but a few months earlier.

Then Goldstrike appeared out of the blue. Munk had a call from Joe Rotman, one of his fellow directors at Barrick, who was in a partnership in a gold mine in Nevada. The partner was S.J. Groves & Company, a big Minneapolis construction company. Rotman's company, Pan Cana Minerals Limited of Calgary, and Groves had a joint fifty-fifty gold mining venture, Western States Mineral Corp. It was a small Nevada mine called Goldstrike, which was producing in the range of 50,000 ounces of gold each year. Rotman's Pan Cana staff and their Groves partners didn't get along. Groves was a construction company, whose main concern was to charge the joint venture rent for bulldozers and trucks, and the rates were too high. Rotman's interest was in deep drilling, but the Groves company didn't want to spend money that way. By 1986, there was a total standoff between Pan Cana and Groves. Rotman turned to Munk for help.

> Joe called me and asked would I be just good enough to get involved and maybe we could buy Groves out. I went down to Bob Smith's office and I said, "Bob, I had a phone call from Joe. I'd like to do him a favour. It's boring. It's not Consgold, it's not a billion pounds, it's not going to double our production. But it's Joe." So we went up to Joe's office. Joe gave our mining people all the information. Since I'm not a miner I just stepped out and left it to Bob.

Pan Cana, in the Western States Minerals Corporation partnership, had bought the Goldstrike property in the 1970s. During Western States tenure, 300,000 ounces of gold had been produced from fourteen pits, the high-grade Post pit had been opened, and gold reserves were sitting at some 600,000 ounces.

Barrick was already a presence in Nevada because with the Camflo acquisition came 26.25 percent in the Pinson mine, close to Winnemucca, Nevada. Pinson, a 60,000-ounce-a-year producer, and the Nevada geological scenario were well known to Camflo's Bob Smith, Brian Meikle and Alan Hill. So when Joe Rotman asked Peter Munk to give him a hand with Goldstrike, Munk had a knowledgeable team ready to go. Mercur's geologists, Larry Kornze, Meikle and Hill, did a quick midsummer inspection trip to Goldstrike and came back with a positive report about what they saw as an underdeveloped operation.

By October, Bob Smith was ready to recommend to Peter Munk that Barrick should attempt to get control of Goldstrike. Bob Smith recalls:

It was small but it was very interesting. I remember Brian Meikle saying, "Here are these seven thousand acres. If you stood on this piece of ground, on one side is Newmont's big Genesis mine producing about 4 million ounces, and 180 degrees up the valley there is the Bootstrap and Dee mines, producing probably another 2 million ounces of gold." Goldstrike was a little "Ma and Pa" organization running on a shoestring with a lot of haywire, but they were making reasonable money at it. I talked to Joe Rotman and said, "Joe, if we could buy Western States would you be willing to sell your half?" and he said, "Sure." And that's when I went to Peter and said, "Let's take a crack at this."

Munk told Bob Smith, "If you can buy it for x dollars, it's worthwhile, but only if you can buy the whole thing. Not half but the whole thing." Joe agreed with that approach because he was convinced that unless Barrick took it over, with their management and mining expertise, Goldstrike would never be developed to its full potential.

One problem was that the Groves group had retained the firm of Burns Fry to sell their 50-percent interest, and in Burns Fry's opinion Barrick should not be the buyer. They wanted to sell to Newmont, because their big mine was only a mile away. Munk offered to pay the asking price of $80 million, subject to some due diligence. Burns Fry were not prepared to make a deal with Barrick unless Newmont didn't want to buy. Newmont took several weeks to decide, but in the end they bowed out. In the midst of this, Peter and Melanie went to a dinner party at Rotman's house, where they met the two principals of the Groves firm. They took an immediate liking to Munk, and by the end of the evening they said they were prepared to sell to him.

By that time, Bob Smith and his staff were quite excited about the potential for deep drilling at Goldstrike. Until then, no one in Nevada had a deep drilling program. The American gold mining culture started from the California panners, whereas Canadians think differently, being pre–Cambrian Shield drilling people. As Peter Munk says, "Bob Smith got quite turned on by the potential of the deep stuff. We decided that even if deep drilling didn't work out, we'd still get our money back, so there was no great risk."

Bob Smith was also confident he could increase the percentage of gold taken out of the Goldstrike property by using the then relatively new process called autoclaving, which uses a high-heat pressure technology to extract gold from ore. He'd had excellent results with it at Mercur.

With the Groves principals ready to sell their 50 percent to him, and full of confidence from what Smith had been reporting about Goldstrike, Peter Munk was ready to negotiate a deal with Joe Rotman's partners in Pan Cana for the other 50 percent of Western States. If he succeeded, Barrick would have Goldstrike. Munk was keen.

> Then I had to go out to Calgary. Northwest was concerned because there was a big negative article about us in *Barron's* because an outfit called Gold Standard had sued us on the ownership of the Mercur mine for about a hundred million dollars. It made the headlines of newspapers in America. And these poor guys in Calgary got frightened.

Munk and his team arrived in Calgary on a Sunday night in December and the next morning met with the Pan Cana board. Munk offered them half the purchase price in cash, to reduce their risk, and Howard Beck explained to them that there was really no meaningful legal exposure in the Gold Standard litigation.

> So the deal was done with Pan Cana after the usual difficulties—and Goldstrike was about to become the biggest find in America.

> Goldstrike, the biggest gold mine in America, is on a 6,870-acre

tract of Eureka County in Nevada at the northern extremity of the Tuscarora Spur. It is in the incredibly gold-rich Carlin Trend, in which there are some twenty significant deposits. The gold reserves in the Carlin Trend are said to be in the range of 100 million ounces. Goldstrike's reserves are now so large that they claim more than a third of that 100 million ounces.

Peter Munk had never seen the gold mine he fought so hard to buy. His decision to go for it was based on his faith and trust in his mining team. As soon as the deal was closed, Munk says,

Bob Smith went out with his people, Dr. Meikle and Alan Hill. They started to drill and they became very excited. They wouldn't tell me how excited they were because I don't know anything about drill holes. At the point Barrick took over Camflo, Bob and his people had little credibility. There was nothing but friction at Camflo. So I had to learn by experience, and my confidence in them grew over the years as they performed and I realized how brilliant they were, and how much integrity they had. But at that time, if they had said to me that we had a billion-dollar mine there in Goldstrike, believe me, I would have run for the hills!

Munk did not run for the hills. As Bob Smith explains, he did exactly the opposite:

Even after we started discovering a fair amount of gold in the deeper parts of Goldstrike, there were a lot of Doubting Thomases and they said, "Hell, we could never mine that because it's under water and we're going to have to de-water the whole thing." Peter never wavered one goddamn moment. He didn't come to me and say, "How are you going to do this?" We chatted, and I said, "We're going to bring a few experts in from Germany. They've done some huge de-watering coal projects over there and we'll get the job done." He didn't question our decision. Peter just said, "Go and do it."

Bob Smith was confident that he could increase the percentage of gold taken out of the Goldstrike property using the newly emerging and costly autoclaving process, and he was able to convince Munk.

Peter never lost faith in us and just let us keep going down that road and, of course, the autoclaving has worked out even better than we hoped.

Peter Munk's dealing in Barrick's gold interests, holdings and subsidiaries was becoming increasingly complex and sophisticated as a result of the interrelated Camflo holdings. Everything had to be simplified for investors to easily understand. By the end of 1986 articles in the press on Munk included charts to enable readers to track Munk's holdings and interests.

In addition to the Goldstrike acquisition by Barrick in 1986, there was the transformation of United Siscoe Mines Inc., which would eventually emerge renamed as Horsham Corporation. By the end of 1985 Siscoe, by then a subsidiary of Barrick, underwent the first Munk-ordained change. In a complicated transaction, Barrick wound up with Siscoe's holding in the Pinson gold mine in Nevada. It was a swap arrangement that negated Barrick's stake in Siscoe and cancelled some of Siscoe's debt, but gave Barrick a direct ownership in Pinson. When 1986 brought the Goldstrike acquisition, which soon became an "elephant" bonanza of the kind every gold prospector, miner and mine owner dreams of, Munk decided that he could now afford to restructure and simplify his entire corporate skeleton. United Siscoe was to be a centrepiece.

Barrick Resources' name was changed by Peter Munk to American Barrick Resources Corporation to give comfort to and encourage investors in the United States. (The name Barrick would continue to be regularly used by the media without the "American.") As a prelude to the reorganization, Munk had successfully completed, in September, a deal with Merrill Lynch Canada Inc. for the sale of C$43 million worth of units of American Barrick's common shares and gold purchase warrants. Each unit offered consisted of one common share and two warrants to purchase gold at US$460 an ounce. For those who had faith (or were prepared to bet) that the price of gold would rise beyond US$460 by September four years later, the enticement was complete. Merrill Lynch had no trouble selling them.

The stage was then set for his strategic corporate restructuring plan.

Munk made the decision to go public with the restructuring at the beginning of December, with a shareholders' meeting for approval scheduled for December 30th. However, the plan never came off. It had to be redesigned, and its implementation delayed until midsummer 1987, because of the swiftly changing circumstances of the Khashoggis, particularly in North America.

In December 1986, Peter Munk was feeling the heat that was beginning to arise from his partnership with Adnan Khashoggi. At a closed congressional session in Washington on alleged U.S. arms sales to Iran, one Roy Furmark, a New York businessman associated with Khashoggi, alleged that Khashoggi had put up his shares in American Barrick as collateral for a $10-million loan to help finance part of the sale of American arms to Iran.

Bill Birchall stepped into the breach. Peter Munk had just arrived in Klosters for the winter. But Munk was in control of how to respond. Birchall immediately told the *Toronto Star* that Furmark was not correct about Khashoggi's involvement in American Barrick. He said:

Horsham is controlled by a Toronto businessman, Peter
Munk, who would have to give his approval for the

Khashoggis to use their interest in the company as collateral. American Barrick shares were not put up as security and the firm, a major North American gold producer, is in no way involved in the arms deal and doesn't want to be implicated.

Adnan Khashoggi's empire in America was about to crumble. Peter Munk and David Gilmour realized it was time to disassociate themselves from their flamboyant partner. The Khashoggis would soon need all the cash they could lay their hands on, which meant that Munk and Gilmour would have to arrange to buy out the Khashoggis' interests in Barrick Investments and, through it, in American Barrick Resources and United Siscoe. That would take some time, and some rethinking of the master plan for the restructuring.

In January 1987, Peter Munk was delighted by what he read in *Fortune* magazine's "The Best and Worst Stocks of 1986." So pleased was he that in case they hadn't seen it he dashed off a quick letter to the "important people"—his directors in Barrick, Norman Short, Joe Rotman, Tony Novelly, Angus MacNaughton of Genstar, David Hinde of Samuel Montagu in London, and the legal workhorse, Howard Beck. Munk's closing line in all the letters was: "I'm delighted that, with your ongoing support and assistance, American Barrick made it to number 33 on the 'Best' list. Let's see if we can't move to the top spot for 1987!"

At the end of February, Peter Munk had a visit from the man who had almost torpedoed the Prudential Bache deal, Dick Thompson, chairman of the Toronto-Dominion Bank and now a respected good friend. Thompson was on a fundraising call. He pointed out to Munk that since Barrick was at last a profitable operation, its (and Munk's) acceptance by the local community would be enhanced by a donation to the Hospital for Sick Children Centre in Toronto.

To Dick Thompson's satisfaction, Peter Munk pledged a Barrick donation of $100,000. This was to be the beginning of a continuing series of charitable donations by Peter Munk, either personally or through Horsham or Barrick or in combination.

After the purchase of Goldstrike, the small mine in Nevada, was completed, Bob Smith's Barrick team moved in to take charge in January. In recognition of Smith's good work Peter Munk wrote a memo to him on March 4, "confirming our agreement whereby you will be using the title 'Chief Operating Officer' exclusively." And Munk would soon be opening the golden-stock-option door for Bob Smith.

When Barrick was listed on the New York Stock Exchange at the end of February, Munk bought 100 shares for each of his five children. He asked Merrill Lynch to produce the share certificates as quickly as possible. On April 14, Peter wrote to Anthony about the purchase that had been made for him. It was Anthony's birthday present. "Dear Anthony: This is the first transfer ever on the NYSE of Barrick stock. The ticker tape paused for nine seconds while your transfer was completed. I can't think of anyone in whose name the first Barrick trade could more appropriately have been made! Love, Daddy." There was a P.S. "My other birthday gift is your trip to Budapest."

At American Barrick's shareholders' meeting in Toronto in May 1987, Munk outlined for the shareholders where Barrick had come from since starting in gold only three years before, and offered a map to the future as he saw it.

He repeated that the move into gold came about because he had anticipated that political unrest in South Africa would mean that European investors would look outside that country for gold investments. He said, "That move spelled to us that the $8 billion or $9 billion that for the past generation had been firmly invested in South Africa gold mines would seek a new home—and that to me was North America."

The Annual Information Form prepared for the annual meeting provided a brief snapshot of the astonishing distance that the focused

Peter Munk had brought Barrick in a short period of time. More particularly, the document showed that Peter Munk had negotiated for Barrick the acquisition of Goldstrike for C$43 million cash and C$38 million in shares, for a grand total of C$81 million. It also referred to Peter Munk's controversial but profitable foray into the Consolidated Goldfields PLC arena.

In the second half of 1986, American Barrick, a newcomer that had existed for less than four years, took a run at the mighty British-based Consolidated Goldfields, a company that had been founded by Cecil Rhodes in the previous century and that was a member of the Financial Times 100 index. With a market capitalization of more than £2 billion, compared with American Barrick's puny couple of hundred million dollars, Consgold was startled, to say the least, at the Canadian company's *chutzpah*.

Munk built a position of 4.9 percent of Consgold with purchases on the open market, but failed to consummate the takeover when the stock price took off in response to his initiative. The gutsy move, however, paid off in the long run. Not only did Barrick end up with a profit of $9.4 million when it sold its position, but the takeover bid attracted the attention of some of the biggest stock-market players in the world—people like the Oppenheimer family and Sir James Goldsmith, who became part of Munk's network and led him to great opportunities later on.

In front of him lay the enormous challenges of the Horsham restructuring plan that was implemented at the end of June 1987, and also of the emerging potential of that small mine known as Goldstrike.

The planned December 1986 United Siscoe and American Barrick meetings had been put off because of the changing situation of Adnan Khashoggi. The friendly Arab was facing financial difficulties on a large scale, and he had a major liquidity problem. Khashoggi had no choice. He and his brother, Essam, would have to be taken out of Horsham Securities Limited and the Horsham plan. In the original restructuring, Adnan and Essam were to jointly hold

22.8 percent of the new Horsham Corporation. Their interests would have to be bought.

By February, the plight of the Khashoggis was increasingly attracting the attention of the world's press. Adnan's Triad America was forced to file under Chapter 11 of the U.S. bankruptcy law. Two of his private airliners were seized for debts in France. His web of wealth was falling apart and he needed all the cash he could get his hands on. Peter Munk and David Gilmour were sympathetic. They would do what they could to arrange an equitable buyout of the Khashoggis as soon as possible.

In a May 25, 1987, letter to the London representatives of Prince Nawaf of Saudi Arabia, who was to remain an investor, Bill Birchall set the scene:

> … I would confirm that we are going to proceed with the
> consolidation into United Siscoe Mines of the control block
> of some 6.35 million American Barrick Resources shares. This
> transaction can now be completed due to the elimination of
> the Khashoggi shareholding in Horsham Securities Limited.

Peter Munk immediately began to look for a superior Canadian executive to take on the role of leader in the new Horsham Corporation. His increasing involvement with Merrill Lynch Canada had brought him into steady contact with Ian Delaney, Merrill Lynch's head man in Canada. By mid-April Munk had decided to approach Delaney, a Canadian, to sound him out. Birchall, who would have to work closely with whoever was chosen, approved of Munk's choice.

Ian Delaney was receptive. It was agreed that Delaney would be president and chief executive officer of Horsham Securities on its emergence as a public company, which would, in effect, be the Horsham Corporation. The stage was now set for the elaborately planned restructuring.

*

In England, another stage was being set by Melanie Munk with the expert assistance and connivance of David Wynne-Morgan, a man who knew his way around London. Melanie had decided that the birthday party to end all birthday parties should be held to celebrate Peter's sixtieth. She called it his "fiftieth" birthday, because at sixty the trim Munk looked to be the younger age. It would be an early celebration, in mid-June when the weather promised to be fine, instead of dreary, cold November 8, Peter's actual birthday.

The site she chose was the palatial Cliveden, the Astor family home outside London (which was famous during the Profumo scandal). Melanie invited Peter's closest friends from boyhood and university days, and colleagues who had shared his business life.

There were to be two celebratory evenings at Cliveden. The first was on Friday, June 19: a private dinner with family and closest friends. On Saturday evening it was the big birthday "bash," with some 150 guests; Howard Beck, dazzled by the magnificent event with dinner, music, loads of bubbly and witty after-dinner speeches, said "it was right out of *The Great Gatsby*." The festivities went through the night with a hearty English breakfast served at 4 a.m.

At the Friday evening private dinner, Erwin Schaeffer presented to Peter, his boyhood chum, a photograph of the two of them together in Budapest at about the age of seven. In that picture, which Peter treasures, are the remarkable unchanged Munk eyes.

This letter from Peter Munk to Erwin Schaeffer, written a few weeks later, gives a glimpse of the feelings he experienced on that memorable evening:

My dear Erwin:

Now that I'm back behind my desk, the first thing I want to do is to thank you for the wonderful speech you made on the first night at Cliveden. It was totally unexpected and so obviously straight from the heart, that you added a very special extra dimension to what was already a wonderful evening.

Although the party itself on the Saturday was spectacular, I shall not easily forget those moments in the library after dinner on Friday, when—surrounded by some of the people I care most about in the world—you made a truly affecting speech and gave me the photograph.

The opportunity to reaffirm friendship comes all too rarely in the kind of lifestyle you and I are forced to lead— and I do want you to know that your words further enhanced what was for me one of the most memorable weekends of my life.

At a directors' and shareholders' meetings of United Siscoe and American Barrick Resources in Montreal on June 30, 1987, shareholders of United Siscoe Mines Inc. approved share issues that gave Munk personal control of Siscoe, which, in turn, held 23 percent of Toronto-based Barrick. Siscoe was renamed Horsham Corporation. Peter Munk and his associates owned 94 percent of Horsham on an equity basis. However, Munk received multiple-voting shares (10 shares for each) and had a majority voting interest in the company. The multiple-voting shares were issued to ensure that the company was Canadian controlled, but more than half the equity was held by non-Canadians, including Prince Nawaf of Saudi Arabia, and Anthony Novelly through a holding company. Most of the 23-percent stake in Barrick that Siscoe acquired came from Horsham Securities.

During the remainder of 1987, Munk focused on raising capital for American Barrick Resources. He left the mining development to Bob Smith and his professionals. Munk and Gilmour, with their expert number-cruncher partner, Bill Birchall, would orchestrate the money mining.

Their success in this endeavour started before the restructuring was complete. On March 13, 1987, an ad in the *Wall Street Journal* announced the sale, worth US$50 million, by Barrick Resources (U.S.A.) Inc. of "2% Guaranteed Gold Indexed Notes due 1992";

redeemable for (a) a cash amount indexed to the price of gold or (b) at the option of the holder, gold bullion, and unconditionally and irrevocably guaranteed by American Barrick Resources Corporation.

In June 1987, American Barrick announced the sale of 1.5 million common shares at US$37 per share ($55.5 million). Underwritten by Merrill Lynch Capital Markets, and Goldman, Sachs & Co., one million of those shares were concurrently offered by the underwriters in the Canadian market at C$51 per share.

The escalating share price of American Barrick left Peter Munk little choice: Barrick shares had had a great run, from C$20.75 at the end of 1986 to as high as $57.25, then back to $47.50 in May. Munk and his board decided the stock had to be split. Shareholders of record as at June 30, 1987, were paid a one-share stock dividend on July 15, 1987, the equivalent of a two-for-one stock split. By mid-October Peter Munk and his team had sold yet another issue of common shares. An October 21, 1987, ad announced the sale by American Barrick of a new issue of 3 million common shares for C$116,250,000. Again it was Merrill Lynch and Goldman Sachs as underwriters with James Capel & Co. in the U.K.

On Thursday, October 29, 1987, Barrick arranged a gold loan of 263,713 ounces from the Toronto-Dominion Bank. This was a major deal that the TD chairman Dick Thompson was pleased to approve, and it allowed his friend Peter Munk to authorize the immediate sale of that gold by Barrick into the market for about C$160 million. The initial interest rate for the TD loan was a phenomenally low 1.65 percent annually.

By this time, the cash in hand and short-term investments of American Barrick were over C$300 million. Peter Munk had funds substantially in excess of the planned capital spending programs for both Goldstrike and Barrick's Holt-McDermott mine in Northern Ontario.

For Peter Munk, at Klosters with Melanie on the eve of the New Year of 1988, there was every reason to celebrate the satisfying achievements of his sixtieth year and his happy "fiftieth" birthday—and when he saw the *Forbes* rating of "Best Stocks" in its October 5, 1987, issue, he must have thought back to his January letter to his close colleagues about Barrick being rated number 33 by *Fortune* magazine on its list for 1986. *Forbes* placed American Barrick seventh among all North American stocks. Not quite the top spot—but getting there.

In December, Goldstrike was coming on strong. Bob Smith and his team were doing a superb job for Peter Munk and Barrick. Smith's responsibility for the development of the Goldstrike property was growing by leaps and bounds. In a December 9 memo, Peter Munk recorded his conversation with Smith that day:

> I told him that the board felt we still only had him as a miner, and, in light of the enormous potential capital expenditure program at Goldstrike, I was advised that he needs top-level full-time backup on his project and more intimate, frequent and in-depth communication between him and myself.

On December 16, Peter Munk, with the concurrence of his directors, granted Bob Smith further American Barrick options to the tune of 200,000 shares. This recognition made the enormously valuable Bob Smith a *de facto* partner of Peter Munk.

CHAPTER THIRTY

GOLD: THE FIRST FREE-TRADE COMMODITY

O ut in Nevada, Smith's team at Goldstrike was making quiet progress in uncovering the actual extent of the gold reserves in the ground. The mine had produced only 40,000 ounces in 1987. But it wasn't the production that was exciting. It was the discovery process, the selective drilling that Bob Smith's team of Meikle, Kornze and Bettles carried out that year. By mid-1987 the gold reserves at Goldstrike had gone from the 600,000 ounces at acquisition time to 15 million ounces, with no end in sight. Alan Hill was given the go-ahead to prepare the Betze Plan (Betze was a combination of *Bettles* and *Kornze*) for the comprehensive development of the mining and processing of the incredible reserves that were emerging under the very feet of Munk's men.

As for Peter Munk, he left the mining to Bob Smith, but in mid-December 1987 he had "suggested" to Smith that a committee of three executives—Smith, Alan Hill and Angus MacNaughton—meet with Munk and his financial man Jerry Garbutt on a regular bi-weekly basis to bring everyone up to date on developments at Goldstrike.

It would be Peter Munk's responsibility to raise the hundreds of millions of dollars necessary to develop Goldstrike. So it was imperative that he be informed not only about the technical details, the type of high-cost machinery and equipment being proposed and all aspects of the Hill plan, but also about the projected costs and budgets. Once Goldstrike was fully up and running he could leave the day-to-day operations to his totally reliable Bob Smith and the financial gate-keeper, Jerry Garbutt.

Just before Christmas 1987 Tony Novelly arrived at Peter Munk's Hazelton Avenue offices to announce that Novelly's Apex Oil Company, his holding company for Clark Oil, was in serious trouble. Apex, based in St. Louis, was one of the largest private companies in the U.S., with 1987 revenues over US$2.5 billion. It also owned, with Clark, two refineries in the Midwest with a combined capacity of 160,000 barrels per day, and 960 gas service stations.

Novelly had joined Munk's Barrick Resources board in 1984 and was a strong investor, with more than half a million American Barrick shares in his portfolio. He told Peter Munk that Apex had just defaulted on its loans and was in receivership. Novelly pleaded with Munk to have Horsham take over Apex. He asked Munk to be one of the bidders when the bankruptcy was adjudicated for the whole Apex structure. "Because the banks need my release ... otherwise I'll sue them," Novelly said, "If you do it my way, you will have a very strong advantage because I won't give the release to anybody else. In return I want a participation with you."

Novelly had Peter Munk's interest but no commitment. Not yet. Munk would have to do a lot of strategic thinking before he could make a final decision to go for Apex Oil or Clark. If he made his move, he would have to have control of Apex as part of the deal. Early in 1988 he brought Bill Birchall and Ian Delaney into the question—should they go for Apex and/or Clark and if they did how would they work the financing?

Delaney and his team determined that it would require US$350 million to do the deal, of which $200 million could be bank-financed. That left the $150 million for Horsham to raise with a joint venture partner. But that number was to be drastically reduced. Horsham would acquire Clark through a new company, AOC Holdings Inc.

Instead of needing $150 million, the new Clark would require only $30 million in equity—$18 million from Horsham and $12 million from Novelly.

It was time for Peter Munk to write one of his memos to colleagues. Munk wrote similar memoranda earlier for Consgold and later for the Trizec and Lac opportunities. It is his pattern of operation when he has made up his mind on any major acquisition or other strategic initiatives, but still needs to persuade and convince "his people." On important issues it is required discipline to put the fundamental reasoning plus all the risks, versus rewards, into a written form. It helps people to think about the proposal, and it can be used years after the deal to review the thinking and check the assumptions.

The memo of May 5, 1988, to Birchall, Gilmour and Delaney demonstrates Munk's ability to persuade and to assess and analyse a business situation. It read, in part:

> In every person's life there comes an opportunity which, if grasped, changes his life. Equally so in corporations; every highly successful entrepreneur has made his corporation successful by recognising and seizing that chance. I strongly feel that the Apex deal is such a chance—a unique opportunity that can change Horsham's destiny. It will do so by moving it to a more rarefied level, allowing its future activities to be more creative and consequently much more attractive to investors, thereby putting it amongst those few corporate "movers and shakers" to whom the right size and quality of deals come automatically.
>
> In addition, it will give us a new concept to sell and, by being seen to move away from its passive holdings in Barrick, will also revive new investors' interest and open the door to a whole range of new constituents—to whom the "Barrick gold story" is now somewhat "old hat."

The following are some of my specifics for urging action now, with top priority, on the Apex deal:

- It is not a hostile but, on the contrary, a friendly transaction. At this size (or even at a fraction of its size) we have always agreed that Horsham could not cope with a hostile transaction. There are not many "friendly" ones of this size out there.
- While it is a very large deal, it is yet one that can be done by "not betting the farm," i.e. at risk is about $40 million of Horsham's funds, which we can easily cover by selling that many shares to new investors—in the wake of the deal!
- It is a deal we are buying out of the bankruptcy courts which, to my instincts, always represented best "values."
- It is a deal in which we have a strong "inside track." I can't think of any other transaction of this magnitude offering us this vital advantage.
- It is a deal in an industry presently in its bottom cycle. Big money was always made by acquisitions at the low point of a cycle.
- It is a transaction that—if it works out well—by its very scope would truly transform Horsham and, as such, is surely worth the effort.
- It is acquiring a "real operation" with its own cash flows from the very start, and its own assets to be geared up—if needed—later for new deals!
- It is a transaction in an industry in which we have a number of friends to help, or join, us. (Peter Bijur, Joe Rotman, the K.I.O., the Venezuelans, etc. just to mention a few that come to mind). Owning Apex will allow us to deal and work with these groups.

- The deal possesses the ultimate "smell test"; the seller is not only our major partner but is putting new funds into the acquisition vehicle!

As Peter Munk noted, the risk to Horsham could be covered "by selling that many shares to new investors," and that is exactly what Munk did. He and Melanie spent weeks on end in New York and Europe, where he used his persuasive power and knowledge to sell, by November 8, 1988, a total of C$29,150,000 (5,300,000 at $5.50 per share) worth of Horsham subordinate voting shares. Willing London investors included Shell International; His Excellency Ashraf Marwan, who had introduced Gilmour to Sadat; Majesty Securities Ltd.; Kuwait Investment Office; and the Banque de Participations et de Placements of Lugano, Switzerland. On November 7 the bankruptcy court approved the Horsham proposal for the new Munk-controlled AOC Holdings Inc. to acquire the assets of Clark Oil & Refining Corporation.

There were still more acquisitions of Horsham shares. The market purchase by the famous American acquisition expert Carl Icahn of one million subordinate shares sent a caution signal to Munk and Birchall. But there was no follow-up by him. On November 15 there was a sale of 1.1 million shares to Airaid Netherlands for $6,050,000, which added nicely to the Horsham coffers.

Chicago real estate investor Sam Zell had been assisting Novelly in negotiating with the banks holding the defaulted Clark debt. Zell kept the banks at bay, assuring them that Novelly would not wind up with control in AOC Holdings. For his part in the deal Zell negotiated the right to buy, and did buy, a 6 percent stake in Horsham for US$20 million.

Apex itself (as distinct from Clark) was to emerge from bankruptcy court in 1990 still controlled by Novelly and with an oil trading operation, oil storage facilities, oil tankers and barges, $35 million in cash for operations and estimated annual revenues in the range of $500 million.

Horsham finished 1988 quite a different animal from the much smaller one that started it. The company now had two main assets: 12.7 million shares representing control of American Barrick, and 60 percent of Clark, worth $235 million. These outstanding figures would obviously improve Horsham's balance sheet.

The massive financing requirements for Goldstrike would come in 1989, but with the gold reserves that were coming onstream at that little mine, gold-secured loans promised to meet all requirements. To begin the Goldstrike financing Peter Munk went to Oliver Baring of the London financial house Warburg Securities at the beginning of September. He retained Warburg to assist Barrick in its negotiation of financing terms and evaluation of alternatives, including the preparation of the information memorandum or any other aspect of the transaction.

Peter Munk has always been highly sensitive about what is said about him or any corporation that he controls or with which he has a significant association. That is why he has from time to time had legal skirmishes with the *Globe and Mail* and certain British newspapers. And that is why he continued in the Egypt years and thereafter to retain the services of David Wynne-Morgan to deal with hostile or erroneous press attacks, and to help shape the attitude of any journalist approaching Munk or his corporations on an assignment. If one looks at the myriad newspaper reports on Peter Munk or his companies written over the decades, a fair assessment is that, notwithstanding Clairtone, the treatment of him by and large has been and continues to be much more weighted to the positive than to the negative.

If there is negative criticism, Peter Munk wants to rebut and challenge it immediately, particularly if the writer has deliberately or negligently used facts that are incorrect or biased toward some negative prejudgement. In mid-December, as he prepared to depart for his winter holiday at Klosters, Munk reiterated a press relations rule he had laid down a year earlier. It was set out in a memo from his assistant, Janet James, and went to Smith, Garbutt and others. It was a rule that made sense.

> Peter feels very strongly that the reasons for our recent rough-housing at the hands of the press, i.e. *Barron's* and *Forbes,* was because the journalists did not have access to him. Even though he is away for a month or so, please ensure that if we do get requests from the media to speak to Peter, that he is given the opportunity to talk to them direct.

There was one more matter for Munk to deal with before flying off to Klosters, where the entire family would gather for New Year's. He instructed Coudert Frères in Paris to apply maximum pressure to the Egyptian government, which was still resisting the International Chamber of Commerce ruling that they pay SPP (ME) US$16.5 million for breach of contract. The legal firm had instructions to oppose all their actions designed to frustrate Munk and Gilmour's claim for compensation.

At breakfast in Klosters on the morning of December 20, Peter Munk reviewed with great satisfaction the fax that had arrived from his financial people, Jerry Garbutt and Greg Wilkins, on the matter of Goldstrike development financing. Munk's team recommended that, of the two banks submitting offers—the Toronto-Dominion Group and the Union Bank of Switzerland Group—the lead mandate be awarded to the UBS group, which offered US$441 million secured against 1,050,000 ounces of gold over eight years, extendable to eleven years. There it was, a commitment for US$441 million, which, according to Bob Smith, would turn the little mine called Goldstrike into North America's top gold producer.

Nineteen eighty-eight was an extremely difficult family year for Peter and Melanie. Peter's mother, Katharina Abranyi, died on August 14, after a long and debilitating illness that saw her less and less able to cope with life and requiring constant institutional care. Her loving son Peter was devastated. He had cared for his mother with an unusual depth of loyalty, affection and compassion that flowed strongly from those early days in Budapest and her later ordeal in Auschwitz.

To make things even more difficult, Melanie's father, David Bosanquet, died that summer. It was a sad season for the family Munk.

However, 1988 also brought many events that gave Peter Munk pleasure. Not the least of these was the privilege of addressing the prestigious Canadian Club in Toronto. Peter Munk delivered his speech on February 29, to a packed house. His topic was free trade—what else?

In late October, Munk replied to a letter about free trade from Jack Lawrence, the youthful head of the major Canadian investment house Burns Fry. Munk wrote:

> In your closing paragraph you asked me to think and speak about the Free Trade Agreement. In my first career (which you are too young to recall!) I have spoken—from practical experience as an exporter of Canadian secondary manufactured products to the United States and the United Kingdom—dozens of times a year, on the need, and the vital importance to give Canadians a chance to tackle world markets and compete. I would refer you to my speech to the Canadian Club on February 29th of this year. I love to speak on the subject—because I so strongly believe in it.
>
> I am ready, prepared and willing to share with you your commitment to our Free Trade Agreement and to provide support on the subject—anywhere and anytime.

Munk's commitment to free trade has not flagged or faltered since those halcyon days of the early and mid-1960s when, as a young star of business, he stumped across the country, exhorting Canadians to export goods and get rid of trade barriers. Even then, Peter Munk was on a straight track that would take him, by the closing years of the

1990s, to the top of a Canadian-based international corporation producing a commodity that since the beginning of man's recorded history has been traded freely and without impediment across every boundary and in every country—gold.

CHAPTER THIRTY-ONE

MUNK'S FIFTY VOTES
A SHARE

In his newly fax-equipped Klosters aerie, Peter Munk ushered in 1989 with all of his and Melanie's children as they skied and partied. There was plenty to celebrate. Horsham was doing extremely well, Barrick's Goldstrike was nothing less than phenomenal and Horsham's Clark Oil was rapidly being turned into a solid profit generator. Peter Munk had a full schedule ahead of him just keeping his many ducks in a row—and properly fed with capital.

His central focus was the development of Goldstrike and the heavy financing required for the state-of-the-art autoclaving units and other equipment needed to maximize gold production at the lowest possible cost. Then there was that thorn in his side, the ongoing attempt to extract compensation out of the Egyptian government. There was the time-consuming litigation over the ownership of Mercur, which Barrick had inherited from Texaco. And there was the potential of a Barrick lawsuit against a London stockbrokerage over their activities during Munk's acquisition of the 4.9 percent holding in Consolidated Goldfields.

As for Horsham's Clark Oil, Peter Munk had set it on a drastic new course, but in the end he would still have Tony Novelly to contend with. Horsham owned 60 percent of AOC Holdings Inc., which had bought Clark Oil for $454 million. The other 40 percent of AOC

Holdings was owned by Novelly and Samuel Goldstein in AOC Limited Partnership.

Munk had installed Ralph Cunningham, a forty-eight-year-old former president and CEO of Tenneco Oil Processing and Marketing, as Clark's chairman and CEO. To watchdog the scene Munk put in his own financial officer, Paul Melnuk, to hold the same post at Clark. The mandate for the Cunningham and Melnuk team was to improve Clark's entire retail operation of 491 basic service stations and 422 upgraded units. The goal would be to convert 100 of these to minimarts and give a general facelift to all retail locations. The team wasted no time in getting into action. Then, in July, Peter Munk negotiated refinancing of Clark Oil, by raising $300 million selling first-mortgage notes through Drexel Burnham Lambert, a major New York financial house.

As Horsham's profits and assets increased, Munk and his advisers could see the opportunity to raise more equity money by the sale of treasury shares. But each new sale diluted Munk's controlling interest. He could be left with less than 50 percent of the votes.

Gold shares collapsed in the aftermath of the October 1987 500-point drop of the Dow. Horsham was getting ready to make an offer for some additional American Barrick shares it did not own. Munk wanted to prevent another "greenmail" like Boone Pickens's move on Newmont.

To ward off predators and ensure that he had unquestionable and total control of Horsham, Peter Munk decided to ask the board and shareholders to approve a by-law that, subject to "sunset clauses," would increase the weight of each of Munk's multiple voting shares from 10 votes to 50 votes. The by-law had a "coattail" provision, whereby any follow-up offer to minority shareholders had to be identical to any offer for Peter Munk's block. The "sunset clauses" made the multiple votes of Munk's special shares non-transferable. If he ceased to be a director, sold any of the multiple-vote shares, became incapacitated or died, each of these shares would immediately be reduced to a single vote.

Several institutional shareholders were reportedly disturbed by the 50-vote-per-share move, but when the shareholders' meeting was held on November 15, 1989, no objection was raised. After the meeting Peter Munk explained that "subordinated shareholders will have the same financial rights and nothing essential has changed. Except the control has been cemented in view of further Horsham takeovers in the resource and industrial areas in the next few years."

Munk now had his 50 votes per share and total control without fear of assault. While he had not disclosed a focus on any particular target, he intended that Horsham should be in a position to use its own shares in making whatever acquisitions might appear and be acted upon.

With Clark factored in, Horsham's net income was $32.6 million, up from $5.1 million for the previous year's period.

Goldstrike was the star of the American Barrick meeting at the Hilton International in Toronto on the morning of January 10, 1989. Peter Munk was in the chair, but the meeting belonged to Alan Hill, with assists from the head financial guru, Jerry Garbutt, and the man now at the top of the gold mining mountain, Barrick's president and COO, the affable Bob Smith.

Hill's proposal for the Betze mine at Goldstrike was exciting—and expensive. His Betze Development Plan had an opening price tag of US$365 million. It had the potential to become the largest producing gold mine in North America. Hill explained the open-pit operations, the proposed autoclaving units, and the details of a mine that he projected would produce some 10.4 million ounces of gold over seven years.

How would this US$365 million be financed? Jerry Garbutt announced the financing deal that had already been made with the Union Bank of Switzerland, Westpac Banking Corporation of Australia and the Royal Bank of Canada. Peter Munk had been assured by Bob Smith that other miraculous events were sure to follow. There were many yet-to-be-uncovered opportunities for mines on Goldstrike's 7,000 rolling acres.

The first of these opportunities came within nine months. In September, a drilling program within a mile of Goldstrike produced three holes with nothing, but the fourth came up with a bonanza, 540 feet of ore grading a rich 0.41 ounces per ton. Further drilling established the mine, which Munk would name Meikle after Dr. Brian Meikle, the brilliant geologist who had played such an important role in the investigation, acquisition and development of Goldstrike.

As Goldstrike's fame grew, so did the international reputation of Peter Munk. In 1989 he was invited to become a director of the World Gold Council, and in June he addressed the World Gold Conference at Lugano, Switzerland. Munk's speech began with a brief overview of gold production in North America, then moved on to make a compelling case for all gold producers to support the World Gold Council, arguing that the demand for gold from the world jewellery market was rising; and suggesting that the ancient, honourable practice of hallmarking by the makers of gold objects should be restored and supported. The Gold Council was on the world stage and Peter Munk was delighted to play a role.

Soon after the Lugano speech, it was reported that Peter Munk's former partner and good friend, Adnan Khashoggi, who had been charged in the United States with aiding former Philippine president Ferdinand Marcos in a massive real estate fraud, had been extradited to the U.S. a few days earlier. The flying Bedouin was grounded. A federal judge set bail for his release at $10 million. He had to stay in the New York area and wear an "unremovable electronic bracelet" to monitor his movements. Peter Munk was greatly distressed by this news. Khashoggi was his friend and Munk would stand by him. He telephoned Adnan in New York to tell him so.

At the same time, Munk was involved with his own court activities in many countries around the globe, but as the plaintiff. He decided early in the year to issue a writ in London against James Capel & Company, Barrick's adviser and broker in the contemplated 1986 raid on Consolidated Goldfields PLC, called Consgold. Munk had information that the British Department of Trade and Commerce had a confidential report on the activities of Capel. The department found that during the Consgold acquisition activities carried out for Barrick, Capel had bought a substantial number of shares for itself and for its clients—some C$86.7 million. The result was that the Consgold share price was driven upwards and out of Munk's reach. He could not complete the Consgold scheme that he, Birchall and Stephen Dattels had put together in July 1986. The litigation was ultimately settled, with a substantial payment going to Barrick.

The plan had been to have Barrick acquire a 4.9-percent share block in Consgold. Barrick could then move to acquire control, sell at a profit, or—the real objective—use the block as leverage to get Consgold to sell its two North American mines, Mesquite and Chimney, to Barrick. That objective was on the verge of being reached after discussions between Munk and Rudolf Agnew, Consgold's chairman. But the price of Consgold shares moved beyond making financial sense, driven so high by the inappropriate Capel intervention that Barrick could no longer compete. Peter Munk does not tolerate being deceived by anyone—let alone professionals whom he has retained to advise and act for him, and who betray his trust. The James Capel Consgold activities were completely unacceptable. It was time to sue.

Meanwhile, American Barrick had again bought into Consgold, which was about to be taken over by a group headed by the British entrepreneur Lord Hanson. By midsummer of 1989 Barrick owned 3.4 million shares of Consgold. Munk calculated that his new substantial holding would get him a seat at the bargaining table if Hanson decided to sell its 49-percent interest in Newmont Gold Corporation, the owner and operator of Goldstrike's immediate neighbour, or perhaps the Mesquite and Chimney mines.

In Utah the litigation Barrick had inherited from Texaco when Munk bought Mercur was moving slowly, but not in favour of Barrick. The plaintiff, Gold Standard Inc., was after a 25 percent interest in Mercur. The case hinged on Gold Standard's sale of the Mercur claim, staked in 1976 by its president, Scott Smith, to Getty Oil, which sold it to Texaco, which then sold it to Barrick. A Utah judge had just allowed Smith to amend his pleadings so as to include a cause of action for breach of fiduciary duty and misappropriation of confidential information against American Barrick. The amended complaint asked the court for an order granting Mercur to Gold Standard and imposing a constructive trust over all its assets. Those assets would include Barrick's Goldstrike mine in Nevada.

Those were simply pleadings that the court allowed in by amendment. They were not findings of fact or rulings of the court. Nevertheless, the court's action set off Peter Munk's alarm system. The Mercur fight was getting nasty. Munk had used no funds whatever from the Mercur mine to buy or develop Goldstrike.

Munk had launched a counter-assault against Gold Standard in 1987. In a New York State libel action, Barrick alleged that Gold Standard and the other named defendants had distributed false and misleading statements, mischaracterizing the facts of the Utah litigation to undermine confidence in the company's business prospects, bring about a decline in the value of the company's securities and coerce a settlement.

If the outcome of any segment of the litigation with Gold Standard was against Barrick there could be a serious negative impact on Munk's ability to raise the enormous amount of capital required to further develop Goldstrike or for other Barrick or Horsham activities.

In November there was yet another American Barrick common stock issue from treasury, 3 million shares, which netted US$90.4 million. Munk was cranking up and being aggressive with American Barrick's hedging programs involving the use of forward sales, "put and call" options, gold loans and other arrangements. By locking in a future price, Barrick could assure its cash flow, regardless of what happened to the price of gold.

In early November word on the street was that Peter Munk's American Barrick staff had hit yet another paydirt find at Goldstrike. The North Claim Block had always looked promising, and the hunch proved right. It was revealed that new mine at Goldstrike would cost upwards of $185 million to bring into production. Betze and Meikle combined would make the Goldstrike property the largest producer of gold in North America.

In November, Peter Munk decided that because of the share price rise since the last split, American Barrick's stock should again be split on a two-for-one basis.

At the end of the year there was still some muttering about Peter Munk's 50-votes-per-share Horsham holdings. Ira Gluskin, an investment counsellor and contributing editor of the *Financial Times* of Canada, commented:

> For years, I used to hear that there was a Peter Munk discount. It was only four years ago that American Barrick was at a discount to its peers because of alleged moral deficiencies of Mr. Munk incurred in the year 8 B.C. Today American Barrick sells at a premium and the very same Peter Munk is a national hero and a credit to his race, creed and lineage. I am convinced that the multiple vote issue at Horsham is just a temporary tempest.

Peter Munk was delighted by Gluskin's words.

CHAPTER THIRTY-TWO

BERLIN AND BRANDENBURG

I n 1990 the Berlin Wall came down, and the unbelievably rapid process of German reunification began. The disintegration of the Soviet Union, combined with apparent return of East Germany to democracy and to capitalism, stirred the strategic as well as the emotional fires in Peter Munk's European soul. As he puts it, "Geopolitical events bring with them major economic changes—and that's the time to make big money." He immediately understood that there would be opportunities to restore Berlin to its prewar grandeur, and to do so profitably. Another possibility was to acquire and develop lands close to and within the social and economic orbit of Berlin.

Peter Munk might have been expected to have some lingering animus against the Germans and the city that had stood at the heart of Hitler's Third Reich. Macklin Hancock remembers Munk telling him, "People will be surprised that I might want to work in East Germany, but I really believe in Europe. I wanted to achieve something in the development of Europe and I thought I had an advantage in the fact that I speak German."

East Germany, Munk knew, was as different from the other East European countries as chalk is from cheese. They had the same recent history under Soviet domination, but once the East Germans were integrated with Germany they became, in terms of currency, as safe as

Frankfurt or Hamburg, where investment was the safest in Europe. From the legal point of view, which was always a big question in new Eastern European countries that did not have property ownership, there was the whole German legal structure. Peter Munk felt he could eliminate the currency risks and the legal risks; he could still buy into Berlin at Eastern European prices and the purchase would be made in Deutsche Marks.

He called on his reliable old friend Pat Samuel to investigate the possibility of a central Berlin redevelopment and invited the master planner, Macklin Hancock, to assist him. Munk's instructions to Hancock were simple: "Whatever Pat wants you to do there, I want you to do. And I want you to conceptualize on how to create the projects." Samuel picked out a huge site and negotiated an option to purchase. Eb Zeidler, the distinguished Canadian architect (who is of German origin), prepared the building designs. Munk says,

> There were two projects I wanted to do. One was a huge urban revitalization project in the heart of Berlin, with a canal system, a little Venice: hotels, shopping centres, office blocks, residences—and the other was outside land development where we looked for the land appreciation that occurs when agricultural land is changed to major industrial use (which was at Brandenburg Park). We withdrew from the Berlin project a year later, after a large amount of effort and money, because we felt the Berlin bureaucrats were playing games as the city became hotter and hotter.
>
> We had an option on the Berlin land, which Pat Samuel had put together, and Eb Zeidler had developed a magnificent plan. But the Treuhandanstalt, an ad hoc agency manned by senior executives of the various large German companies, were a clique. When it came to really valuable things that they were advertising abroad, they *said* they wanted French and Canadian and American investors. But they were keeping the

best for themselves. Germany was for Germans, not for us Canadians. We had the prior claim, but it was clear we could never put it together.

So I went to Berlin with our Canadian ambassador and raised hell. We went to talk directly to the head of the Treuhand, who told us "Maybe you think you're unfairly treated, but every morning I have another ambassador sitting here telling me the same thing. I'm a German. My job is to do what I think is right. Thank you for joining us, Mr. Ambassador," and we were both kicked out—and I was a potential $200-million investor with a brilliant plan and millions spent on putting it together, with the full encouragement of the mayor and his whole planning department. The Treuhand did not want us. They took three little pieces of land from our plan, just enough to make it impossible for us to put together the deal.

Peter Munk walked away from Berlin, but not away from the Brandenburg development opportunity that Pat Samuel had uncovered for him, 580 acres thirteen miles south of central Berlin. He was discouraged by the Berlin rebuff, but he believed that his analysis of the economic future of East Germany was correct. Munk said in 1995:

Nothing was surer than that land values would increase. It was only a matter of the zoning, planning and Macklin Hancock's expertise. The land was at the corner of the Berlin Ring Road, which is their peripheral road, like our 401. The government agreed to build a connecting road from central Berlin, and we agreed to develop the land at our cost, put in all the infrastructure, power, water, roads, and do what Canada and Britain do so successfully, bring in integrated business parks. It was a very good scheme; it worked out well and I'm very proud of it today. It's part of Trizec's international program in real estate. We've got Ford, Coca-Cola, McDonald's there. Brandenburg's got the best names. And we've made money.

Throughout this period, when Peter Munk wasn't speaking at a conference or an annual meeting or on an offered podium, he was engrossed in the major matters of Horsham, American Barrick and now Clark Oil. After a relatively short time at Horsham, only three years, Ian Delaney decided to set up his own business, and Peter Munk responded by appointing himself chief executive officer of Horsham. He also moved Jeremy Garbutt, his vice president and chief financial officer at American Barrick, up and across to Horsham as president and chief operating officer. Peter Munk also made another personnel change, the first of many upward moves by Gregory Wilkins, whom he named chief financial officer of American Barrick, succeeding Jerry Garbutt.

The year 1990 was to be filled with noteworthy Munk-initiated events. On January 15, 1990, the Horsham Corporation was listed on the New York Stock Exchange under the symbol HSM. At Goldstrike in February the first of six autoclave units was commissioned after Bob Smith forecast that American Barrick would produce 565,000 ounces of gold in 1990, of which 330,000 would be from Goldstrike alone. On the legal front Barrick won a significant legal skirmish in the battle with Gold Standard over Mercur, with potential hooks into Goldstrike. A Utah judge granted a Barrick motion for summary judgment, ruling that Gold Standard's claim to a share in the Mercur mine was only 15 percent and not 25 percent as claimed. And Munk was still hard at the hedging of Barrick's production. By March the company had hedged 95 percent of its 1990 production at US$421 an ounce, well above the US$345 market price for gold.

At an annual meeting, Peter Munk told the ever-growing crowd that "my job has increasingly become one of a contemplative philosopher"; and "Barrick today has a market capitalization somewhat in excess of the Bank of Nova Scotia. And I like the Bank of Nova Scotia!" The range was $2.5 billion for Barrick against $2.3 billion for the bank. He saw his duty as to "reflect on your behalf and my behalf, on what can possibly go wrong. I certainly have had my share of setbacks and problems in my life, and that's a tremendous asset because of the experience it provides."

In the Midland Walwyn Capital review of the top ten Canadian stocks for 1990, two remarks were made that reflected professional opinion on the efforts of Peter Munk in his leadership of Barrick. The opening sentence was: "American Barrick is Canada's premier gold producer." The research report closed with this: "We continue to regard American Barrick as possessing the best combination of financial, managerial, technical and resource assets within Canada." Peter Munk, his team and Goldstrike would soon change the words "within Canada" to "within North America."

After receiving an honorary Doctor of Laws degree from New Jersey's Upsala College in the spring of 1991, Peter Munk was in London for negotiations with the legendary international financier Sir James Goldsmith, who died in the summer of 1997. By this time, May 1991, Jimmy Goldsmith owned a direct 42-percent interest (plus a further 7 percent indirect) in Newmont, Goldstrike's next-door neighbour. With its autoclave coming onstream, Munk's Goldstrike was proving to be a hugely profitable operation, whereas Goldsmith's Newmont was not living up to expectations. Munk had the team that could get Newmont going. An anonymous competitor contributed to the growing Barrick legend, saying, "If Bob Smith can find gold and dig it out, Munk will show you how to turn gold into profits."

Munk and Goldsmith sat down to discuss the advantages of a merger. If they could put Newmont and Barrick together, it would get rid of the problems created by the complicated boundary between the two in Nevada, and would allow the joint development of the Deep Post ore body, which Newmont and Barrick shared. Munk and Smith were projecting Barrick production at 530,000 ounces for 1991, heading for 1 million ounces in 1992. With Newmont in their hands, the potential would be enormous.

But there was no merger. Munk and Smith would take Barrick forward on their own.

After his many sessions with Goldsmith, Munk decided that American Barrick stock should have a full London listing, a move that was enthusiastically welcomed in that city's business press. The mining correspondent of *The Times*, Colin Campbell, wrote positively about Munk's profitable hedging activities and the discovery of the ore body called Purple Vein at the potential dump site. He quotes Bob Smith saying that the geological formation containing Goldstrike and Newmont, the Carlin Trend, is so rich that "they will be mining this place when I'm six feet under looking up ... and even then they will still be digging down."

In the fall of 1991, Munk decided the time was ripe for yet another American Barrick treasury issue. This time it was 4 million shares that netted C$113 million in early November, just two days before the stock market took a drastic dive. It was a move that saw Munk called both "smart" and "lucky."

The smart and lucky Munk was also forging ahead with the Brandenburg project. All the pieces had come together. Over many months, Munk continued to make eloquent speeches in German before the local governmental officials, mayors and bureaucrats, convincing them that he had a superb industrial park plan and that they ought to allow him to proceed. On September 26, Peter Munk announced the purchase of the site for US$12 million from Treuhand, the state agency responsible for privatizing East German assets. He told Horsham's shareholders that with the combined support of the local community and the state government, Horsham was finalizing plans to build a multifaceted business park on the Brandenburg site. He assured them that Horsham's initial investment and risk would be limited; the project would have to finance much of its own growth.

Munk also gave his Horsham shareholders a 1991 snapshot of American Barrick and Clark Oil, saying that American Barrick Resources Corporation, founded with an initial outlay of less than $30 million in the early 1980s, had since become one of the largest and most financially successful gold mining companies in the world with its market capitalization approximating $4 billion. Yet despite its exceptional growth, there was still much to look forward to at Barrick. In 1992, it expected its gold production to well exceed a million ounces, from only 34,000 ounces in 1984. Gold reserves were over 25 million ounces, all in North America. Munk said that since Horsham had acquired Clark it had generated net income of nearly $90 million to Horsham's account.

Horsham finished the year with net earnings of $61.4 million, and cash and short-term investments of $376.2 million. The value of Horsham's 20-percent interest in American Barrick was approaching $1 billion. American Barrick itself had net earnings of $92.4 million; and cash and short-term investments at $252.1 million with stated total assets at $1,306.3 million. The graphs of all those Barrick numbers were heading rapidly upward as the pace of production and discovery at Goldstrike escalated.

But there was another escalation. It began in August 1991, when Munk had to exercise certain expiring American Barrick stock options that he had been granted during the corporation's infancy. Munk's options were exceptionally valuable. He exercised them, then sold the shares into the market.

The resulting publicity forced an explanation from the principal founder of American Barrick.

CHAPTER THIRTY-THREE

THE OPTION STORM

In October 1991 the Barrick team staged a quarterly information meeting in Toronto for investors and analysts to keep them abreast of Barrick's good news. These were now an integral part of Barrick's corporate culture, and were organized by Isabel Mulligan, a highly regarded investor relations professional. When the presentations by Bob Smith, Greg Wilkins and others were over, Munk took the podium. The final item was, as he described it, "a personal issue, the exercise of his stock options then estimated to be at $36.6 pretax millions." Munk talked about the income tax considerations that had forced him to move. He told his audience, "Let me look boldly into your eyes and tell you that my intellectual and moral commitment has not changed." His performance was described in *Canadian Business* as "vintage Munk and quintessential Barrick."

With that, Peter Munk hoped he had heard the last of the carpings about the Barrick stock options. In the following few months, all was quiet. There was no investor backlash and no public comment. Then the commotion began. On April 7, 1992, an article appeared in the *Globe and Mail* under the headline "OSC suggests new executive-pay rules." The then-chairman of the Ontario Securities Commission, Robert Wright, was mulling over the virtues of the American system of compelling disclosure of executive salaries of listed corporations.

But it was the subheading that got Peter Munk's undivided attention: "Wright's compromise would require disclosure of unusual salaries like Munk's." The so-called unusual salaries were explained in the fifth paragraph:

> Mr. Wright is not proposing to import the U.S. system, even after [the] disclosure that one Toronto executive, Peter Munk of American Barrick Resources Corp., pulled down an unheard of $32.3 million (Canadian) in salary, bonus and stock option gains in 1991.

The facts were: Munk had refused a salary for himself until the shareholders were paid a dividend. When American Barrick started as a public company, Munk also refused to accept any stock options. His view was that options should go to the executives, not the original founders or investors with an existing stock position. Therefore, Munk didn't get his options when all the other executives (e.g., Dattels, Garbutt, Smith, Hill and others) got theirs, but only in 1987, a few years later, when share prices had moved from $1.40 to $10 or $11. Had he taken those options in the initial plan, the payout would have been a multiple of the $30 million. He had no choice but to exercise in 1991. Munk thought it was misleading to make the public think that he had a salary of $32 million. He would explain his situation at the upcoming American Barrick annual meeting.

Munk's concern about the public's perception was valid. Newspapers and journalists jumped on the story. Peter Gzowski conducted a three-person panel on his CBC *Morningside* show the very next day. The participants, Christopher Waddell (Toronto), Diane Francis (Toronto) and Giles Gherson (Ottawa), were asked "Does Peter Munk, the chairman of American Barrick Resources, actually make $32 million a year?"

In the ensuing discussion the panel had one thing straight—that Munk's yearly salary was "only about $700,000"—but it was Diane

Francis, the editor of the *Financial Post*, who put the situation in perspective:

> One thing also on Peter Munk's seemingly obscene amount of money this year: let's not forget that Peter Munk started that company; he found all those gold mines and he started another company. American Barrick's revenues are about US$350 million and it made a net profit of over $100 million.
>
> This is a staggering amount of money, and his is a pent-up stock option over a number of years. Quite frankly, none of those shareholders would have made a dime if this guy hadn't wagered his own bankroll initially and started this whole company. It's all owed to him. His case is very different; he's the founding entrepreneur.

Even the news magazine *Maclean's* had a shot at Peter Munk. In its April 20, 1992, edition, in a piece headlined "The pay perks of the rich," *Maclean's* ran a photo of a smiling Munk that read: "1990 pay $791,521; 1991 pay $32,618,150."

Munk stood at the podium before a full house of American Barrick shareholders on the morning of April 23, 1992. After duly reporting on the year's growth in gold production, reserves and profits, and outlining plans for the future, Munk turned to the controversy:

> Barrick is my life—it is something that I created, that I conceived, and I have lived. So to me it's more than just a job. And it is in that context that you must allow me to speak about ... my annual income or personal salary which, in most people's minds, is almost obscene. I think that it deserves, in fact, it needs, touching on.
>
> When I was given those options only six or seven years ago, the total value of this company was $80 million. The

company was engaged or embarking upon a brand new business, and had zero credibility in mining. And so it should have. The chances or the odds that anyone would have given you that the company would be around nine years later in the gold business, let alone double its share value, would have been very small indeed. The fact that those share values have gone up twenty times is a miracle. It's a phenomenon that will go down in the annals of business history.

At that time, we deliberately and with full recognition of the entrepreneurial spirit—a fundamental component of the American Barrick philosophy—said to ourselves that the important thing in our business is to buy the time during which we can prove right our concept and our approach. Time, in business, is a function of how much money you have and how soon you run out of the ability to write a cheque. So we said, let us all, the handful of key executives, take the minimum amount of salary. Let us make sure that we don't spend our money—giving us the time to prove our principles.

When the company's value moved from $80 million to $3 billion last year to close to $4 billion today, I received my share. I am proud of having done that and I'm thrilled that there was $3 billion out there that was earned by institutions, by investors, by people who believed in us. In the process, close to 2,000 jobs have been created, and stockbrokers and truck makers, mine suppliers and contractors have all benefited as we built facilities, as we expanded our activities from Kirkland Lake in Northern Ontario down to Utah and over to Nevada.

And it is just misleading, in my mind, for some to have represented these exercised options as an annual salary—but it's not their fault; it is the reporting system that adds bonuses, salaries and options together to show an executive's total annual remuneration. But this is not, of course, an annual salary, but that's the impression the public gets. I, as a

Canadian, a voluntary Canadian taxpayer, came back from
Britain to pay my taxes here because I love this country.
There's nothing more I could wish for Canada; there's nothing
more, as I see it, that could help in the short term, to cure the
ailments we have than to have twenty-five more Peter Munks
start twenty-five more Barricks every single year.

So far as Peter Munk was concerned, he had set the record straight
on his option exercise. No shareholder had complained, no backlash
came from investors. That controversy was now behind him.

In his chairman and chief executive officer's letter to the shareholders, Peter Munk had plenty to write about—production records,
for example. Barrick produced over 1.3 million ounces. Operating
costs were down to $164 an ounce and dropping. Reserves were up to
27.2 million ounces. Net income rose 89 percent to $174.9 million.
The hedging program realized a price of $422 an ounce, $77 above
the average spot price for the year. Munk expected Barrick's annual
production to hit 2 million ounces by 1995, well ahead of schedule.
The Meikle mine (formerly Purple Vein) would begin production in
1996, with an anticipated output of 400,000 ounces per year. But as
Munk wrote to his shareholders,

> exciting as these developments are, Barrick remains an entre-
> preneurial company. We remain on the lookout for opportu-
> nities to increase reserves and production, but only at prices
> that will add additional value for shareholders.

Munk's eyes were now on companies like Lac Minerals Limited
with its gold mining operations in Chile. It was only one of the many
candidates for acquisition that the Barrick executive team, with Munk
and Birchall in the lead, would be scrutinizing. The goal was an ever-
increasing pot of gold reserves for Barrick Gold.

Meanwhile, in Europe, Peter Munk's vision for Brandenburg Park was finally becoming a reality. Horsham Properties GmbH had planning approvals for the first 220 acres. Munk had officiated at the ground-breaking ceremony that launched the construction of the roads and other services. The first buyer had signed on the dotted line. Coca-Cola purchased a 25-acre site for a regional office, distribution and bottling plant, a real opening prize. Horsham's investment in Brandenburg was $34 million. Munk's plan was for the park to pay its own way and produce substantial profits for its Horsham parent.

In 1992 that Horsham parent and Peter Munk also had to deal with Anthony Novelly and his holdings in Clark Oil. Munk talks about his serious problem with Novelly.

It became obvious that it was the wrong partnership. We had 60 percent of Clark but we could never really call the shots because every time we wanted to do something, like going public when we put together a prospectus the first time around in 1992, he sued us to stop us. We went to the board for approval—we had control of the board—but he said, "I'm not going to approve this unless I get some money from the underwriting." I said, "Look, the underwriting is being organized so Clark can go public, but the main object isn't the money we raise for ourselves—it has to go into the treasury of the company first and foremost." We had just started building a strong company. I wanted it to be well financed.

I told him we shareholders should only benefit and only cash out once the company is strong. I mean us getting $20 million individually doesn't help the company. If we take the money out, then the shareholders and we are both holding something that could be less valuable because it can go under. So I insisted on all the money going into the treasury and that's how the prospectus with Goldman Sachs was issued. But Novelly said, "Unless you add $25 million minimum to the issue, which is for me, I won't approve it." I said, "But that's not the deal. If you take out $25 million as a 40 percent owner then we should be taking out $30 million for our share. That's $55 million!" His response was, "Well, that's your affair." I said, "We're not prepared to raise money from the public unless that money goes into the company. Once the company does well then every shareholder has got the right to sell shares." And what did he do?

Novelly sued us even though we had the majority on the board. By suing us when the prospectus was just approved by the SEC, Novelly made it impossible for Goldman Sachs to raise the money, because they had to wait until the court adjudicated. So we asked for an accelerated decision or hearing, which we got in Delaware. We won the case hands down, of course. But by that time the market had realized there was a fight between the directors and soured on the issue.

And so because of Novelly, Clark remained private, which it still is today. We missed the boat. We did not improve our balance sheet, and Novelly and my people became very incompatible. We started to negotiate to buy him out, which we did, finally, at the end of '92.

The name of P. Anthony Novelly appears for the last time on the list of directors in the 1992 Annual Report of American Barrick.

The Munks were once again in Klosters for a stretch of time that had become the pattern—from just before Christmas through until Easter, when they were back to Toronto and the comforts of 19 Highland Avenue. The period at Klosters would be broken by board and other meetings in Canada and Europe, road shows for investors, the Davos Conference and other events that required the Munk presence.

More and more, in his solo strategic thinking sessions at Klosters, Peter Munk was focusing on the opportunities that an increasing share price and cash balances in both companies offered.

CHAPTER THIRTY-FOUR

TRIZEC

If Peter Munk had any reservations about whether he had been accepted by his Canadian peers after his return to Canada early in the 1980s, the honour bestowed upon him at the beginning of 1993 ought finally to have put those concerns to rest. He was appointed to the Order of Canada, the nation's top civilian award. The citation included references to his outstanding business achievements and his generous philanthropic activities. With other new members, Peter Munk was invested as an Officer in the Order by the Governor General, Ray Hnatyshyn, at an elaborate ceremony at Government House. For Peter Munk 1993 was the period of calm before two storms, called Trizec and Lac, which would break in 1994; they would be the direct result of what the chronicler of Canadian business Peter C. Newman has described as his "incredible intuition, his sixth sense of knowing when and where and how to move."

Knowing how to move has not always helped Munk in knowing what advice to give his eldest son. In the early 1980s, after completing his university education, Anthony Munk wanted to find employment with a financial or investment house. And he wanted to stand on his own two feet and make his own reputation. After periods with Guardian Capital and First Boston, he accepted an offer from Gerry Schwartz, the principal of Onex, probably the most successful leveraged-buy out firm in Canada. Eventually, he also served on the Horsham board of directors.

In late 1994, Peter and Anthony Munk decided that, notwithstanding the pitfalls and usual difficulties of a son working for a strong-willed, highly opinionated, extremely successful father, Anthony Munk should make the move out of Onex and into the Horsham executive group. By the fall of 1995, however, Anthony was back with Gerry Schwartz and Onex. "He went back to Onex," explained Munk. "He came and said, 'I'm very sorry but I'd like to go back.' He liked the atmosphere more at Onex because they make more deals and he loves the deals. And that's where his real expertise lies."

Peter Munk did not stand in Anthony's way.

Gerry Schwartz and Anthony and those guys look at six deals a week! I hate deals. When I do deals, it upsets me, makes me nervous. I always feel that I'm going to make a mistake. I do them to attain my strategic objectives. It sometimes takes a few deals to get there. But I never do a deal per se. I hate it! It's a totally different mentality. Yes, I did Lac, but God save me from another Lac. And yet I'll do one next year again— maybe because I have to—for getting Barrick in position. But it's a different mindset. Their business is to look at deals, like investment bankers. Gerry's background was as an investment banker. Anthony had some time at First Boston, the investment bankers. I like people like Bill Birchall and Greg Wilkins and Bob Smith, who have run a business for twenty or thirty years and build permanent entities and value for their shareholders. Different mentality.

Peter Munk's other son, Marc-David, is Linda's child. Marc's father is a man to whom she was married for a brief time after divorcing Peter. Peter and Melanie later adopted Marc-David as their own. He explains:

Linda and Melanie get along very well. No animosity there. And then my two kids with Linda, Nina and Anthony, have two half-sisters, Natalie and Cheyne, my children with Melanie. On their mother's side they equally have a half-brother, Marc.

The kids don't differentiate between full- or half-siblings. They grew up together, were treated equally, spent holidays together. So when Linda got divorced from Marc's father and moved back to Canada, it was simply natural to bring Marc into the fold. Linda was concerned that Marc didn't have an active father. Melanie and I never thought twice about it. We said, "Of course he's just like the others. He's our children's brother." We just treated Marc like the others. How could you not?

Peter Munk is the beneficiary of an unusual friendship between two women, the one who was and the one who is his wife.

Linda and Melanie have had an ongoing, close relationship from day one when they met thirty years ago. The two are great together. When Linda was sick two years ago it was Melanie who took her to the hospital, and Linda would do the same for Melanie.

In 1994, when Melanie had to be brought home from the hospital and I was away, it was Linda who picked her up and brought her home. When Nina got engaged and Linda was away, Melanie helped plan the wedding.

It's a normal, healthy family friendship. We trust each other and have totally common interests. I would look after Linda's father when he is sick just as I looked after Melanie's father. Linda's father is still my ex–father-in-law but the more important thing is that he's my kids' grandfather. He played a major role in my being in business, more than my

own family. He was great to me. How can you forget those
things? You can't.

By the end of 1993 the North American real estate market was at a fifteen-year low. Among the real estate companies still alive was the
Calgary-based Trizec Corporation, one of the largest publicly traded
real estate companies in North America. Trizec had been established
in 1960. Over its thirty-three-year life it acquired, built, owned and
managed forty-one office buildings in Canada and the U.S., and
forty-four American retail centres (54 million square feet), including
department stores in sixteen states.

The retail property portfolio was segmented into three separate
groups, the main one being the Hahn Company of California, which
had malls in major metropolitan areas that catered to upper-income
customers. With sixteen retail centres in California and one in each of
five other states, Hahn was a major component of Trizec.

By 1993 Trizec had accumulated a long-term debt of C$4.8 billion. Against the massive Trizec debt the corporation showed total
assets at the end of 1993 of C$5.7 billion and net losses for 1992 of
C$544.1 million, and C$312.1 million for 1993. With a falling cash
flow from operations (to C$67.5 million in 1993 from C$146.8
million in 1992) and real estate values declining throughout North
America, recapitalization became an urgent priority if Trizec was to
survive. Then, after trying and failing to keep its subsidiary
Bramalea out of bankruptcy, Trizec defaulted on its bank debt.

Trizec's management sought outside help to assist them in looking
at every aspect of the company's activities. Out of this review came
two approaches. The first was a recapitalization plan, the second was
a new business plan.

Tony Fell, the tall, brilliant head of Dominion Securities, was
retained by the banks, as a result of the default, to design and implement a different recapitalization plan which, translated, meant "find
a new investor or group of investors" willing to put up hundreds of

millions of dollars to refinance the failing North American real estate giant.

Fell put in the first of many long telephone calls to Peter Munk in Switzerland. Munk was definitely interested. He had Fell fax over all the Trizec information he needed to make a basic decision to go or not to go. If his decision was to go, then he would have to persuade his colleagues in Toronto and elsewhere that a move on Trizec was the thing to do.

In his Swiss home, Munk pondered the Trizec statements. Horsham had a pile of cash on hand, and Munk was confident he could find a partner to come on board with him. It would take a hell of a lot of work and negotiating, but Munk was ready.

I made a pitch to all my guys. They called me back and they said, "God, it's a great thing. Let's go!" It was simple to acquire Trizec, because we had over half a billion U.S. dollars in the bank then, in cash. I wanted to go into something where we would be a major, more than just a bit player. And I wanted to do something that was in the bottom of the cycle. Trizec had those characteristics. We could negotiate it without a fight. Trizec had a major franchise value. It was a dominant player in the real estate field and I could get control. Trizec was one of five or six big decisions in my life, in my business career. But those decisions do not get implemented until all of us—management and directors—sign off on it. Our job is to make an unassailable case.

Usually when I'm in trouble, in deep trouble, when I feel that I'm at a dead end or that I'm going the wrong way ... it doesn't happen very often ... then I don't sleep for a long time and I really feel that something has to change. Then at three or four in the morning or at six in the morning, I just start to formulate an idea and then that idea germinates. Then from germination it goes into maturity and then I become fanatical.

The reality check is that I call my colleagues. That used to be Gilmour, now it's also Birchall, always, for the last thirty years. It's also Greg Wilkins, and others whose judgement we trust. Certainly when it comes to Barrick it's Smith. Then I pitch them and then usually they go along. But after all, their destiny is tied up with their decision so they are just as involved as I am. Then we have another meeting and we have a fifth meeting and eventually we come up with a platform and a position. We listen to each other and talk, and then boom, we go. That's how it works.

And that's how it worked for the Trizec deal.

By the magic of the telephone and the fax machine, Munk and his colleagues worked the Trizec acquisition. The amount of cash and securities that Horsham had in hand to do the Trizec transaction was $970.4 million, close enough to a billion to sound phenomenal for a company that started in business just a little over a decade earlier.

By March 28, 1994, the Horsham team announced that it planned to make an equity infusion of C$600 million (approximately US $440 million) in Trizec. The complicated transaction would give Horsham 43 percent of Trizec's common shares.

Next Munk focused on bringing a fellow investor into Trizec. This was the Argo Partnership L.P., consisting of O'Connor Capital Inc. and J.P. Morgan & Company Inc. from New York.

On June 10, 1994, Horsham announced the Argo deal. In addition to the original Trizec arrangement, Horsham would make an offer to purchase C$300 million (representing a 28.5-percent fully diluted interest) from all holders of new common shares of Trizec. Argo would acquire, at Horsham's cost, 35 percent of Horsham's total investment in Trizec, subject to the condition that Horsham's investment in Trizec should not be less than 40 percent. The plan would give Horsham 46.5 percent, Argo 25 percent and remaining shareholders 28.5 percent.

On July 20, Mr. Justice Gregory Forsyth of the Alberta Court of Queen's Bench approved the restructuring plan between Trizec, Horsham and Argo. That was the final condition of closing.

In the end, Horsham and Argo put approximately US$750 million of new equity into Trizec. Existing investors then swapped their debt of $1.4 billion for cash and equity (shares). Trizec still carried a debt load of $2.4 billion, but the interest payments were reduced by about one-third, to approximately $170 million. The result was that Trizec had a positive cash flow of $91.5 million in its first Horsham year.

In a reflective mood in 1995, Munk talked about his family life, his turbulent business history, and his style of life—Klosters, Toronto, Georgian Bay and wherever.

> Melanie sometimes calls me a workaholic, but I still manage to get away to enjoy life.
>
> Not in '67 when I was fired, or when I had no money in '68, or when I was at the height of success have I not spent a month up at my island. The moment I got up there, it was the wind, it was how you tied up your boat, what happens when the waves hit your boat? How do you get the damn food out there? What do you do when the generator breaks down? I used to sail in those days. We used to water-ski and it was always dangerous and exciting, and it was always in water, and it was camaraderie with your neighbours. It's a community.
>
> I bought my island in 1958. Linda and I drove up there, and Everett Anderson, who ran Georgian Bay Waterways at Parry Sound, was our guide and he showed us an island. I was interested in Crown islands, because you could buy them in those days for $300 an acre and the commitment was that you had to build on it within eighteen months, a building for a minimum price, which depended on how big an island you

bought. In my case my island is four acres and I had to put up a building for $9,000, which I did and I lived in it until three years ago. I never had staff up there and my kids learned how to wash dishes, and didn't have any of that nonsense of having help. And we had no hydro until a few years ago so they had to pump the water. They had to wash in the lake. It's a very healthy kind of life. It makes you very Canadian and very nature-dependent. And you don't have to worry about your goddamned colds, because up there the weather took care of you.

Melanie and I came back to Canada in '80. I was by that time in my early fifties and I suddenly had these little kids again and washing diapers and all that stuff. Things had changed, but the dishes had to be done and people dropped in. So by that time I was in a different position. I owned a big company and we had fifty hotels. So after five years we brought in the hydro. It was a wrenching thing because I used to pump the water, and I had candles, and I cut my wood, and I used to do things on my own. I still do. When we're there we cook, make the beds, do the dishes, we do everything. It's quite a contrast. When you start running a million, or a ten-million, or a billion-dollar company and you go to big hotel suites and have planes and all that, it's important that just because your business goes up and down, your personal life maintains certain standards as a touch of reality. Especially for your kids. You can't bring up kids any better— and the island does that. The island is very egalitarian. Then in 1993 Melanie finally prevailed. We had five grown-up kids who'd started marrying, and so we added on to the old house. We put on a whole kitchen extension and a little sleeping cabin for the kids. The old cabin had just the living room, in which there was a kitchen and a big fireplace and then one bedroom up and a bathroom. The kids slept over the old boathouse. I spent thirty years there, very happily, and developed some very close friendships. Just like I did in Klosters.

When you're up in Georgian Bay you don't worry about the bankers. The island is a wonderful, forceful way to shock you out of falling into the trap of thinking of nothing else but your business problems and it also puts your problems in context. After Friday night's storm up at the island, I mean, when the lightning hits and your boat tips over and you barely make it to shore, that's living, that's what life's all about. It helps put things in perspective.

CHAPTER THIRTY-FIVE

THE TORONTO HOSPITAL AND LAC

Over many years of meetings and discussions, Peter Crossgrove had convinced Peter Munk that he should make a public service commitment by joining the board of the Toronto Hospital, of which Crossgrove was chairman.

Their association began when Crossgrove, as president and CEO of the major gold mining firm Placer Dome, and Fraser Fell, its chairman, were approached by Munk, "with the thought of merging Barrick and Placer Dome, which was an interesting idea," Crossgrove says. "That didn't go very far because the directors of Placer Dome weren't interested in entertaining it." Then Crossgrove tried to get Munk interested in the Toronto Hospital, and "we started to have lunch quite a bit, and the hospital and the mining business became intertwined because Munk was in a learning curve in the whole mining industry. He had actually invited me on his board way back then. So when I stepped off the Placer Dome board, I immediately went on the Barrick board."

Peter Crossgrove had to be patient with the man he wanted to involve in the Toronto Hospital.

Peter is an emotional, caring person. He's been beaten up pretty badly in his life in one way or another. In getting into this charitable area of the hospital he was very focused. The whole process took several months. He was very careful how he did it, and he chose to focus on the Toronto Hospital and subsequently his involvement with the University of Toronto.

For the Toronto Hospital, he donated the first $5 million to get the new cardiac centre established, to which he is totally committed, and not only financially. He has come to understand that the Toronto Hospital is one of the few things we could probably pass on to the next generation as good as or better than it was when we received it, which is unusual today. It's a struggle to keep it in good condition, to keep the doctors, to keep the research funded, to keep the capital there. Five hundred and seventy thousand patients a year go through there, plus all the people that come with them. I mean, a hospital wears out. Peter understands it deserves support. But he did the research before he became involved, which was quite amazing. A lot of people just jump in, but he stood back, and thought it through. And, of course, he's become an outstanding board member. If he's over in Europe on vacation, he will leave his vacation and fly back for a board meeting. His commitment is incredible to the hospital. He chairs the planning committee, and he's very creative, very thoughtful, and right into it just the way he's into his business. It's wonderful to see.

Peter Munk's initial gift of $5 million was soon increased by a further $1 million, in Melanie's name, for the establishment of a chair in cardiovascular surgery. The total of $6 million is the largest single gift the Toronto Hospital has received.

On Wednesday, May 11, 1997 at 11 a.m., at a ceremony attended by Peter and Melanie in the lobby of the Toronto Hospital's thirty-five-year-old Gerrard Wing (redecorated under Melanie Munk's supervision), Premier Mike Harris of Ontario pulled aside a drape on the wall to reveal the sign bearing the name of the newly established $25-million centre where the acclaimed heart surgeon Dr. Tirone David and his colleagues will perform some 2,500 open-heart operations every year.

The name is the Peter Munk Cardiac Centre.

Peter Crossgrove's observations on Peter Munk's character reflect his knowledge of the man.

> He's not a patient person. Once he's sorted out what he
> wants to do he wants it yesterday. And that, some days, has
> to be a problem. It takes him a while to get comfortable with
> somebody. But once he does it's an open book. He listens. A
> lot of business people that I know on the boards that I sit on
> are so insecure that they're not able to delegate, for whatever
> reason, whether they're afraid that if they delegate some-
> body'll become too strong and take over, or it'll be perceived
> as a sign of weakness. Peter delegates, he trusts his people,
> and he's very careful. He has insecurities. I mean there's no
> question.

Peter Munk started to focus on South America in the spring of 1994 as part of Barrick's new strategy to expand beyond North America. There was an obvious strategic fit with Lac Mineals' assets in South America.

On July 7, 1994, the world of Lac Minerals and Peter Munk's interest in it began to change. It was on that day that Margaret Witte, the president of Royal Oak Mines, launched a bid for Lac. Munk had little choice. If he wanted Lac, he had to come in with a bid, and the bid had to be better than Witte's.

Peter Allen resigned as chairman and CEO of Lac, his family's company, on July 22. He was suceeded by James Pitblado. Pitblado, a sixty-two-year-old financial wizard and amateur marathon runner, had joined the Lac board in January 1994. As a chairman of Dominion Securities from 1981 to 1992, he brought with him a formidable background in dealing with takeover situations from both sides of the boardroom table.

If they were to make a bid, Munk and his colleagues would have to deal with Pitblado. They were prepared for that. They had respect for the new Lac point man. When he retired from Dominion Securities, he was succeeded by none other than Tony Fell, the man who had just persuaded Munk and his Horsham team to buy Trizec. That mammoth deal was scheduled to close (and did) on July 25, just days after Peter Allen resigned.

Another key element was in play in Munk's decision to make an offer for Lac. It was the defence document the Lac board published, setting out in detail its assets, and in particular its increased gold reserves. As Bob Smith describes it, the defence document was prepared by the Lac board to establish values for the company's production capability and its reserves in order to get the best price for Lac. When Smith and his Barrick team first made an assessment of Lac based on previously published information only, Smith told Peter Munk no. It was only after Lac produced their defence document, in which they announced their additional reserves and resources that the advice to Munk was changed to "Yes, we'd better go for it." The fact that RBC Dominion, Wood Gundy and Goldman Sachs were financial advisers to Lac and had input to the defence document added credibility to its contents. As Bob Smith says, "It's interesting to speculate that if they had not published that document, Royal Oak might have garnered enough support to take over the company; or Lac might have survived."

Munk, Smith, Birchall, the rest of the Barrick gang, investment advisers Bunting Warburg, Kidder Peabody, and a team of Tory, Tory, Deslauriers and Binnington lawyers, headed by James Baillie, worked to put together a bid for Lac. At the same time, the details and machinations of the closing of Trizec also required the supervision of Munk, Birchall and Wilkins. On July 25, Trizec closing day, Munk launched the American Barrick bid for Lac.

His offer for each Lac share was $4 cash plus 0.31 of a Barrick share, putting a value on Lac of $13.38 a share. The Barrick offer would be open until August 26.

Peggy Witte sat down with her bankers and made her expected move on August 8. She sweetened her bid to match and better the Barrick numbers. Her new offer was $5 in cash plus two Royal Oak shares for each Lac share, putting a value of $16.25 on each Lac share. The Royal Oak offer was open to August 16.

Meanwhile, Peter Munk and his team had hit the road to sell the institutional and other big holders of Lac shares in Canada and the United States on why they should take the lower Barrick offer instead of the Royal Oak offer. The road show was absolutely essential if Munk was to be successful.

The message he was getting from those shareholders after Royal Oak sweetened its offer was simple: We like Barrick as an operator much more than Royal Oak … but you'd better come up with an appropriate sweetener of your own.

Barrick and Royal Oak actually joined forces at a hearing before the Ontario Securities Commission. They'd come to ask the OSC to dissolve a Lac "poison pill." The pill gave the directors the power to block a hostile takeover bid by selling new shares out of treasury at a 50-percent discount to existing shareholders. That action would dilute share ownership of a company trying the hostile bid. After a two-day hearing, the OSC ruled on the evening of August 19 that if the holders of 66 percent of Lac's outstanding shares accepted either Royal Oak's or Barrick's offer, the commission would dissolve Lac's poison pill.

Next, Munk called a board tactics meeting on Sunday, August 21. Munk and Bob Smith were getting antsy. The two of them had decided the time was ripe to approach James Pitblado to see if they could cut a deal. The Royal Oak offer was about to expire, but Barrick's would go on to August 26. At the board meeting all agreed that Pitblado should be approached; all, that is, except the quintessential corporate lawyer, Howard Beck. Beck was the last to voice his opinion. He said that since they were in the centre of a hostile takeover fight, Barrick would be in a much better negotiating position with Pitblado if they gave the Royal Oak bid a realistic chance to fail. Beck spoke so convincingly that Munk changed his mind, as did the rest of the group.

Howard Beck was right.

In the late afternoon of Tuesday, August 23, the break came in the form of a telephone message from none other than Tony Fell, acting in his capacity as financial adviser to the Lac board. When the call came, Munk was *en route* from New York, where he'd been meeting with institutional shareholders of Lac. As soon as he was back in his office, Munk arranged to meet with Fell at 8:30 that night. Fell arrived at the Barrick offices accompanied by RBC investment banker Gary Sugar. Greg Wilkins was with Munk. Fell asked Munk if Barrick would put more cash on the table if it meant that the Lac board would recommend Barrick's offer to sharehold-ers. Munk's answer was in the affirmative. He would have to decide how much more cash.

The Barrick board convened immediately that night and approved Munk's recommended increase in the price.

At 9:30 the next morning, Fell and Sugar, with their lawyers, were back at Barrick's offices, where they met with Munk and his team. The group got right to the point and agreed to an improved package that was equal to about $1.46 more per share. The deal was done. Pitblado arrived about 12:30. The documents were signed shortly after 1:00 p.m. At a press conference held at 2:00 p.m. the new bid was announced. Munk said he was delighted with the "all win-win situation," as he called it.

Munk's bid as accepted by the Lac board was $5 cash plus 0.325 of a share at $29.75—a total value of $14.67. The bid was open until September 6.

There would be no rest for Peter Munk and Bob Smith between August 25 and September 6. As Vince Borg, Barrick's vice-president of public affairs and communications, told the press, "Peter Munk will continue to meet with Lac shareholders, and so will Bob Smith. We're not taking anything for granted. They will return to New York some time next week for meetings with big institutional Lac shareholders to pitch them on the value of the company's new and improved cash-and-share offer."

Peter Munk and Bob Smith were successful salesmen. As of 9:30 p.m. on September 6, some 84 percent of Lac's shares had been tendered to American Barrick. Munk then extended the offer until September 19 in an effort to obtain the remainder of the Lac shares.

In acquiring Lac, Peter Munk had made Barrick the largest gold producer outside South Africa. The company now had dominant positions on the three richest gold belts in North and South America: the El Indio Complex in central Chile; the Goldstrike property on the Carlin Trend in Nevada; and the Doyon/Bousquet Complex on the Cadillac Break in northwestern Quebec.

In Barrick's third-quarter report for 1994, gold production for the nine months was 1,508,079 ounces, 28 percent above the previous year's levels. Net income for the period was US$184.1 million. Having completed the Lac transaction, Barrick had in hand cash and short-term investments of US$647.8 million.

Peter Munk had long been an admirer of Brian Mulroney, the former prime minister of Canada who is highly regarded around the world as an influential leader of statesmanlike quality. Mulroney has the charm, the wit, the blarney and international experience that allow him access to the top level of government in virtually any country in the world. Thus, when Peter Munk was doing some strategic thinking and moving Barrick onto the international stage beyond North America, it was Brian Mulroney who came to mind. Mulroney's reputation in Canada and the slings and arrows he continually endured from his fellow countrymen while he was in office were of little or no concern to Peter Munk.

After consulting with Smith, Gilmour and Birchall, and then with the whole board, Munk approached Mulroney in the fall of 1993 with an invitation to join the boards of both Horsham and Barrick, in an active international advisory capacity. Munk made the offer palatable by including an option on 250,000 common shares of Barrick.

At the November meetings of the boards of both companies, Brian Mulroney was welcomed as a new director, as was Peter Crossgrove. Peter Munk wrote in his February 24, 1994, letter to Barrick's shareholders that "Mr. Mulroney is highly respected by world leaders in government, banking and industry; as American Barrick prepared to enter world markets, he is providing the Company with invaluable guidance and counsel."

Mulroney was involved in bringing together Paul Desmarais's Montreal-based Power Corporation and Barrick to form Barrick Power Gold Corporation, which would test the gold mining opportunities in China. Munk's long-time colleague Neil MacLachlan was named president of the new company. In November 1994, also with Mulroney's active involvement, Barrick Power signed letters of intent with China's gold agency, China National Gold Corporation.

Mulroney was increasingly in demand. He and Peter Munk sat down to work out an arrangement that would make Mulroney an officer of Barrick, as chairman of an international advisory board; it would be his role to recruit a top-level panel of leading figures from the nations in which Barrick was doing business or intending to do so.

Meanwhile, at Horsham, Peter Munk made a major financing decision for Clark USA, Inc., the private U.S. company that owned Clark Refining and Marketing Inc., the operating corporation. On September 19, shortly after Barrick completed its takeover of Lac Minerals, Horsham announced that Clark would raise US$250 million by selling one-third of its equity and US$100 million in new high-yield notes. The proceeds would be used to redeem some existing debt and provide the bulk of the cash needed to close the Clark purchase of a large Texas oil refinery owned by Chevron of San

Francisco. However, Munk later advised his Horsham shareholders that because of "industry conditions and weak public markets the offering was withdrawn." Clark did not "go public."

There was one last note on the Lac acquisition. Dick Thompson, Peter Munk's now long-term friend and supporter, couldn't resist the publication in late September 1994 of a discreet ad that said that the Toronto-Dominion Bank and the Royal Bank of Canada had provided to American Barrick Resources Corporation interim financing in the amount of $600 million for the purchase of common shares of Lac Minerals Ltd. It was noted that the whole deal had been: "Structured, Arranged and Agented by the Toronto-Dominion Bank."

With all the massive corporate acquisition activity that had been led and orchestrated by Peter Munk in 1994, it was not surprising that the man was getting the editorial attention of major business magazines and newspapers in North America and Europe and, for that matter, around the world. And the international recognition and positive publicity were a mark of something else that was of the utmost importance to Peter Munk—respect for his considerable and remarkable achievements.

The Prime Ministers' Night at the National Archives building in Ottawa was a special occasion, with an extra dimension for Peter Munk. He had been invited by the chair of the National Archives, Dr. Jean-Pierre Wallot, to co-sponsor a publication program dedicated to honouring Canada's prime ministers. The program, known as "Canada's Prime Ministers 1867–1994," was given a festive launch at the National Archives on the evening of October 24, 1994. The master of ceremonies and principal welcoming speaker on the same platform as all, save one, of Canada's living former first ministers, and Prime Minister Jean Chrétien, was a man who had at one time aspired to be prime minister. It was Peter Munk at his eloquent and forceful best. On the stage as he spoke were Pierre Trudeau, Jean Chrétien, John Turner, Joe Clark and Canada's first woman prime minister, Kim Campbell. (Brian Mulroney was out of the country on Barrick business.) It was a symbolic event for Peter Munk, who was no longer bedevilled by the question of his acceptance by his fellow Canadians.

The Hungarian American Foundation awards dinner was held on December 12, 1994, at New York's Waldorf Astoria Hotel. Peter Munk, with two prominent Hungarian-born Americans, was given special recognition for his outstanding achievements. It was a glittering black-tie affair in the Waldorf Astoria's ballroom. Munk and Melanie's special guests included his children Nina, Natalie and Anthony; his boyhood chums Steven Friedlich, John Kis and Erwin Schaeffer; David Wynne-Morgan; and Alan Sullivan, the consul general of Canada. Brian Mulroney, the former prime minister, made a splendid introduction of Munk, who gave a moving acceptance address.

CHAPTER THIRTY-SIX

CANADA'S GOLDFINGER

Peter Munk had been thinking for some time about changing the name of American Barrick. Now that the Lac deal had launched him into South America he had decided to make a change. Pat Garver, Barrick's in-house legal counsel and a vice-president, was given instructions to get government clearance for the name Barrick Gold Corporation and to take all necessary steps to have supplementary articles of association issued to change to that name. And at the same time Peter Munk decreed that Barrick should have an appropriate golden logo. By mid-January 1995 the entire process was completed to Munk's satisfaction, including the design of the logo which was three tick-mark-shaped gold bars above the name BARRICK.

The month of February is a heavy-duty travelling month for Peter Munk as he takes his road show around North America and Europe selling institutions, financial houses and other investors on the wisdom of holding even more Barrick and Horsham (now TrizecHahn) shares. And, of course, there are the appropriate board meetings thrown in.

After a sensational year of takeovers—with Lac folded into its golden bosom, Barrick was now the world's most profitable gold producer and was heading toward being the largest—Munk was now much sought after by the press. In Zurich in early February 1995 there were two interviews scheduled with leading publications; and in Paris there was another with Ed Carr of *The Economist*, arguably the leading international weekly newsmagazine focusing on world politics and economic matters.

Franz Schneider of *Finanz und Wirtschaft* had reported an earlier interview with Munk in October 1988 when the entrepreneur explained to the sceptical Schneider his strategy for turning Barrick into an international leader in the gold mining industry. After the 1995 interview, Schneider happily reported:

> A little over six years later, in February 1995, we spoke again with the head of Barrick. Nowadays, when Munk talks to Zurich's financial community he has nothing more to prove. Barrick is number one in North America and, in terms of profitability, the world leader.
>
> Conditions are favourable for the continued ascent of Barrick shares. Since 1987 they have seen three 2-to-1 splits. Even with an excellent P/E of 20, they are the first choice among gold shares.

Peter Munk had indeed arrived at the centre stage of the world's gold mining industry.

It was the interview with Ed Carr of *The Economist* that attracted the most attention, titled as it was "Canada's Goldfinger." Carr noted his total control of Barrick and Horsham; his thumping of the lectern while speaking; his disassociating himself from the day-to-day running of his firms. Carr saw that Munk's "biggest problem of all is succession." If there was any synergy in Munk's companies, it was himself. But for investors, to say nothing of those jockeying for position, the question of who will replace such a forceful man is the one strategic issue that will not go away. There may be a system behind Mr. Munk's luck; but it is not infallible, and can certainly not be inherited.

As time moves on beyond the horizon of this writing, there is no answer to the question "Who will replace such a forceful man?" It is likely that the succession issue will not be resolved until it is forced and made unavoidable by the incapacity or demise of Peter Munk— unless he has plans not yet revealed.

Peter Munk decided that Horsham would have to sell a portion of Clark U.S.A. Inc. to obtain the financing necessary to complete the US$203-million acquisition of Chevron Corporation's Port Arthur, Texas, refinery. Paul Melnuk, Clark's president, had been Horsham's president, but Munk had moved him to Clark in St. Louis, Missouri, in April 1994, and made him CEO and appointed Greg Wilkins as president of Horsham. Melnuk worked a deal with Tiger Management, a New York hedge fund manager, for an equity investment of US$135 million that would drop Horsham's interest in Clark to between 60 and 64.4 percent after the deal closed on February 27, 1995. At the same time Munk and Melnuk negotiated a US$400-million letter of credit facility from a group of banks led by Bank of America. With the new 185,000-barrel-a-day refinery, which would double Clark's capacity, Munk was satisfied that Clark was positioned to improve its performance and grow. It had made a 1994 profit of only US$7.8 million, while losing $16.1 million the year before.

As he was preparing for the Barrick Gold Corporation's annual meeting, Munk got some good news from the *Report on Business* magazine's April edition. Barrick was ranked third in Canada in the category of "Leaders in Investment Value"; ninth out of the twenty-five "Best Run and Most Respected Corporations"; fifth-best in "Long-term Investment Value." Not bad, but Peter Munk would expect his Barrick team to do even better the next year.

The *Financial Post* magazine for May published a list of fifty Canadian companies, ranking them for top profit margins. Munk's Barrick Gold Corp. ranked fifth, just 2.7 percentage points behind the

Ontario government's liquid cash cow, the Liquor Control Board, with its 1994 profit margin of 29.5 percent.

His speech at the annual meeting was delivered with typical Munk fire as he went over the many positive points of the Lac acquisition and how "the Good Lord had smiled on him and Barrick." He also complimented Peggy Witte and said he found her to be gracious. When she lost out to Barrick on the Lac deal, she congratulated Munk and wished him well.

Brian Mulroney's priority assignment as a Barrick Gold officer and director had been to assemble its international advisory board. There had been a great deal of speculation as to whether Brian Mulroney would be able to entice his friend and fishing buddy, the former president of the United States, George Bush, to serve on the board. The answer came on May 3, 1995, when Barrick announced the formation of the International Advisory Board. President George Bush would serve as honorary senior adviser and provide counsel on evolving international issues.

The International Advisory Board comprises outstanding representatives of business, commerce and politics from North and South America and Europe. Its members include Brian Mulroney (chair), Senator Howard H. Baker, Jr., the Honourable Paul G. Desmarais, Sr., Vernon E. Jordan, Jr., A. Andrónico Luksic of Chile, Karl Otto Pöhl of Germany and José E. Rohm of Argentina.

Getting George Bush on board was quite a coup for Mulroney and for Munk. This was Bush's first corporate position since he left office in early 1993. At a Toronto Club dinner given on May 30, 1995, by Peter and Melanie Munk for the members of the new Barrick International Advisory Board, former president Bush said that in 1941 he had almost decided to come to Canada and to join the Royal Canadian Air Force. Instead, as history tells us, he went into the U.S. Navy, became a pilot and with a submarine's assistance survived a crash in the Pacific.

Earlier in May, Peter Munk chaired Trizec's first annual meeting since he had completed the difficult restructuring necessary to keep the company afloat. Horsham now held 47.9 percent of Trizec, and the Argo Partnership 25.8 percent. The remaining 26.3 percent was held publicly. Munk's objective was to enhance, sell and buy assets to achieve growth, even though he also wanted to get its debt-to-capital ratio down from 68 percent to between 50 and 60 percent. First-quarter earnings of US$10.1 million indicated that Trizec was solidly in recovery.

The short form of the citation for the conferring of an honorary doctorate upon Peter Munk by the University of Toronto's Chancellor Rose Wolfe at Convocation on Wednesday, June 7, was this:

> Peter Munk (B.A.Sc. 1952), chair and chief executive officer of Barrick Gold Corporation and the Horsham Corporation, for contributions to business, philanthropy and higher education.

To Peter Munk's great joy, U of T president Robert Prichard had invited a special person, a fellow 1952 graduate and one of Munk's closest and dearest friends, Steven Friedlich, to be the Beadle for the Convocation. Bob Smith, also an alumnus, was in attendance as well.

Shortly after invocation on that sweltering June morning, the appropriate honorary degrees were conferred on Peter Munk and the other recipients. The Chancellor then called upon Peter Munk to address Convocation.

Peter Munk spoke of his own beginnings, his failures and to his successes. Then he told graduands that

> you have to be *courageous*; you have to learn to take advantage of *change*. Be *non-conventional*; don't fritter your energies—*be focused; remember to share*. Most important, use the biggest weapon of all weapons, the least appreciated yet the most

important tool for success and this is *moral integrity*; and *don't be afraid to dream and don't be afraid to dream big!*

Munk had been encouraged, invited and gently pressured by the U of T's engaging young president to make a multi-million-dollar contribution to the university. The plans called for this announcement to be made in the fall of 1997.

That summer at his Georgian Bay island home with Melanie, Peter Munk planned shifts of policy and direction for Horsham and its holdings over the next few months. Barrick was booming. It had a record half-year profit to June 30 of US$146.5 million and was on track to produce 3 million ounces of gold in the year. The profit expectation for '95 was US$300 million. After the C$2-billion Lac deal Barrick's only debt was the $170-million loan acquired with Lac against cash in hand of $322 million. Revenue from gold sales was moving toward US$3.6 million a day. Munk planned to spend $30 million in 1995 actually exploring for gold in Peru, Argentina, Mali and Niger, but he pronounced that "I'm not very optimistic about China." Horsham, however, was a different matter. The Trizec acquisition was on track and Brandenburg Park was doing well, but Clark U.S.A. Inc. continued to be a problem. Perhaps it was time to reduce Horsham's exposure in Clark and maintain the move toward real estate.

Munk made the decision to unload all or as much as possible of Clark. That was made public on October 16, 1995. By November 7, Clark had two new equity owners, Occidental Petroleum and Gulf Resources, reducing Horsham's stake from 60 to 40 percent.

Meanwhile, Munk was working to shore up Barrick's ability to make yet another Lac-type acquisition if one was to appear. This time he went to the institution that had given him such a hard time eleven years before when he wanted to buy Camflo, the Royal Bank of Canada. With the Royal in the lead and a syndicate of transnational banks behind it, Munk arranged a five-year US$1-billion revolving credit facility that was in place as of December 5, 1995. Peter Munk was ready for yet another big deal.

In mid-October 1995, an article in *Barron's* by Cheryl Strauss Einhorn opened with "Admirers of Canadian tycoon Peter Munk liken him to the legendary Warren Buffett." Munk's reaction?

> Warren Buffett is like the god of investments. Buffett has made $4 billion. He's the most successful investor of our generation. It's like in skiing, when you start getting compared to Jean-Claude Killy you know you are going to come out as a loser.

Einhorn noted that the gold mogul had no gold around his office and didn't wear any. And some of the windows of his office environment on the 39th floor of BCE Place on Bay Street were thoroughly blacked out. Instead of taking in the view of Lake Ontario, Munk prefers to focus inward, concentrating on building his empire.

CHAPTER THIRTY-SEVEN

THE ROAD AHEAD

At Klosters on January 28, 1995, Peter and Melanie Munk gathered a star-studded dinner party of Canadian and international personalities, most of whom had a heavy-duty stake in Peter's adopted country.

One of them provided this report:

January 29, 1995

Last evening, I had the pleasure once again to attend one of Peter and Melanie Munk's delightful dinner parties in Klosters. The gathering, in Munk fashion, brought together a most interesting group of people, among them George Soros, Karl-Otto Pöhl, Conrad Black, Tom and Sonja Bata, and Premier Bob Rae. Peter, ever concerned about the effects of government fiscal profligacy on world markets, had inserted into our dinner menu the attached quotation from the *Wall Street Journal*. I suggested to Peter that Finance Minister Paul Martin would do well to read it. Peter said, "Good idea—and for greater effect, let's sign it!"

Most of us indeed did sign it (Bob Rae declined) and I reported on this incident to Paul Martin upon my return. The Minister listened, but did not comment. But did it have the desired effect? Of this I have no doubt.

QUOTE OF THE DAY
"Yet the growing doubts in Congress about his $40 billion Mexican loan guarantee demonstrate that Mr. Clinton is now the weakest president since the declining Nixon, and maybe since Hoover, especially within his own party. If Mr. Clinton were a currency, he'd be the Canadian dollar."

The signatories included not only Munk, but also Conrad Black, Barbara Amiel, Sonja Bata, Tom d'Aquino, Andrew Sarlos, Maurice Strong, Angus MacNaughton and William Thorsell. Quite a crowd.

The question was put to Peter Munk in 1995: What are your business objectives for Barrick now?

> Well, I haven't finished yet. Barrick is a great company. It's one of the great Canadian companies. The raising of the billion-dollar line of credit is part of the next phase. The first phase was becoming the predominant gold producer in North America, which I think we have achieved. We had narrow limits, narrow focus, and a highly specific set of objectives. We didn't move outside the geography. We had a fixed program. We didn't borrow money. We have achieved that, maybe a bit better than what I was initially hoping for, with luck.
>
> We are now in the second phase. I am not going to allow Barrick to coast and live off its success. That path is so often the end of a beautiful, exciting beginning. Barrick has to be challenged. This company has to have a set of goals as attainable, as specific and as exciting as the first set was.

Munk explained that in the future Barrick will be operating globally—in Latin America, where for political reasons nothing new in gold mining has been done for thirty years, and Southeast Asia. He's going to let somebody else deal with South Africa. He doesn't want to be everywhere.

As Munk says:

In the old, big global mining companies, the boards approved an annual hundred-million-dollar exploration budget given to the head man of the exploration company, who looked at their global exploration. The man in charge of African exploration got 17.6 percent. The guy in North America got 21.3, the guy in Malaysia got his percentage. And their job was to spend the money. That's not the way we're going to operate. We'll take our money and we're going to get the money leveraged the way we've done it already—in line with business principles, not traditional mining practices. I want Barrick to be the universally accepted global leader in the gold business.

Munk had another set of objectives for Horsham, which had Trizec as a base. He says he didn't buy Trizec just to ride the cyclical wave of real estate. He sees Trizec as a vehicle of growth in three world areas, South America, Europe and Asia. From Munk's perspective, what all three areas have in common is that their young people are the new middle classes.

They're the young men who have been given jobs in Barrick's mine in Chile or the dozens of other mines that have opened there recently, the new accountant in Singapore who now has to use computers because his software company has to comply with the New York Stock Exchange regulations, and hundreds of others. These young people have suddenly emerged from the subsistence classes to the middle classes, just as they did in Canada and the U.S.A. after the Second World War. There was the Depression in the thirties, the war in the forties, then

in the fifties and sixties a revolution took place after a generation of poverty in Canada. The young soldiers came home.
They had children and the baby boom began. They wanted
material wealth, Frigidaires, a new bicycle and a new motor-
bike, a new car, a new radio, a $600 stereo set, a new house.
Everybody was acquiring things. Homes were being built.
Every homeowner wanted to have more broadloom. It's not
like that in Canada any more. But it's like that in those new
areas because people are becoming wealthier and their
economies are growing. And the wonderful thing is that
because of American television, American movies, and satellite
broadcasting, the desires of the kids in the Slovak Republic, in
Bratislava, are identical to the desires of the kids in Bangkok
or Buenos Aires. They want Reebok shoes, the latest sunglass-
es, the latest T-shirts, the latest roller skates. The parents want
a taste of a better life as well. But the shopping facilities in
those areas, in Bucharest, in Budapest, in Bangkok, in Buenos
Aires, are still geared to the shopping habits of the way they
were fifty years ago, the momma and poppa shops. There are
no Yorkdales, no Eaton Centres—not yet.

But if anybody knows how to build them it's the
Americans. There are three companies in America who could
do it and Hahn is one of them. Hahn has got the franchises
and the relationships with the Gaps and the top-line mass
retailers who cannot expand anymore in North America. The
new rich happen to be in Lima, in Santiago, in Bangkok and
in Bratislava. And that is where they want the Gaps, the
Disneyland shops, the theme restaurants, all those things that
belong to the classical American shopping mall. And in the
next ten years, I'm going to take the Hahn company, developers of shopping malls in California, international. That is
where I see the future of Hahn and that business. We've
got the vision. We've got the balance sheet, the credibility.

We've got the track record, and we have the strategic plan
for Hahn.

Then what about Clark? Munk recognizes what oil refining and
marketing is for the Exxons and the Shells. It's a big man's game. Clark
does billions of dollars a year in business, but it is such a regional, tiny
force that when Exxon and Chevron and Shell reduce their prices
Clark hasn't even got a voice. Munk knows that if the markets go
against Clark it could have a dramatic effect. It's better to be the dominant player: Barrick in gold, Hahn in shopping malls, and Trizec in
office buildings. In October 1995 Horsham announced that Clark
was not a core asset.

At Klosters in January 1996, Peter Munk put the finishing touch-
es to his plan of personnel changes designed to put some additional
fire and initiative into Barrick, with its new South American operations, its billion-dollar (U.S.) line of credit and its annual cash flow of
more than half a billion dollars. Munk had decided that he was going
to have to spend more of his time on corporate development at
Barrick. He informed his executive team that he intended to be far
more involved than he had been and would take on a more active role
in the "conception and execution of the international strategies of
Barrick." He had talked Bob Smith out of resigning in 1996. Smith
would stay on as president and be part of a six-man executive team
headed by Munk, who was now going to assume direct responsibility
for the company's expansion strategy.

Part of the Munk strategy was to establish a portfolio of gold
exploration and mining companies, while undertaking corporate
finance initiatives. The corporation would aim at acquiring companies with potential gold mine projects.

From Barrick at the end of January 1996 came news that the corporation was going to spend more than US$300 million to con-
struct the Pascua open-pit gold mine in Chile. Barrick reported its
1995 profit at $292.3 million on revenues of $1.3 billion. The 1994

profit had been $250.5 million and revenues were $936.1 million.

Meanwhile Horsham raised US$275 million through debentures to bolster its cash resources.

With Peter Munk vowing to be more actively involved, there would be 1996 acquisitions and corporate moves that would make him Canada's top business newsmaker of the year.

CHAPTER THIRTY-EIGHT

AREQUIPA

Peter Munk's pledge to become more deeply involved in the affairs of Barrick and Horsham was taken by some observers, including members of his own management team, to be akin to carrying coals to Newcastle, or gold to Goldstrike. The man was already the "soul in control," not of the day-to-day operations of his companies, but of the strategic decision-making processes that were necessary to keep fire in the bellies of his shareholders, his executives, and the tens of thousands of employees who produced for Barrick, Horsham, Trizec, Clark and all their constituent enterprises.

During his long skiing and thinking session at Klosters in the winter of 1996, Munk was relatively content with the state of Barrick. But he could not be totally content. As he perceived the reality of the gold mining business, Barrick had to constantly increase its reserves and cash flow if it was to achieve and then maintain his objective: that in the short term, Barrick should become the world's dominant gold producer. That objective could be approached in two ways: by a well-financed and successful exploration program carried out in geologically and politically attractive regions of the world; and by the acquisition of part or all of smaller companies that had discovered significant reserves, or owned substantial producing mines.

To go the acquisition route, Barrick would have to have cash in hand and a major line of credit well in advance of the appearance of a potential purchase. Munk had already positioned Barrick to be able to move quickly on any such target by arranging a billion-dollar line of credit. That amount, coupled with cash in hand in the range of $200-million and the highly valued Barrick shares, gave Munk and Barrick a powerful war chest.

Horsham, on the other hand, was troublesome. In Munk's opinion it was not producing an appropriate increase in value for its share-holders. He would have to do something to kick-start both Horsham and its two major holdings (apart from Barrick), Trizec and Clark. The decision to unload Clark had already been made and steps had been taken to implement it. But what to do with Horsham and Trizec? At Klosters, Peter Munk was pondering that question. The answer was not immediately obvious, but finding that answer was Peter Munk's self-appointed task.

Nineteen ninety-six was to be one of Peter Munk's most challeng-ing and productive years as an entrepreneur. It would be a year in which he attracted a high level of attention. This would be the year of Arequipa, TrizecHahn and Bre-X, in that order.

In 1993 Catherine McLeod, a young stockbroker, daughter of a Vancouver geologist, Don McLeod, joined forces with a senior geolo-gist, David Lowell, who had extensive knowledge of Peru. They took public some promising Peruvian exploration properties that they had acquired. Their shell company was later named Arequipa Resources Ltd.; its share price began to move upward with the very first drilling results out of Pierina.

Bob Smith and his people had kept their attentive eyes on Arequipa from the time those first results were published. The second batch of results (from only nine drill holes) was made public on July 5, 1996. It was decision time for Munk, Smith and Barrick.

The Toronto press reported that Barrick "stunned the market" on Thursday, July 11, with a C$915-million bid for Arequipa Resources, a small Vancouver-based company "with promising gold and copper properties in Peru."

What was stunning to the market was that Munk would make such a big-dollar move (C$27 per share) on the basis of limited information. Barrick geologists, however, had visited the Pierina property earlier. They had a handle on the little company's drilling program on the initial anomaly, and they also knew that the property contained four more anomalies.

From the information in hand, Bob Smith and his team quickly developed their own estimates—3.5 million ounces of gold and 1.5 million in gold equivalent or silver. Smith immediately went to Peter Munk with the recommendation that Barrick should "go for it." Munk, the non-miner, agreed. He ordered the Barrick financial team, headed by Randall Oliphant, the chief financial officer, and Bill Biggar, the head of investments, to come up with a proposal to Arequipa's management and shareholders that would give Barrick control.

The Arequipa offer was ready by the morning of Thursday, July 11. Peter Munk had given his approval to the numbers and timing. It would be a cash offer, through a drawdown on that as-yet-unused billion-dollar line of credit that had been organized by Barrick treasurer Jamie Sokalsky.

The stage was set. Barrick's main player, Peter Munk, would not appear in the negotiations—at least, not in the opening scene.

Munk designated Alan Hill, Barrick's executive vice-president of development, and Bill Biggar to meet with the Arequipa executives to present the offer.

As luck would have it, both Arequipa's chairman, David Lowell, and its president, Catherine McLeod, were in Toronto to pitch their company's prospects to institutional investors. Their road show was set for July 11, with a packed schedule of meetings. That day, the Barrick team telephoned McLeod at the King Edward Hotel at 7:30 in the morning. She explained that unfortunately she was "too busy" to meet with them—too busy, that is, until she grasped that

Barrick was making a C$915-million offer for Arequipa. They wanted to get together with her and David Lowell as soon as possible to explain the details.

A surprised Ms. McLeod had no objection. The meeting at the King Edward that morning was cordial and informative. McLeod and Lowell were noncommittal. It was too early in the game. For McLeod the opening stakes were enormous. Barrick's offer would make her personal shareholding in Arequipa worth some C$8.9 million, to say nothing of Lowell's stake, which was a multiple of that.

As the deadline of August 19 approached, Arequipa shares were regularly trading at a market price in the range of $2 above the Barrick bid. It was time for him to take centre stage. Munk telephoned his Arequipa counterpart, David Lowell, on Tuesday, August 13, and told him that he would adjust the offer in exchange for Arequipa's support. Bob Smith, Bill Biggar and Alex Davidson, the exploration chief, would fly to Vancouver the next day to meet with Lowell and McLeod. The deal was hammered out, and was accepted by the Arequipa board. Barrick increased its offer to C$30 a share, or gave Arequipa shareholders the option of receiving 0.79 shares of Barrick plus 50 cents cash for each Arequipa share. For the many Arequipa shareholders who had paid only pennies for their stock, that option would allow them to avoid paying capital gains taxes—until they unloaded their Barrick shares. The revised Barrick bid was to expire on August 26.

By the time the offer had expired, 93 percent of the Arequipa shares had been tendered to the Barrick offer, and the remaining 7 percent were acquired within eight weeks. Barrick issued 14 million shares to those who opted to exchange and paid out about C$512 million in cash.

The Arequipa deal was done. When Catherine McLeod said, "I think it has almost been a Cinderella story," she was right.

CHAPTER THIRTY-NINE

TRIZECHAHN

eter Munk stood at the podium in the Royal York Hotel on the afternoon of May 9, 1996. The company's annual meeting had been held in Montreal in the morning, and he was now speaking to the gathered shareholders of Horsham Corporation at the follow-up Toronto information session.

In his speech that day Munk did something he had rarely, if ever, had to do before. As chairman and CEO of Horsham he apologized to his audience for the flat share-price performance of the company. He admitted that he and the company's executives had failed "in the most fundamental responsibility that a public company has toward its shareholders, to show performance. We shall not live with it and we shall do something about it."

With Horsham's shares languishing and Trizec's trading down at C$9 from the C$12.50 they were purchased at, Munk was agitated.

His first moves were to move the Trizec headquarters from Calgary to Toronto and shuffle the Trizec management team, starting at the top. On March 7 he gave his young lieutenant and protégé Greg Wilkins some additional responsibilities on top of being president of Horsham. He would also be president and COO of Trizec. Willard L'Heureux—who had been in that post since 1994, when Munk and his partners had rescued Trizec from the brink—was given new duties.

He would be in charge of Trizec's new international expansion program. That program was already in Munk's plans for implementation in Europe and South America and as a major engine for growth for Trizec. And Brandenburg Park, the first Munk venture in Germany as Horsham Properties GmbH, was gaining momentum.

Peter Munk's main focus for Trizec's international growth was not on the firm's core commercial office buildings but on the potential of its wholly owned retail subsidiary, the Hahn Company. Munk recognized that in the Hahn executive suite he had people with expertise and experience that would be invaluable in realizing his strategic goal of pursuing global real estate opportunities in general, and retail shopping malls in particular. Munk envisioned those opportunities first in Central Europe and then in South America and Southeast Asia.

The result of Munk's strategic planning and thinking was the merger of the Horsham and Trizec corporations, which gave the Trizec operation, among other things, access to the power of Horsham's financial resources, including its cash kitty of over US$500 million.

The proposed merger was announced on September 10, and by the end of September Horsham's offer to acquire the 52 percent of Trizec it didn't already own was approved by the boards of both companies. The stage was set for approval of the merger by the shareholders.

The information circular produced for the special meeting of Trizec shareholders held on October 31, 1996, included this background formal account:

> In the early summer of 1996, Horsham, Argo and Trizec considered various business combinations of Horsham and Trizec that would have required complex reorganizations of Horsham, but these alternatives did not prove practicable. Argo subsequently approached Horsham to reconsider the possibility of a merger of Trizec and Horsham. Argo had become familiar with Horsham's assets, management and corporate strategy as a result of the Trizec Recapitalization and

the subsequent discussions, and had developed an understanding of the potential benefits of a merger transaction....
Extensive negotiations took place between Horsham and Argo during the month of August 1996, culminating in Horsham formally presenting the proposed terms of the Arrangement to Argo in late August. In early September, Argo confirmed its intention to support the Merger on the terms outlined herein. On September 9, 1996, Horsham's proposal was submitted to the board of directors of Trizec and the Special Committee was appointed.

For Horsham, this was the opportunity to realize value by becoming an operating company. On October 31, the Trizec shareholders approved the merger, and Munk's new creation, TrizecHahn Corporation, was born full of cash and real property.

Munk later explained that, "Trizec's fatal flaw was the fact only US$200 million worth of its shares are available publicly. That's too small a float to attract big institutional investors. The merged company will have a float of $1.8 billion."

And what about Munk's essential principle of never relinquishing *control*? The merger into TrizecHahn Corporation produced a total of 129.8 million subordinate voting shares in TrizecHahn and 2.8 million multiple voting shares, each of which carried 50 votes. And Peter Munk owns all of the multiple voting shares, giving him a total of 140 million votes. That, in anybody's language, means control.

There were other players in the development of the merger. In particular, Jeremiah O'Connor's Argo Partnership of New York held a 26 percent interest in Trizec, having partnered with Horsham (48 percent) in the 1994 acquisition of Trizec. Merger talks involving O'Connor had started informally in the summer of 1995, but were unsuccessful. When the merger deal was about to be finalized in October 1996, O'Connor commented that Peter Munk in the early stages was "trying to do some things with his company that didn't pan out. I may have called him the last time, but all credit should go to Mr. Munk."

The newly created TrizecHahn, with Greg Wilkins at the presidential helm, accelerated its pace of activity by picking up three new buildings in the United States by year end for a total price tag of $330 million, and unloading $230 million worth of properties.

Meanwhile, Peter Munk's skiing friend Prince Charles visited the site of Horsham Properties' proposed new outlet mall at Ludwigsfelde on the outskirts of Berlin. The architecturally minded Charles lauded the retail development plan that had been prepared by British town planner John Thompson, under the direction of Philip Jones, another Briton who was running the activities of Horsham Properties in Germany, Hungary and elsewhere in central Europe.

The Ludwigsfelde project would be the first to directly combine the skills of TrizecHahn's U.S. retail development experts and those of Horsham Properties with local real estate and political expertise, but it would not be the first introduction of the Hahn Company expertise into a European project. Munk had already involved Hahn in Budapest.

Earlier in the year, Munk had accepted a proposal to cooperate with Hungarian national television, which wanted to do a one-hour Munk biography. He travelled to Budapest, where, in the presence of the TV cameras, he and his half-brother, Dr. Paul Munk, visited his father, Louis, and grandfather Gabriel's old residence, from which the family had departed in the evening of June 29, 1944, and which Paul, born in Switzerland, had never seen. It was a time for meeting people he had not seen since those days; for nostalgia and for reminiscing. It was also a time for Peter Munk to discuss on camera the range of his life, his failures, his internationally acclaimed successes and his plans for real estate in Budapest.

Munk had decided to invest personally in a joint venture with Polus Investments (or Granit Polus Rt) of Budapest, a company controlled by his friend Sandor Demjan, one of Hungary's most successful businessmen. As part of his arrangements with Demjan, the Hahn Company arm of Trizec was retained as a consultant to Polus in the development of Polus Center, on the outskirts of Budapest at a site that had formerly been a Soviet military base. It was to be Budapest's first major modern shopping mall.

The development was completed in November 1996. Peter Munk was front and centre at the grand opening, cutting the ribbon on behalf of Andy Sarlos, who could not be there because of a heart condition.

In late 1997, TrizecHahn made a joint-venture agreement with Sandor Demjan and his Granit Polus Rt to build two more shopping malls in Budapest, five more in large Hungarian towns, and seventeen in Poland, Romania, Slovakia and the western part of the Ukraine. All would be within a seven-hundred-kilometre radius of Budapest, where the development headquarters would be set up.

Had Munk's focused efforts increased the value of the shares of Horsham, now TrizecHahn, as he had pledged to his Horsham shareholders in May? In a few short months, the stock had moved from C$18 to more than C$29. The pace of activity at TrizecHahn, as dictated by its chairman and controlling shareholder, Peter Munk, has not been a brisk walk but a full-speed, all-out sprint, a dash for a world record. From merger day to December 31, 1996, TrizecHahn had acquired at least US$330 million in commercial real estate in the U.S.

In November and December, $250 million was laid out for the Allen Center in Houston, one of the largest office complexes in the Southwest. This period also brought the US$80-million acquisition of two office properties (Atlanta and Columbia, South Carolina), the sale of three office buildings (Los Angeles and Montreal) and five shopping centres (Modesto and Santa Barbara, California; Billings, Montana; Holland, Michigan; and Kingsport, Tennessee) and the refinancing of Bankers' Hall in Calgary (C$130 million). And in the negotiating works was a US$210-million purchase of a 50-percent interest in a 2.7-million-square-foot portfolio of properties located in mid-town New York between Times Square and Grand Central

Station, including the landmark Grace building on 42nd Street. That deal was a purchase from the Weiler-Arnow Investment Company of New York, with the Swig family of San Francisco retaining their 50-percent stake. The TrizecHahn purchase closed in late February 1997.

In March, TrizecHahn was selected by the Los Angeles Community Redevelopment Board to negotiate exclusively to redevelop a 4.4-acre site, including a venerable Hollywood landmark, Mann's Chinese Theatre and the Walk of Fame. Negotiations were expected to be concluded in six months for construction of a 425,000-square-foot, four-level complex of retail, entertainment and food outlets, to begin in 1998.

From New York to Hollywood to Budapest to Germany—with Peter Munk's flying entrepreneurship there seemed to be no limit to where he and his TrizecHahn team would touch down to do a profitable deal. And Munk's deals were not of the "flip" type, aiming only for a short-term profit. For the benefit of his shareholders he was interested in long-term developments and investments. And he was now prepared to enter into partnership arrangements with other carefully selected players, but on one basic condition. He would never give up *control* to anyone.

Peter Munk is as knowledgeable as anyone about the enormous fundamental differences between Europe and North America in the matters of business, politics, culture and the massive grab-bag called *society*. As a Canadian citizen of European origin, he found it entirely natural to turn his personal attention to the opportunities that he could so clearly see emerging on the European continent—especially as his personal real property focus and TrizecHahn involvement escalated.

He was comfortable in leaving all the major day-to-day decisions for North America in the hands of his most able young president, Greg Wilkins. Crossing the Atlantic, however, into quite another set of business and cultural environments was a different matter—it might be asking or expecting too much of Wilkins. Even so, Peter

Munk placed Wilkins in charge of all of TrizecHahn's operations, in Europe, North America, Asia or wherever. And he was proving to be skilful at handling the myriad details of the rapidly expanding international net that Munk was throwing across the world.

Nevertheless, as his direct involvement in European investments grew, Munk began to focus on the obvious need to have Europeans involved as equal members of his hard-driving, ever-enlarging team. He has said, "You can't have a global presence unless you have global partners—people who eat, breathe and sleep in the country they operate in." In keeping with that rationale Peter Munk moved to expand TrizecHahn in Europe and simultaneously to acquire not only new real estate assets but also the services of the strong, stellar German entrepreneur who would bring a range of new assets into TrizecHahn with him: Dieter Bock, a fifty-eight-year-old lawyer and financier with a proven track record. Bock had made a name for himself in England in the mid-1990s when he pulled off a major corporate coup in the executive offices of Lonrho PLC.

In 1974, ten years after graduating from law school in Munich, Bock made his first significant investment foray into real estate in that city. By the end of the 1980s he was making property investments in the United States and South America, eventually gathering his holdings into a company named Advanta Management AG. In 1992–93 Bock's Advanta bought an 18-percent interest in the British conglomerate Lonrho, at the behest and with the encouragement of its then chairman, the colourful Roland (Tiny) Rowland, a huge man who was appropriately nicknamed. Bock immediately joined the board of Lonrho.

Lonrho had interests in gold, oil and gas, and hotels, mirroring the interests of Peter Munk; the conglomerate also had involvements in platinum, agriculture and industrial equipment.

In 1995 Dieter Bock and Tiny Rowland locked horns in a widely publicized boardroom battle for control, which Bock won decisively. Rowland was out, and the German entrepreneur was elected chairman and CEO of Lonrho. Throughout these events Peter Munk was an uninvolved but admiring and respectful onlooker. He and Dieter Bock had met socially many times over the years but had never done any business together.

Then, in 1996, Munk learned that Bock had decided to get out of Lonrho. Like Munk, he wanted to be his own man, and he felt that the Lonrho responsibilities did not allow him enough freedom to manoeuvre. Bock sold his Lonrho holdings to Anglo American Corporation of South Africa for the satisfying sum of US$424 million, and resigned as CEO, retaining the nominal post of non-executive deputy chairman.

His relatively brief association with Lonrho had not stood in the way of significant realty activities by Bock's Advanta Management AG in the development of commercial sites—notably, the rebuilding of the Adlon Hotel in Berlin and the historic Taschenbergpalais in Dresden. Of particular interest to Peter Munk was the fact that Bock had developed the Kempinski Hotel in Budapest.

At the time of his departure from the Lonrho executive suite Bock had several real estate developments under way, all of which Munk saw as fitting neatly into TrizecHahn's European objectives. As would Dieter Bock himself, if only Munk could persuade his younger German friend to both sell and participate. Convincing the independence-minded Bock was no easy task, but eventually the focused and highly persuasive Munk prevailed.

TrizecHahn announced on March 5, 1997, that Dieter Bock had agreed to sell a large portion of his real property interests in the U.K. and Germany to the Canadian company. There were several ingredients to the deal, the most important to Peter Munk being the infusion of Bock's considerable talents at the top level of TrizecHahn's executive and at its boardroom table.

TrizecHahn acquired from Bock's Advanta its showcase 13,000-square-metre office-retail development at 1 Poultry in central London, three mixed-use retail and office projects (two of them in Berlin) and a planned Baltic Sea tourist resort. The consideration for this deal was about US$147 million for Advanta's development projects—approximately 5.5 million shares of TrizecHahn valued at US$20.75 each or $115 million (a stake of about 4 percent of TrizecHahn) and an assumption of $32 million in construction financing.

But there was more than a 4-percent interest in TrizecHahn inside the consideration package that Munk offered to his friend. Munk also named Dieter Bock president and chief European executive of the Berlin-based TrizecHahn Europe, and a director and vice-chairman of the parent TrizecHahn Corporation.

The talented German entrepreneur accepted, and the deal was a *fait accompli*. In one deft move Munk had parachuted into TrizecHahn Europe a like-minded, highly successful, battle-hardened, independent thinker who could carry out Munk's strategy for the growth and development of TrizecHahn Europe. And Bock brought eighteen experienced Advanta employees into TrizecHahn Europe with him.

Meanwhile, there was a frenzy of activity in North America, so much so that one newspaper blared "Cash-rich TrizecHahn on a roll."

First, there was the late-March announcement that Munk's corporation had gone Las Vegas, entering into an agreement with Aladdin Holdings LLC to develop a 450,000-square-foot retail and entertainment complex that would be part of the redevelopment of the Aladdin Hotel and Casino. TrizecHahn had another project on in Nevada. It was developing the 400,000-square-foot Fashion Outlet, with its 1920s Times Square theme.

That was followed by an announcement that TrizecHahn was adding US$173 million to its war chest of $1.3 billion as it accelerated the pace of its acquisitions and property developments. To raise the funds, Munk opted for equity rather than debt, with a new issue of 8.6-million subordinate common shares. At the same time TrizecHahn had agreed to acquire a 25-percent interest in a new group buying the Citicorp Center and Seventh Market Place in Los Angeles for US$125 million. The prospectus for the share issue disclosed that in 1997, in addition to the two Las Vegas projects, TrizecHahn was to begin construction on a shopping centre in Denver and a major reconfiguration of Prestonwood Town Center in Dallas. The total price for all four would be in the $550-million range. In addition to building, Peter Munk was capitalizing on a need and decision by U.S. insurance companies and foreign investors to reduce their real estate holdings in the United States by some $15 to 20 billion in 1997. It was a buyer's market that Munk couldn't resist.

Also in March, TrizecHahn was finalizing a US$200-million credit facility, using its unencumbered Barrick shares as collateral. At the end of 1996 TrizecHahn owned 58.5 million shares of Barrick, of which 28.2 million were unencumbered. The value of those shares at that time was in excess of $800 million.

Then came the CN Tower project announcement. TrizecHahn signed a letter of intent with the Crown corporation Canada Lands Company to lease, develop and operate the CN Tower and the adjoining lands for entertainment-related activities. The transaction was valued at more than C$100 million.

That was Munk's North American TrizecHahn news. Elsewhere on the planet he had his corporation working with a consortium of Asian developers and investors called Fort Bonif001o Development Corporation, and he had entered into a consulting agreement for the creation of a "city within a city" shopping centre in Manila. In Taiwan there was yet another joint venture. This was with Breeze Development Co. Ltd., a local firm, to develop a North American–style retail and entertainment centre in Taipei's shopping district. And in Budapest, TrizecHahn (now under Bock's eye), through its interest in Tri Granit Development with Sandor Demjan, had obtained the right to redevelop, adjacent to the city centre, the landmark West End Railway Station, built by Eiffel in the 1880s, into a major mixed-use office/retail/residential project.

Peter Munk and his cash-rich TrizecHahn were indeed on a roll, across three continents and with deals in the works wherever Munk's young corporate creation could do profitable business. Was Munk's ambition outstripping his ability? Would he, Birchall, Wilkins, Bock and their teams be able to exercise effective development, financial and management control over a flurry of projects taking shape all over the map? Would they be able to deal with all the different currencies, environments, societies, cultures and time zones?

Peter Munk, the architect and chief executive officer of TrizecHahn, has total confidence in the abilities of his people and the success of his projects. As Greg Wilkins said in early April 1997:

> This flurry may sound haphazard, but we've been cultivating these opportunities for some time, and the decisions to go forward happened to come together at the same time.

One thing that did not come together was Barrick's search for a home run. Munk was preoccupied throughout this period by a small Canadian exploration company named Bre-X, which claimed to have discovered the world's largest gold deposit.

CHAPTER FORTY

THE BRE-X SAGA

Peter Munk's involvement with Bre-X Minerals Ltd. began with a few hesitant steps back in early 1993. At that time he had decided that a prudent way to hook into the gold exploration that was gathering momentum in the most promising sectors of the globe was to buy into small companies that were out there on the ground prospecting and getting results.

The first company pursued by Barrick in Indonesia was Bre-X. Two Barrick geologists, Larry Kornze and Paul Kavanagh (who later joined Bre-X as a director for his geological expertise), visited the Busang site in October 1993. Drilling had begun just days earlier. Kornze and Kavanagh recommended that Barrick begin discussions with Bre-X, and their company did so.

In November 1993, Bre-X chief David Walsh proposed a deal to Barrick, involving money to finance exploration by Bre-X, whose shares were selling for pennies. But the proposal didn't fly. Bre-X really didn't want to dance with Barrick, at least not on Barrick's terms, which included Munk's unalterable principle that down the line he had the right to assume control of Busang.

Barrick instead began to increase its interests and involvement in Indonesia through Yamana Resources Inc. and other participation vehicles. Yamana had secured exploration rights on 2.7 million hectares of property in Kalimantan on the Island of Borneo, on the same land mass as the Busang discoveries. Barrick's deal was a loan to Yamana of US$14,666,000 which was convertible in whole or in part into shares. On January 15, 1996, Barrick converted $7,166,000 of its loan into 3,005,310 units of Yamana, representing 14.65 percent of that company's issued and outstanding shares.

Because of a local custom that foreign firms have Indonesian partners, Barrick, having examined a number of alternatives, decided to form a business association with Citra Lamtoro Gund Group, an engineering and construction firm controlled by President Suharto's eldest daughter, Siti Hardijanti Rukmana, but known as Tutut, the most powerful and influential of Suharto's children.

By the end of 1996, through deals such as Yamana and International Pursuit Corporation (headed by Stephen Dattels, who had become a Munk millionaire, then left Barrick to do his own thing), Barrick had direct or indirect land positions on some 22 million acres for exploration in Indonesia. Its holdings were mainly in the provinces of Kalimantan and Irian Jaya. COWs (Contracts of Work) were eventually granted to Barrick by the government for drilling on some five of these exploration sites in the spring of 1997.

Through the first half of 1996, Barrick's team continued to monitor and keep a watchful eye on Bre-X's reports as the company began to publicize its finds and the market price for its shares started up the steep price path, pushed further with each new announcement.

According to Bre-X its drilling program began to produce results that indicated resources of 30 million ounces, then 47, 57 and possibly 100 million ounces of gold. Bre-X shares worth 53 cents in 1993 went to more than $280 and, following a 10-to-1 split, enjoyed a 52-week high of $28.65 in 1996. Barrick, or any other major player, would have to have been interested in a stake in Bre-X. For its part, Bre-X said it was prepared to sell to a mining company with the operating experience necessary to build a mine. The price would be in the billions.

Peter Munk explains the Barrick position as the Bre-X reported resources began their climb in early 1996:

Barrick is the premier gold company, and certainly has been for the past three years, by any criterion. And when you are number one in the capital markets you've got to make sure you remain number one. That imposes a requirement on being there when major resources are found, particularly when major resources are found by companies who don't have the wherewithal or interest to develop it themselves. More often than not, of course, you only find out about these resources when a company like Freeport McMoRan or RTZ or Newmont announces it. Based on Bre-X's public statements we thought Busang was an excellent resource, and we were interested in acquiring Bre-X. We relied on public information and we were going to make an offer for Bre-X or, if that offer was not going to be accepted, then make a bid. We believed that a large number of their shareholders felt that they'd gone as far as they wanted in Bre-X's specula- tive value increase. They were a bit uncomfortable and might be very happy to take in exchange a stock of a major company, which had more liquidity, more stability and lots of money to develop the site. So we were assured by our investment banking advisers that if we couldn't make a friendly deal, then a bid would succeed.

But the Bre-X people wouldn't talk to us. All the stuff we read in the paper back then that Bre-X doesn't like us didn't make sense. When it comes to that kind of money, personali- ties shouldn't come into it. They were the stock market dar- lings. I decided then that we'll just have to pursue a bid. We started our due diligence, but, of course, access to information can be restricted. As far as the resources were concerned we got all the published geologists' reports. There was no financial position to do due diligence on because they were an exploration company, a penny stock. They had no balance sheet, and essentially only the one asset, the Busang gold deposit. And the asset turned out to be huge in contrast to anything we had ever looked at.

It turned out that they did not own title to their only asset. The market thought that they owned the Busang deposit, we thought they owned it, but in the main zone, they did not even have a COW, they only had an application for one. The markets promoting their shares appeared to be operating on the basis that Bre-X owned the deposit, but they had only an application and the application was affected by many other apparently serious problems that were not generally known in the market.

Indeed, Munk's lawyers had discovered a motherlode of problems when they tried to confirm Bre-X's title to its only assets. It quickly became apparent that the Indonesian government had never approved the transfer of the original Busang COW to Bre-X. That COW also appeared to have expired (although it was later renewed). The Australian and British parties that had sold the Busang concession originally to Bre-X were questioning the sale. Bre-X's Indonesian partners in the original Busang discovery were claiming that Bre-X had illegally cut them out of the rich new Southeast Zone, and were now asserting a 40-percent interest. And, ominously, the title documents filed by Bre-X with the U.S. Securities and Exchange Commission, when examined by Barrick's lawyers, did not appear to be genuine. Barrick had carefully done its diligence on all its prior deals, including Lac and Arequipa, but it had never encountered anything like this.

In light of all this, and the signals it sent out, we came to the conclusion that we could not even contemplate making a bid. I then stepped back and said if Bre-X is not the owner and we can't buy Bre-X, we'd better promote ourselves to the real owner, i.e., to Indonesia, since the gold belongs to the government of Indonesia. What else could you do?

My personal presentation to the government was that you, the government, as owners, have a responsibility to decide who is going to do the best job for your country. My pitch was always the same. Of all the gold mining companies in the world, we are the most qualified. We pointed out that this Busang development was going to produce at least 2 million ounces of gold a year, and no single gold mining company, apart from Barrick, actually had the experience of putting a 2-million-ounce producer onstream with the latest technology. We'd done it on budget, on time, and with a number of environmental awards in the process at Goldstrike in Nevada, the toughest regulatory environment in the world. We also highlighted what we had done to help build a community, Elko, which has been selected as "the best small town in America," with schools and hospitals and a host of other facilities.

One of Munk's really big guns weighed in in support of Barrick's achievements. George Bush wrote a letter to President Suharto dated September 20, 1996.

At the Barrick International Advisory Board meeting in Elko, President Bush spent the day looking at Goldstrike, visiting the schools, and talking to the mayor and the miners. In the evening he spoke at a reception and said that he had never seen a greater achievement by a corporation in a shorter period of time.

At the advisory board meeting, one of the projects talked about was Barrick's involvement in Indonesia.

George Bush said to me, "Peter, you have done such an outstanding job helping to build this whole community—do you think it would be helpful to you if I were to drop a note to President Suharto about it?" I said, "Sir, that's up to you. It can only be of help to us." He wrote to Suharto and sent me a copy of the letter. He had seen first-hand what Barrick had accomplished in Nevada and that added a great amount of credibility to my pitch. And while my pitch is good because it's based on fact, every company has a good pitch, and we could use all the extra credibility we could get.

The Republic of Indonesia realized, as did Bre-X, that Bre-X needed a senior partner, and they made statements to the international press saying that no COW would be issued until Bre-X brought in a major mining company and sorted out its ownership disputes. Walsh wanted to let Bre-X go to an auction, but not until he could present the full facts about the extent of the Busang resources. That way they could postpone the "evil day" of a major company's involvement and the consequent on-site due diligence practically as long as they liked. As long as John Felderhof held out the hope of more and more reserves, it might have been another year or two. Walsh wanted to delay, and Felderhof and the rest of his team kept on giving him the ammunition—"Bre-X has only 40 million ounces, but it may have 100 million, so how can we go to auction *now*?"

The government position was that "an auction may be good for you people, because you want to get the maximum price for the shares, but what we want is the best solution for Indonesia. We want some benefits for the people of Indonesia now: jobs, taxation, foreign exchange. We want the investment of $1.5 billion—sooner rather than later." The government wanted to be sure that they were dealing with a mining company that had its finances in place, a company that had an impeccable environmental record and that was keen and able to move immediately. Munk was keen to make contact with Walsh.

We got a phone call from Mr. Walsh's people in Toronto. We met with them in July and from then on we tried to make a deal. David Walsh eventually hired J.P. Morgan as his adviser and we hired RBC Dominion Securities and Goldman Sachs.

When I first met David, I apologized for what he had perceived as an insult, but which in fact was not an insult, back in '93 when Barrick and Bre-X were negotiating. I said, "Listen, I knew nothing about it. I never came across the word 'Bre-X' until much later. I'm not in the business of following juniors. There are nine thousand juniors. Whether we offered an exploration deal to a small company called Bre-X in '93 or not—and on what terms—believe me, my people didn't have to check with me." He and I got along quite well. But Bre-X kept on giving reasons why this was a major find and growing enormously and it was too early to do a deal. We couldn't understand why Bre-X would not do what the government clearly wanted them to do, and what would have been so beneficial to their shareholders, by eliminating all that uncertainty about getting their title—their COW. Our deal was structured so that their shareholders would have directly benefited from increasing reserves and production. The auction they wanted could not realistically take place because the ultimate determination of who should bring this auction had to be made by the government, who owned the resource.

And this dance went on and the government got more and more frustrated because they wanted the mining and job creation and investment to start. But all they saw was the continued increase in Bre-X share price which offered no benefits whatsoever to Indonesia or to its people.

On October 28, 1996, in a belated move intended to tie down a clear path through the Indonesian bureaucracy, Bre-X hired Suharto's eldest son, Sigit, as a consultant. The fee to his company, Panutan, was estimated by some to be as much as $1 billion, which included lucrative supply contracts as well as a 10-percent interest in the Busang mine and a monthly retainer of $1 million for 40 months, all of which was subject to Bre-X getting the required approvals. It looked as though Bre-X had the Indonesian situation locked up.

They signed up with Panutan, against my advice; I begged them not to. But they signed up and from that day on the thing was totally off the rails, because the newspapers began characterizing the issue as a battle between the President's children. There is an enormous amount of self-imposed discipline amongst the papers there. They generally do not attack the Suharto family politically. But when it comes to commercial issues there are no holds barred. And suddenly a major dispute had surfaced.

We were prepared to put a billion and a half dollars into the project and then share the profits with Bre-X, but of course we needed control. We're not going to put up that kind of money unless we control our destiny. We had been negotiating here in Canada hundreds of hours on how to allocate the proper financial benefits between the Bre-X shareholders and Barrick and so on. But once they signed up with Panutan the negotiations stalled.

The Indonesian ministry was above reproach and they said we've been to Canada, we're satisfied, in nickel we have Inco; in gold for this deposit, which is of national significance, we must have the best, which is Barrick, as Bre-X and its financial advisers had previously acknowledged.

In the meantime Felderhof was adding fuel to the fire by holding out the sugared carrot of enormous further resources. The brokers were so deep in that they believed in it. Barrick was widely perceived to be the bad guy as the story took on classic David-and-Goliath proportions, with the stand-off between a big major and a small minor.

As a direct result of the enormous local publicity, the issue of gold began to arouse Indonesian nationalistic instincts and became perfect fodder for those wishing to attack Suharto and his regime. It was a give-away by the government to foreigners. Finally, the ministry decided to bring the matter to a head and summoned both Munk and Walsh to Jakarta.

When word arrived from Jakarta that the meetings had been arranged for November 14, Peter Munk was in Budapest opening the largest shopping mall in Central Europe. He was scheduled to be back in Toronto for a black-tie roast for his friend and Barrick president, Bob Smith. He changed his plans immediately. He would go to Jakarta. Smith would have his roast without Munk.

Munk, speaking for Barrick, made his presentation to Mines Minister Sudjana, setting out his company's established track record in developing gold mines, along with its environmental and social policies. David Walsh explained Bre-X's position as the finder of the enormous Busang deposits and its recognition of the need to find a partner with expertise to build and operate the mine and its plant.

Sudjana heard both sides, then gave the government's judgement on the matter, reading from a document, which had obviously been prepared in advance, decreeing that Barrick would get 75 percent of Busang, and Bre-X 25. Walsh was devastated. The minister also asked the Canadians if they would consider setting aside a further 10 percent for the government. The parties had until November 20 to work out a development agreement. Munk comments that

> it appeared that the government took the position that after months of trying, they couldn't deal with Bre-X and didn't want them to have any say in the future development of the mine at Busang. So Bre-X got reduced to 25 percent. We hadn't asked for 75 percent, we just wanted control. But that's

what the government decreed. So we had to revise the terms
we previously discussed with Bre-X to give them full compensation in the form of an extra billion and a half dollars in royalty rights. This was done through detailed negotiations with
J.P. Morgan, so the economic benefits of Bre-X shareholders
would be maintained despite the changed percentages.

On Wednesday, November 15, the Barrick team (minus Munk)
reopened face-to-face negotiations with Bre-X. The negotiations were
tough. The Bre-X side was bitter, feeling shafted. Walsh had expected, after giving away a lucrative deal to Sigit, to take his monster
gold mine to auction among the world's biggest producers, and to
do it when *he* chose to and not sooner. Instead the government
made it clear that Indonesia—not Bre-X—would finally determine
which company was most qualified to develop this national treasure. The unhappy negotiations snailed on, patience thin and often
broken on both sides. But they couldn't leave the game. The stakes
were astronomical. Or so some at the table believed.

The deadline of November 20 ground by with no deal. Sudjana's
second-in-command, Umar Said, granted a new deadline of December
4, saying to the participants in no uncertain terms "I expect to hear
only one word from you. Agreement!"

But when we were about ready to sign, Walsh once again
became convinced that this was not the right thing to do
because the deposit was still growing—Felderhof would be
able to show them untold ounces. And if they got a billion
now they could get two billion a year from then. I think
Walsh was acting on the belief that he was protecting the
shareholders' interests. I imagine Felderhof said to Walsh,
"Why give it away?" So Walsh yielded to him and didn't sign.
And that's when the headlines said "Indonesian deadlines are
spurned by both parties."

In Toronto, Munk was in constant contact with Barrick's team in Jakarta. There was still no public confirmation by Sudjana of his astonishing decree of November 14 in Barrick's favour. It finally became public on November 26 in the form of a letter from the Government of Indonesia to Barrick and to Bre-X. Walsh put out a press release announcing the government's directive.

Observers were stunned by Barrick's Bre-X achievement, which the *Globe and Mail* called "masterful" and "a triumph of international intrigue." Newspaper headlines spoke of "Munk's Indonesian coup"; "Munk nears top of gold heap"; and "Mystery surrounds Bre-X/Barrick story."

Seventy-five percent to Barrick? Why? the press and public asked. Especially the Bre-X shareholders.

In person and by conference call, Munk convened his Barrick board of directors the next day, November 27, for a full briefing on a deal that would make the company what Peter Munk had dreamed it should be from the time of its minuscule beginnings in 1983: the world's largest and most profitable producer of gold.

Munk, talking in his lucid, staccato tones, gave a snapshot history of Barrick in Indonesia and of the intense meetings in Jakarta from November 13 to 16.

Doubts and warning signs were emerging, however, from any number of sources. In Toronto, Jean Anes, vice-consul for investments with the consulate of Indonesia, said that Barrick did not have a complete lock on the Bre-X gold find, but was the preferred investor. The government was only "making a recommendation" and Bre-X could find another partner. And an Indonesian businessman, Jusuf Merukh, was claiming 40 percent of the Busang gold find and threatening litigation.

The media and others were distracted and were in an uproar about whether and how George Bush and Brian Mulroney, of Barrick's International Advisory Board, had influenced the Indonesians.

The Bre-X imbroglio kept growing. Bre-X shareholders were furious when they thought Barrick had cut into their treasure trove. As one financial-house analyst said, "It's got to be a fair deal. Barrick can't screw Bre-X shareholders or there will be hell to pay." Another commented, "Everybody can sort of hold their nose and say 'This thing smells, but it doesn't smell too badly.' But if Barrick takes advantage of its favourable position and doesn't treat Bre-X fairly 'then it smells very, very bad.'" But, as November 1996 ended, no one, least of all Peter Munk, had any idea how badly Bre-X would smell by the time the next April Fool's Day arrived.

However, on November 30, in the early days of the Bre-X saga, the *Globe and Mail* was so impressed by Munk's Indonesian coup (as the front-page headline read) that the authors were able to claim that

> nothing matches his latest exploit in Indonesia ... If he gathers up the loose ends in the next four days, his Toronto based company, Barrick Gold Corp., is a cinch to become the leading gold producer on the planet.

To be the leading gold producer in the world would have been a coup indeed: 1995's gold output had South Africa's Anglo American at 235 tonnes and Gold Fields of South Africa (GFSA) at 105 tonnes, with Barrick snapping at GFSA's heels with 98.

The *Globe* writers of November 30, impressed though they were, wondered whether it was Bre-X's alliance with Suharto's son, Sigit, that had sunk them in the end. Barrick's association with Tutut, Sigit's big sister, cast the whole conflict in terms of a rivalry between the President's children. The *Globe* quoted Amitav Acharya, a specialist in Southeast Asian politics, who called Tutut "the most prominent and the most influential, both in business and politics, of Suharto's children."

Two questions to be answered at that moment were: Could Barrick and Bre-X work out an arrangement? And would Tutut's father put the seal of final approval on it?

The admonition of Umar Said, that an agreement had to be

reached by December 4, wasn't enough to force the parties to an accord by that time, despite his ominous caution that, "if the negotiations are not concluded by that date, the Indonesian government will take the necessary steps to prevent a delay in the development of the Busang gold deposit."

At this point the executive team of Placer Dome Inc. went public with the information that they had been in negotiations with Bre-X for two months. John Willson, president and CEO of the Vancouver-based company, was doing his best to break up the "sweetheart" deal of Barrick Gold and the Indonesian government. In an interview on December 2, Willson said:

> We were very disappointed to see the auction process pre-empted. We regret that the opportunity for Bre-X shareholders to determine the value of their holdings, and to exercise their natural right to determine their partner, was taken away.

For Peter Munk there was good reason to take Willson's position seriously and move with whatever steps were necessary to fend off his efforts to break up the Bre-X deal that was slowly coming together. After all, Placer Dome was a major player. It had eight thousand employees and was operating sixteen mining sites around the world, and all but 11 percent of its gross revenue flowed from gold. To add to Munk's problems, Placer Dome's intervention was soon followed by similar statements from Teck Corporation of Vancouver and Newmont Mining of Denver.

However, Munk was still confident that Barrick's position with the Indonesian government was secure, even though his experience with the governments of Nova Scotia and Egypt had taught him some harsh lessons that might have made him suspicious.

On December 3 Bre-X stirred the negotiation pot a little more by releasing a statement that said drilling had increased estimates of potential resources at Busang by another 10 million ounces, to 57 million.

But the hard-nosed negotiations in Jakarta were beginning to show some results. The basics of a deal had been hammered out by December 4. David Walsh told reporters that day that Barrick and Bre-X had the outline of a 75/25 joint-venture deal. At the same time, a Bre-X press release from Jakarta stated that although an agreement had been reached on matters raised by the Indonesian Ministry of Mines and Energy, "several points remain outstanding," and that Bre-X expected to receive "clarification" from the Ministry "in due course."

Peter Munk was disturbed by a press interview with Umar Said that same day to the effect that Bre-X's rights to or claim to ownership of Busang II and III were in serious question. Said harshly criticized Bre-X's dealings in its property and its failure to meet Indonesia's disclosure requirements, and said that Bre-X did not have a contract of work (COW) for the richest parts of Busang and had not informed the government of its discovery. He also indicated that COWs by Bre-X were not among those awaiting final approval by Suharto, and that Bre-X had not made proper disclosures when it first became involved in the Busang deposit.

Then, on Friday, December 6, Said confirmed that Barrick and Bre-X had met the Indonesian government's terms and conditions and had met the December 4 deadline, even though nothing had been signed. Said also stated: "The deal is very positive and the next step will be for them to make an agreement with us and set up a joint-venture company."

In Jakarta, the Barrick team had gone as far as they could with the dragging discussions. Munk told them they had done a great job for Barrick but enough was enough. It was time to send in a fresh team from Barrick's deep young bench. His new emissaries included his top financial man, Randall Oliphant, who arrived in Jakarta for the next round with Bre-X that began on Monday, December 9. As usual, all of the Barrick strategy and tactics were hands-on—conducted and run by Peter Munk out of his Barrick Toronto office. He was on the telephone day and night. Faxes flew to and from Indonesia. This appeared to be the most golden opportunity of Peter Munk's life, and he could not pass any part of the responsibility for its success or failure to anyone else.

On Thursday, December 12, the Indonesian government unexpectedly announced that it was cancelling parliamentary approval for Bre-X's application for contracts of work (COWs) on Busang. The mines and energy minister, Sudjana, stated that "the Bre-X contract of work will be processed from the beginning." Umar Said explained:

> We have obtained a series of documents through our lawyers that show that Bre-X said it owned Busang II and III. Maybe that was meant to push up the price of its shares. We are checking with Bapepam [an agency of government] to see if this is criminal.

The Indonesian ministry's position was that, first, Bre-X had never obtained government approval for its acquisition of the original Busang COW, and second, it would be inappropriate for Bre-X to say it "owned" the gold deposits, because under Indonesian law ownership rights belong to the nation, and foreign companies are restricted to mining under licence, for limited periods and with restrictions on operations. Furthermore, Bre-X did not even have a contract for Busang II.

There was chaos on the TSE. Bre-X investors bailed out in droves. Trading was halted for Thursday, the 12th. When it traded again the next day, about 8.6 million shares were exchanged in Toronto, more than four times as much as the next most active stock.

An article in the *Far Eastern Economic Review* had revealed that

> Suharto has met with two unnamed, prominent businessmen, one from the United States and the other from Indonesia, who asked him to review the government order that forced

the Barrick negotiations ... the two men expressed concerns over the impact on foreign investment if an unfavourable deal is forced on Bre-X.

Was this report true? And, if so, who were the two men involved? It seemed that anyone with direct access to Suharto could foul up any deal that Barrick and Bre-X might make. Preliminary answers to these questions were delivered the next day in the *Globe and Mail*, which reported that the two men were Mohammad Hasan, "a businessman with publishing interests and a close friend of Suharto," and James Robert (Jim Bob) Moffett, chairman of Freeport-McMoRan Copper & Gold Inc. of New Orleans."

Munk was now getting reports from his people in Jakarta and reading with concerned amusement about the latest flip of position by Sudjana. Now Sudjana said Bre-X's "cancelled" COW applications were still valid, but would be automatically cancelled when Bre-X and Barrick formed a joint venture and made a new COW application.

Sudjana also informed the world that a tentative agreement between the parties had come unglued. After a meeting with Suharto he told reporters:

Until Dec. 12 afternoon, they had said they had agreed. But last night there was a 180-degree change. I don't know the situation. Who influenced whom we don't know. They don't agree with what has been agreed to with the government. I will wait for them. This is also the advice of the President ... give them a chance until the end of December. I forget the date, but there is a limit.

The parties would not need until the end of December to agree. On December 16, Barrick put out the following terse press release:

Toronto, December 16, 1996 ... Barrick Gold Corporation

announced today that Barrick and Bre-X Minerals Ltd. have jointly submitted a proposal to the Government of Indonesia for the development of the Busang Project.

The Government of Indonesia is expected to advise Barrick and Bre-X of its response in due course.

In Jakarta, Umar Said stated: "The government takes 10 percent. Bre-X will have 22.5 percent and Barrick 67.5 percent."

Also in Jakarta a source close to the negotiations said that Bre-X wanted to clarify the status of its local partner PT Askatindo Karya Mineral, which had a 10-percent interest in the Busang discovery. The reason for the request for clarification was that the partner, PT Askatindo, apparently had its signature on the contract of work application for Busang II and III which had been initialled and agreed to in principle by the government.

Details of the agreement with Bre-X that had been submitted to the Indonesian government were not made public, and in Jakarta, on December 23, Sudjana claimed that he was in the dark about the deal between Barrick and Bre-X. "They haven't reported to me yet. If they do, I will ask them to make an announcement." In fact, the joint submission had been delivered on December 16 to Umar Said.

Meanwhile Barrick was into its due diligence, which had commenced in late November after the confidentiality agreement had been signed with Bre-X. However, Barrick had not had access to the property for drilling.

In mid-December Peter and Melanie Munk departed for their customary winter sojourn at Klosters. On New Year's day 1997, Peter Munk was still waiting for word from Jakarta, but after a "nothing" position statement by Sudjana to press people at a ministry New Year's celebration, a protracted period of silence ensued. The minister said he was waiting for the parties to officially announce their ownership proposals to company shareholders before he could respond.

Questioned about the government's actions, Sudjana responded vaguely that if the government played too overt a role in the negotiations the parties "may say we compelled them. So we must be careful." With regard to a deadline for a final deal there was none, only "as soon as possible." Those gobbledegook Sudjana statements made it obvious that something was amiss. Was there unseen sand in the governmental Bre-X–Barrick gears in Jakarta? or was it that there was an as-yet-unseen cat among the Busang pigeons?

There was a ton of sand, and the biggest cat in Indonesia: none other than Suharto's golfing buddy Mohammad (Bob) Hasan, a forestry magnate and confidant of the president, the same Hasan who, with Jim Bob Moffett of Freeport-McMoRan Copper & Gold, had personally lobbied Suharto to open up the bidding.

On January 11, it was reported that the ultra-wealthy Hasan had a direct interest in the Busang scenario because he had recently acquired a 50-percent interest in that pivotal Indonesian firm PT Askatindo Karya Mineral, the signatory applicant on the forms for the Busang COW. Under Indonesian law, Askatindo (read now: Hasan) would participate in any proposal to explore and develop Busang.

The report also stated that Bre-X had achieved its 90-percent interest in the so-called motherlode, Busang II and III, through a pre-Hasan partnership deal with Askatindo.

Other sources said that Hasan had also obtained a 50-percent piece of PT Amsya Lyna, which held the mining licence for the Busang Northwest property, close to the motherlode. Hasan conveniently acquired the Askatindo and Amsya interests from the Syakerani family. The acquisitions were not by Hasan directly but by the Nusamba Group, which he heads. Of interest is that three foundations headed by Suharto own 80 percent of Nusamba, 10 percent by Hasan and 10 percent by Sigit Harjajudanto, Suharto's eldest son.

With these reports in hand, it was not difficult for Peter Munk to figure out—instantly—that the caller of the Busang shots was not any of the previous players, not Said or Sudjana, but Mohammed Hasan, and that Suharto would confirm, endorse and gold-stamp whatever direction Hasan wanted to go.

Just before the government responded to the mid-December submission, Bre-X released on January 13 what was described as some stunningly rich Busang assay results. They claimed that one of Bre-X's drill holes showed 396 metres of ore grading one third of an ounce of gold. That was 5.5 times richer than the average grade of the deposit. These were absolutely staggering results, which apparently no one publicly questioned.

Meanwhile Jusuf Merukh launched a US$2-billion lawsuit in Alberta against Bre-X, claiming 40 percent of Busang II and III. An added party to the action was, not unexpectedly, PT Askatindo.

That suit was launched on January 14, the same day that John Willson's Placer Dome Inc. made a C$6.4-billion merger offer to Bre-X that included a 40-percent equity participation for Indonesia—in essence, offering the whole of Placer Dome for a 60-percent stake in Bre-X.

Peter Munk watched these shenanigans carefully because he now knew full well that Suharto and Bob Hasan were in control of the situation.

> Barrick and Bre-X received letters from the ministry saying that they had thirty days to finalize the agreement and we have to get the approval of the minority. The minority was Hasan.

For public consumption, Bob Hasan went on the record welcoming the Placer Dome bid, and saying the process should be opened up to other companies. As to the development of the Busang gold deposit, he said, "I think it should be done by people who really are in the business like Bre-X, Placer Dome or any other company that is at home in this field. Not necessarily Barrick." Hasan, in the United States to compete in the Bob Hope Chrysler Classic golf event, was careful not to call attention to the huge company run by his close pal Jim Bob Moffett, the chairman of the giant Freeport-McMoRan firm. Why should he? The Placer Dome bid was nicely orchestrated and encouraged in order to open the door for Jim Bob's corporation, in which Hasan meanwhile acquired a 9.9-percent stake from the Bakri family in Jakarta. It was reported that Hasan had met with John Willson of Placer Dome in Jakarta before Christmas and, for his own purposes, had encouraged Willson to make his enormous bid.

Peter Munk went on the record saying that Barrick's proposal for control of Busang offered the least risk for the Indonesian government. In a telephone interview from Switzerland with the *Financial Times*, Munk said he was "more confident than I was a while ago" that the Barrick/Bre-X proposal would go ahead. Even so, he indicated that he might well fly to Jakarta to press his case.

Sudjana's threat was clear to Barrick. The letter was signed by Sudjana, but the gun to the Barrick/Bre-X heads was being held by Bob Hasan. The "legal partners" that Barrick and Bre-X had to settle with were the two companies that Hasan controlled. The condition that there had to be a settlement with Hasan was, in fact, impossible, because Hasan had plans that did not include Barrick.

Hasan told the press that he doubted the Barrick/Bre-X deal was firm. He said, "I don't think there is a deal because we have not even been talked with. We are the actual licence holder ... they have to talk to us." In Jakarta on January 21, a spokesman for Sudjana stated that the government "encourages people such as Bob Hasan to join the battle for ownership of the Busang project."

Bill Birchall was in Jakarta and wanted to find out what was really behind that shotgun letter of Sudjana's. It would be Birchall's call if Munk was to go to Jakarta. He would go only if the situation was critical and Birchall needed him, or if Barrick was in real danger of losing out.

There was speculation in the press that Bre-X was ready to tell the Indonesian government that it couldn't come to a deal with Barrick and that the rights to build the mine and develop should be auctioned off. In a press release, Bre-X stated that it would work "diligently with senior executives of our Indonesian partners, PT Askatindo Karya Minerals and PT Amsya Lyna, to resolve outstanding matters." And "We remain anxious to join forces with local and foreign partners acceptable to the government of Indonesia."

There was no reference, either direct or indirect, to Barrick in the Bre-X release.

All the warning flags were up. Was there a mighty plot on in Indonesia to get Barrick excised, totally out of the deal? David Walsh, who was in Jakarta, said, "I don't think I've made any secret that I think that an auction process would have been more ideal." Birchall's urgent advice to Munk in Toronto was to get to Indonesia as soon as possible to personally attempt to settle the mess once and for all.

Munk was airborne, arriving in Jakarta on January 27, to meet face to face with Jim Bob Moffett's partner, Hasan.

The discussion with him was extremely difficult. It was evident that Hasan believed he held all the cards. Munk suspected that he had already made up his mind against Barrick. In Munk's words:

> The meeting was up and down. He invited me for lunch but it was Ramadan and we didn't eat. He had a Canadian there, his right-hand man, Jerry White. And Hasan's banker was there.
>
> I told him what I'd done for the past year. Because he was the new guy, and I'd never met him before, I told him "We've got the money lined up. We've made a fair deal with Bre-X and now we're also prepared to protect your minority interest."
>
> I also told him we couldn't put out a billion and a half dollars of our shareholders' money unless we had control. They could have benefits, they could have royalties, but the control must be Barrick's. Hasan got that loud and clear.

I told him that we insist on having the final say in environmental standards and that the project would include a full college education program for all the workers' kids—hundreds and hundreds of kids, which was news to him. He was interested in health care, and I said we intend to start our own hospital because we have to have the same health standards and safety standards in Indonesia as we have in Canada and anywhere else. He asked me, "Why couldn't I do it myself?" I said, please, you don't take a billion-dollar gold mine and just build it by yourself. These are not products you take off a shelf. No bank is going to give you project finance or credit, because you've got no track record of putting a mine onstream. I told him, if you are the minority partner, you get your share of what we earn. I think we can prove to you that no gold company can do it better and we have a long list of partners with whom you can check.

That was the end of the meeting with Hasan. He told me, "That's fine. Leave your people behind to negotiate." So I went to London, then to Klosters. I left Bill Birchall and Randall Oliphant behind to negotiate. But they couldn't get anywhere with Hasan.

On February 5, Barrick's chairman held one of his regular year-end-results conference calls from Klosters to mining analysts in eager Toronto. He spoke confidently about Barrick's credentials for winning the Busang war. However, he also said that under Indonesian law the ownership of natural resources such as gold belongs with the nation, and the final decision as to who would develop the Busang mine would be made in the national interest.

And as much as this doesn't fit in with our North American understanding of the mining law, mining rights [and] mining ownership, I am afraid in today's world that power is shifting and sovereign nations in Asia are becoming very self-assured of their own rights and their own laws. I think we must respect those laws.

There were only twelve days remaining before the February 17 deadline. Not much was happening in Jakarta during the week of February 3 because Bob Hasan was away that week on a fishing trip— reportedly with Suharto. Further contact when he returned to his office on February 10 did not result in any progress.

The Barrick board met on February 12 to assess the increasingly dismal situation and counsel Munk on what should be done next. Perhaps a new offer—or had the barn door been shut by Hasan?

On February 13, the *Globe and Mail* reported that Bre-X had reached a deal with Hasan and would soon announce its partner for the development of Busang. It would be Hasan's nominee. The Indonesian government was expected to approve of Hasan's selection early in the week of the 17th. If the *Globe and Mail*'s report was accurate, Barrick had lost. It was out. The largest gold find in the world had slipped through its fingers. The axe fell on Barrick's position on the deadline day, February 17, when it was announced that Bre-X had done a deal with Freeport-McMoRan Copper & Gold and, of course, with its chairman Jim Bob Moffett's pal Bob Hasan. The deal was to create a new company to develop Busang II and III. It was to be 45 percent owned by Bre-X, 30 percent by Hasan's companies, 10 percent for the government of Indonesia and 15 percent by Freeport-McMoRan, which already operated a substantial gold and copper mine in Indonesia. It would build and operate the mine and pay US$400 million toward construction costs.

When the arrangement was announced, Hasan proclaimed that he personally, not the Indonesian government, had chosen Freeport-McMoRan, and that he had selected Jim Bob's company as the "best solution for my country, its people and Bre-X, the company responsible for finding this incredible deposit." It went without saying that the solution was also best for Bob Hasan, who had increased his stake from 10 to 30 percent without putting up any funds for the proposed development or payment of any kind to Bre-X—or their shareholders.

The Barrick loss was immediately described in the press as a major blow to the company and to Peter Munk who had built the firm from the ground up over the previous decade. He was said to be known to take defeat very hard.

He does, no question. The proud Peter Munk is hard on himself, and a defeat is hard on the reputation that he treasures. And to suffer a loss so publicly, with such notoriety; to come from the pinnacle of achievement, when he emerged with 75 percent of Busang, down to the low point of being ignominiously eliminated by Bob Hasan—it could not have been easy.

Peter Munk answers the question about how he felt when he heard the news that Hasan had chosen Freeport-McMoRan instead of Barrick:

Very bad. I must say I was frustrated. I'm not very good at losing. In life when I really, really want something badly I focus and I can usually get there somehow. I do it for my company, which pays me. I was able to bring to bear almost all my mental and financial resources, and I was convinced, as I am today, that there could have been no better partner for Bre-X shareholders and Indonesia than Barrick.

I spent the bulk of my time during the year on Bre-X. Nineteen ninety-six was the only year I didn't spend even a week at Georgian Bay. That never happened before, not even in the Clairtone days. If necessary I wouldn't have gone to Switzerland. I've never done that, ever. Ever. But it was a matter of getting involved in sixty million or more ounces of gold, or letting somebody else do it. Not only would we have lost it, but title of the premium gold producer would go to somebody else. And I don't get paid to let that happen.

On the other hand the Freeport solution was okay for me because I knew that with Hasan owning 30 percent, Freeport owning 15, and Bre-X owning 45 percent, nobody could become the premier miner because there were going to be fights and such arguments over cash flow, and division of the benefits—it would have been a mess. I had been concerned that Placer Dome could have had it, or Newmont could have had it, and if that happened Barrick would have been a secondary player for the next decade. I don't like that. I just couldn't afford to lose it. But I believed I had.

I really was in bad shape for a couple of weeks. And I took it to my shareholders—I had to be the one to tell them. I'm the boss. It was my responsibility.

In short, the proud Peter Munk was crushed. But as he would soon learn, the loss of Busang was probably the most fortunate defeat of his career.

On February 19, to keep the share sale hot pot boiling, John Felderhof, Bre-X's vice-chairman and head of exploration, went public with more extravagant claims: "If you asked me what is the total potential, I would feel very comfortable with 200 million ounces." Felderhof, it was known, had already made a 1996 profit of C$42.4 million in his trades of Bre-X. At the same time, David Walsh and his wife, Jeannette, hauled in C$34.9 million. This would make those hauls pale by comparison.

Four days after Barrick's ouster, Peter Munk put his reaction into words. At this point the world had no idea that Bre-X was anything but the biggest gold deposit ever found, and Hasan had just been quoted as saying that he chose Freeport "at the last moment" largely because he was a friend of the company's president, Jim Bob Moffett.

Munk expressed astonishment at Hasan's words, and added that in view of this revelation of Hasan's "thought process," he was pleased Barrick had not sweetened its bid further by offering to dilute or give up control of the Busang project. To do so, he said, would have made no sense. It would have been "totally contrary to the founding principles that Barrick was built on."

Peter Munk and Barrick Gold were out of the Busang gamble. But to Munk and everyone's astonishment the Bre-X Busang game was far from over and was about to be exposed as one of the most amazing gold mining fiascos of this or any other century.

On March 19, 1997, Michael de Guzman, Bre-X's chief geologist at Busang, was reported to have committed suicide by jumping from a helicopter *en route* to Busang from Samarinda. Suicide? *Maclean's* magazine's Jennifer Wells wrote, in an article that appeared on August 18, 1997, and deals with the rumours surrounding the corpse said to be that of de Guzman, "The closer one gets to the deceased de Guzman, the more one believes that he is very much alive."

For Munk and others affected by Bre-X and Busang, the strange news about de Guzman was the first hint that the find might well not be what Walsh and Felderhof were claiming.

As the months went by, the Bre-X mystery was pursued by a justifiably aggressive press.

At Barrick Gold's annual shareholders' meeting on May 1, 1997, Munk admitted to feeling "a high level of personal loss and a high level of personal embarrassment" over losing Busang. But Munk also told his listeners that he was pleased to be out of Busang by then.

The deal was only available to us by giving up control of our investment in the operations and most importantly our cash flow ... this is contrary to the principles that built our wealth, and so we had no hesitation in walking away.

But defeat soon turned to delight, notwithstanding Peter Munk's protestations of loss and embarrassment. Four days later, on Monday, May 5, 1997, the headlines blared the truth: "Bre-X find biggest scam in mining history: report." And "Bre-X samples false, tests show."

The public report of the independent consulting firm retained by Bre-X, Strathcona Mineral Services Ltd., was devastating not only for what it said but also for the blunt and brutal terms in which its principal author, Graham Farquharson, stated the findings:

> We very much regret having to express the firm opinion that an economic gold deposit has not been identified in the southeast zone of the Busang property, and is unlikely to be.
>
> The magnitude of the tampering with core samples that we believe has occurred and resulting falsification of assay values at Busang is of a scale and over a period of time and with a precision that, to our knowledge, is without precedent in the history of mining anywhere in the world.

Peter Munk was appalled when he read the Strathcona report. The damage inflicted on Canada's national and international mining industry was beyond what anyone would have thought possible a few short weeks before.

For his part, in early August 1997, Felderhof issued a carefully crafted statement proclaiming his innocence in the Busang affair. Peter Munk had no comment on Felderhof's claim.

Falsification, misrepresentation, tampering. Those were the operative words in the Strathcona report that stamped Bre-X as the biggest scam in mining history. For Peter Munk, the news explained "the irrationality of Bre-X's actions over the year."

> I am an engineer, and I'm a black-and-white person. I couldn't understand how they defied the government, defied J.P.

Morgan, defied their lawyers. Why? What were they after?

Now it makes sense. And once it makes sense you feel good because you can understand why you lost. Now I do.

CHAPTER FORTY-ONE

MUNK'S FUTURE

Peter Munk has amassed a considerable fortune. Much of his wealth is in the form of shares and share options in Barrick Gold Corporation and TrizecHahn. As one might expect from a man as well organized, counselled and advised as Munk, all his plans for his estate are in place. Peter Munk has had the benefit of the experience of being poor, and he has also seen what can happen when wealth is handed from one generation down to the next. Inherited money became identified in his eyes with a less successful fulfilment of life's objectives. Moral strength, moral values, a model for the accomplishment of personal objectives and the development of self-confidence based on individual achievement, he believes, are a far more valuable inheritance than money could ever be.

Peter Munk doesn't believe in leaving his family money. "I believe in leaving them a strong set of moral guidelines. I think that I was influenced by the fact that I saw my grandfather, at the age of seventy-four, kicked out of Hungary by the Nazis with only a knapsack. So to me that can happen again in a lifetime. If you've got the moral guidelines, the self-confidence and the determination, you'll start again and will make it. But if all you have is the money and the money is taken away from you, then you are finished."

Over the years, Munk has committed himself to bringing up his children to be honest, moral, generous and socially responsible. On the other hand, he has tried to give them the opportunity to work hard and take risks, and to become wealthy not through inheritance but through their own efforts. His commitment to Canada is his own personal affair. His children can choose their own direction.

Then what will happen to the immense wealth Peter Munk has accumulated? There are two parts to the answer. As Munk sees it, the business is a living entity that has a societal obligation to its stake-holders: people create the wealth and put their time, intellect and their efforts into a business to build it, and his business will carry on, whether under the leadership of Peter Munk or anyone else. It will be up to the directors to decide that when the time comes, in the interest of all the stakeholders. The fact that one's name is Munk should not qualify that person any more than the name Smith or Jones. So says Munk.

A condition of his estate calls for all of his Barrick and TrizecHahn shares to go into the Peter Munk Foundation. Its objectives are to promote the concept of free enterprise, liberty and freedom. The trustees are a group of five people: his lawyer, his accountant, Melanie and his two oldest children. He changes the trustees every five years, and he intends eventually to refine that concept so that it cannot be abused; he admits that he hasn't spent enough time on the structure.

However, the strategic mission of his foundation is very clear: it will be to teach young people the benefits of self-reliance and the benefits to society and the economy that derive from free enterprise. The media and academic society, in Munk's opinion, are too removed from the free enterprise that created the wealth of the modern world, and do not understand that in this century mankind was effectively saved twice by the spirit, the wealth and the creative power of the most successful free-enterprise system in history: North America. Two tyrannical systems run by murderous dictators, Nazism and Communism, might have overpowered Europe and the Americas, might have taken over mankind, and if they had won, would have set civilization back by a thousand years. But they did not win, and in Munk's opinion their defeat was due to the power of America and the spirit of the free world, a power and a spirit that owe their existence to the unbridled free-enterprise system that flourished in America and the British Empire in the century prior to the Second World War.

And what does Peter Munk himself aspire to do in his remaining years? He intends to use his best efforts to increase the wealth of his shareholders, and to use to the maximum his renowned ability to think strategically and dream big, to savour the acceptance and respect of his peers in Canada and internationally. He can also relish accolades such as that in the February 1996 edition of *Barron's*, in which he is described as: "The world's most influential mining executive"; or in *Time* magazine's Global Business Report of February 1997. *Time* profiled a dozen of the key players from around the world who could make a difference in 1997. Munk, the only Canadian included, was described as "one of the world's most successful gold tycoons." Once again, Munk disclosed the secret of his incredible success: "I'm not exactly an Einstein, so I compensate by being more focused."

Peter Munk, the golden phoenix miraculously risen from the ashes of Clairtone, has lived a life and enjoyed good fortune light years beyond anything that red-headed boy of sixteen could possibly have imagined, let alone aspired to, as he rode the sway-backed horse to the Columbus Street siding in Budapest on the darkening evening of June 29, 1944.

INDEX